The Content Analysis
of Dreams

The Content Analysis of Dreams

CALVIN S. HALL   and

ROBERT L. VAN DE CASTLE

BOTH OF THE INSTITUTE OF DREAM RESEARCH

 New York

APPLETON-CENTURY-CROFTS

DIVISION OF MEREDITH PUBLISHING COMPANY

ACKNOWLEDGMENTS FOR TABLES

Acknowledgment is gratefully made to the following authors and pub-
lishers who have granted permission to use tables from copyrighted pub-
lications.

15-1 through 15-5. Edith Sheppard. *Dream rating scales*. Mimeographed.
July, 1964, 1-55.

15-6. A. T. Beck and M. S. Hurvich. Psychological correlates of depression. I. Frequency of "masochistic" dream content in a private practice
sample. *Psychosom. Med.*, 1959, *21*, 50-55.

15-7. E. Polster. An investigation of ego functioning in dreams. Ph.D. dissertation. Western Reserve University, 1951.

15-8, 15-9. Claire F. Rabe. A study of sexual attitudes as revealed by symbols in dreams. M.A. thesis. Western Reserve University, 1949. Reprinted
as Research Report No. 2 of the Institute of Dream Research, 1963.

15-10, 15-11. J. Rychlak. Recalled dream themes and personality. *J. abnorm. soc. Psychol.*, 1960, *60*, 140-143.

15-11, 15-12. J. Rychlak and J. M. Brams. Personality dimensions in recalled dream content. *J. proj. Tech.*, 1963, *27*, 226-234.

15-13 through 15-19. R. M. Whitman, C. M. Pierce, J. W. Maas, and B.
Baldridge. Drugs and dreams II: Imipramine and procholorperazine.
Comprehen. Psychiat., 1961, *2*, 219-226.

15-21. J. L. Framo, J. Osterweil, and I. Boszormenyi-Nagy. A relationship between threat in the manifest content of dreams and active-passive behavior in psychotics. *J. abnorm. soc. Psychol.*, 1962, *65*, 41-47.

15-22. I. T. Lott. Identity formation in the manifest dreams of late adolescents: an exploratory study. Honors thesis. Brandeis University, 1963.

15-23. G. W. Domhoff. A quantitative study of dream content using an objective indicator of dreaming. Ph.D. dissertation. University of Miami, 1962.

15-24. G. M. Goldenberg. An investigation of primary-process thinking in the manifest dream report. Ph.D. dissertation. Wayne State University, 1963.

15-25. C. Perry. A manual of procedures for analyzing manifest dream content into narrative elements and for classifying such elements with respect to distortion from reality. Mimeographed. Department of Psychology, The University of Sydney, 1964.

15-26. K. M. Colby. Sex differences in dreams: a contribution to the masculinity-femininity problem. In *A skeptical psychoanalyst*, New York: Ronald Press, 1958, 107-145.

15-27. W. Reis. A comparison of the interpretation of dream series with and without free association. Ph.D. dissertation, Western Reserve University, 1951. Abridged version in *Dreams and personality dynamics*. M. F. De Martino (Ed.), Springfield, Ill.: Thomas, 1959, 211-225.

15-28. Dorothy Eggan. The manifest content of dreams: a challenge to social science. *Amer. Anthropologist*, 1952, *54*, 469-485.

15-29. R. M. Griffith, O. Miyagi, and A. Tago. The universality of typical dreams: Japanese vs. Americans. *Amer. Anthropologist*, 1958, *60*, 1173-1179.

15-30. C. H. Ward, A. T. Beck, and E. Rascoe. Typical dreams: incidence among psychiatric patients. *Arch. gen. Psychiat.*, 1961, *5*, 606-615.

To the basketball team

Brett, Lance, Keith, Craig, and Drake

Preface

Throughout recorded history, man has been keenly interested in his dreams and has felt that they contained important but mysterious messages. Their origin has been attributed to such diverse sources as the absence of bed covers or the presence of spirits. Considerably less mystery has been attached to dreams since Freud formulated his well-known theory to account for the peculiar visual idioms manifested in dreams and provided a clinical method to unravel their apparent meaning. Freud's qualitative approach to dreams is illustrated with elaborate detail in his *Interpretation of Dreams*.

The study of dreams has changed but little in the sixty-five years that have followed the publication of Freud's monumental work. It is true that others have advanced different theoretical interpretations of what constitutes the hidden message within dreams, but the methodology of investigating dreams has remained fixated at a qualitative stage of development. Freud himself decried the stagnation characterizing the field of dream inquiry.

The hypothesis might be offered that no radically new approaches were possible as long as attention was focused exclusively on the latent content of dreams. With such an emphasis, there could be no substantive dream data but only a clutching at elusive shadows which constantly changed their shape as one approached them in the privacy of the therapeutic sanctum.

We feel that the time for a new approach, a quantitative one based upon analysis of the manifest content, has arrived. Although some investigators before us have used quantitative methods for analyzing dreams, no one has ever attempted to devise a system encompassing the breadth of analysis to be found in this book. Many books have appeared which offer suggestions on how to proceed with qualitative analysis of dreams. This book is unique. It is the first book devoted to describing how the investigation of dreams can be approached in an objective quantitative fashion. We hope that it will do for dreams quantitatively what Freud's book did for them qualitatively.

The need for a book such as this one is heightened by the recent discoveries of objective indicators of dreaming by Aserinsky and Kleitman, and by Dement and others. These discoveries have touched off a chain reaction of research in laboratories throughout the world. The major emphasis in these studies to date has been on physiological parameters of dreaming, and little has been done with the psychological variables that are to be found in the dreams themselves. We attribute this one-sided development in dream research to the lack of appropriate methods for analyzing dreams. Now that dreams have entered the laboratory in such a dramatic and unexpected manner, new ways of treating them are required which are just as objective as the indicators of dreaming themselves.

Several original contributions to dream research have been incorporated within this book. We have attempted to make a theoretical contribution by delineating some of the problems involved in applying content analysis to reported dreams. It might be considered that the book provides a bibliographic contribution since the work of others who have devised scales for dream analysis has been fairly exhaustively surveyed. The main contribution of this book is, however, a methodological one. For the first time, a comprehensive system of classifying and scoring the contents of reported dreams has been described and made available to the dream investigator. An important empirical contribution is provided through the extensive normative material based upon 1,000 dreams that is included in this book. An explanation is given of how our scoring system may be transferred to IBM type cards so that dream content can be mechanically processed and statistically evaluated in the same manner employed with other scientific data. If by means of this book, dreams can make the circuit from couch to computer, we will have achieved the fulfillment of one of our fondest wishes.

Preparation of this book was made possible by a grant (10207) to the Institute of Dream Research from the National Institute of Mental Health of the United States Public Health Service. We would like to acknowledge the secretarial assistance of Mrs. Sharon Clark in preparing the manuscript for publication.

C.S.H.
R.L.V.d.C.

Contents

1

The Methodology
of Content Analysis

In this introductory chapter we propose to discuss some of the issues which have been raised in connection with the methodology of content analysis, limiting our discussion to those issues which appear to have relevance for the analysis of dreams. A more extended discussion does not seem warranted since the domain of content analysis has been mapped by Berelson, (1952), surveyed by Cartwright (1953), and expanded by contributors to the volume, *Trends in Content Analysis* (Pool, 1959). Recently, a practical handbook of content analysis intended primarily for the use of political scientists has been prepared by a group at Stanford University (North, Holsti, Zaninovich and Zinnes, 1963). Content analysis has even acquired a critic (Stephenson, 1963).

Why does one do content analysis? Nearly all writers on the subject agree that it is done in order to quantify that which is qualitative. Content analysis converts verbal or other symbolic material into numbers in order that statistical operations may be performed on such material. This purpose is accomplished by formulating classes, tabulating frequencies, and figuring rates. Osgood (1959) notes that content analysis consists of "methods in which the bias of the analyst is at least minimized, in which the essential operations can be made explicit and the conclusions

1

thereby more easily replicated, and in which the findings can be communicated in meaningful numbers" (p. 34). Berelson (1952) defines content analysis as "a research technique for the objective, systematic, and quantitative description of the manifest content of communication" (p. 18), and Cartwright (1953) states that "the fundamental objective of all content analysis is to convert phenomena, i.e., symbolic behavior of people, into scientific data" (p. 466). Scientific data must display four characteristics, according to Cartwright. These are (1) objectivity and reproducibility, (2) susceptibility to measurement and quantification, (3) significance for systematic theory, either "pure" or "applied," and (4) generalizability.

The specific research objectives for which the content analysis of verbal and other symbolic material has been employed are many and varied. They include propaganda analysis studies (Lasswell, 1927), classification of the figures of speech in Shakespeare's plays (Spurgeon, 1935), use of an adjective-verb quotient (Boder, 1940), analysis of personal letters (Baldwin, 1942), assessment of tension in written documents (Dollard and Mowrer, 1947), analysis of values in Richard Wright's autobiography (White, 1947), comparison of metaphors in the novels of Jane Austen, Emily Brontë, and George Eliot (Schorer, 1949), thematic analysis of movies (Wolfenstein and Leites, 1950), and studies of literature as an expression of the writer's personality (McCurdy, 1961), not to mention the numerous content studies of projective test protocols (Murstein, 1963) and psychotherapy (Auld and Murray, 1955). Among recent developments in content analysis should be mentioned a computer system for content analysis and retrieval based on the word as a unit of information (Stone, Bales, Namenwirth, and Ogilvie, 1962). This system has been employed in the counting and comparing of themes in folktales (Colby, Collier, and Postal, 1963). Also using the word as the unit of analysis, Harway and Iker (1964) have been attempting a computer analysis of content in psychotherapy.

In general, psychologists employ content analysis of verbal material in order to say something about the personality of the individual who has produced it.

OBJECTIONS TO QUANTIFICATION

The application of quantitative methods to written material does not meet with universal acceptance even among psychologists who as a group are trained in the rigors of quantitative analysis and who are taught to equate science with measurement. A seemingly endless dialogue goes on between those who prefer words (qualitative description) and those who prefer numbers (quantitative description). The members of the dialogue are sometimes called artists and scientists, sometimes clinicians and statisticians (or experimentalists), and sometimes humanistic psychologists and rat psychologists. Whatever their labels there seems to be widespread mistrust and fear of numbers, particularly when they are used to describe and characterize the works of writers and artists. Since we are going to be dealing with material in this book which resembles the creative productions of writers, it is not irrelevant to examine briefly some of the apparent reasons for this antipathy toward quantification.

Quantity (numbers, mass) has debased quality in modern society, particularly in the United States. If words can be classified as good or bad, then there is little question in which categories the words "quality" and "quantity" would be placed by the majority of people. Quality signifies that which is well made, durable, expensive, and in good taste. It denotes superiority. Quantity (mass) signifies that which is mediocre, commonplace, cheap, poorly constructed, and in poor taste. It denotes inferiority. Negative feelings about quantity are expressed in many ways. It is said that mass production has displaced the honest craftsman, mass culture has reduced art to the aesthetic level of the lowest common denominator, mass education has resulted in watered-down learning, and mass man has replaced the individual. Since quantity is associated with numbers, numbers are held suspect.

Numbers are cold and impersonal in comparison with words. A love letter cannot be written in numbers; nor can a poem.

Numbers are hard. They are used for such impersonal things as money, prices, checks, licenses, addresses, taxes, and time. Words are soft and warm and intimate. They can be combined in pleasing ways, spoken with feeling, or sung to music. It is not surprising, therefore, that people should be repelled by a methodology whose aim is to transform words into numbers. Anyone who would reduce a poem to a set of figures is capable of tearing a butterfly to pieces.

A person's identity is lost when he is given a number. Many people are disturbed by the increasing use of numbers in our computerized society. Pleasant telephone exchange names like Mohawk, Hillcrest, Madrona, and Cherry are being replaced by two-digit code numbers. A customer receives a number when he enters his favorite bakery. Birthday telegrams can be sent by number. Most outrageous of all to many people is the growing tendency for one's social security number to take the place of one's name. Reacting against this "numbers" game, people complain of feelings of depersonalization, alienation, and regimentation. Their objections to being treated like objects rather than like human beings does not make them very sympathetic toward the proposal that greater use of numbers be made in all fields of inquiry.

Mathematics is a "hard" subject. Compared to most of the other subjects in the high school curriculum, mathematics is considered to be difficult. So are physics and chemistry in which a great deal of mathematics is used. Many people have a hard time understanding anything that is expressed in numbers; they are puzzled by equations and other mathematical expressions and operations. A table of figures repels many readers, and any sort of statistical analysis is a perplexing mystery to the vast majority. Moreover, mathematics and physics are held responsible for such ugly realities as the atomic bomb. The mathematician, engineer, and scientist are often pictured as inhuman zealots, e.g., Dr. Strangelove.

Thus, for all these reasons—the debasing influence of quantity, the cold, impersonal character of numbers, the depersonalization and regimentation that results from being numbered and treated as a statistic, and the difficulty people have in trying to learn mathematics—quantitative analysis of qualitative material is looked upon with disfavor in many quarters.

OBJECTIONS TO CONTENT ANALYSIS

The above reasons might be considered sentimental or emotional objections to the symbolic properties of numbers. Content analysis as a method of quantifying verbal material has been attacked on other grounds by serious students of human behavior who feel that it has definite flaws and limitations. These criticisms have as their major tenet the thesis that numbers can serve only as signs and cannot convey, as effectively or efficiently as words, the actual complexity of real events. Some of these rational objections to content analysis will now be presented.

Content analysis is reductionistic. By reductionism is meant that a large body of material is compressed into relatively few categories. For example, one might reduce all the statements in a set of recorded interviews to three classes: positive evaluations, negative evaluations, and neutral statements. The major complaint against reductionism is that there is a loss of data whenever classification is performed. This is necessarily true because in the act of compressing material, something is always going to get squeezed out. The pertinent question is whether what is squeezed out is significant for the problem under investigation. If the investigator suspects it is, he should revise his classification system so that it will include everything he deems relevant.

Qualitative analysis, on the other hand, does not avoid the alleged harmful effects of reductionism and may even compound them, by permitting these effects to proliferate under the imprecise use of verbal generalizations.

Content analysis ignores the unique. This criticism has been forcefully made by Alexander George (1959) in his discussion of quantitative and qualitative approaches to content analysis. He points out that an event which happens only once may be of greater importance than a frequently occurring event. It does not take much imagination to think of examples which support George's contention. But there is nothing in the methodology of content analysis which prevents one from formulating categories whose frequencies turn out to be one, or even zero. In fact, absence of any entries in a category may signify more than their presence. For example, it would make us curious if, in a long dream series, the person never reported a dream in which his mother appeared. In this case, as in many others, an appreciation of the singular or of the absent depends upon a knowledge of what is usual, that is, upon norms obtained by quantitative content analysis.

An expert using qualitative analysis can classify people or describe their behavior as well as or better than a group of trained people using quantitative content analysis. Undoubtedly, this is sometimes true but the problem is to find the expert who can do it and who has the time to do it. Moreover, as Cartwright (1953) points out, science does not consist of a body of knowledge which is closely guarded by a group of experts. Scientific knowledge should be widely disseminated for the good of the science.

An expert may use intuition, sensitivity, insight, empathy, and a feel for the material as well as a fund of exact knowledge. Intuition does not operate in a vacuum, however. It operates with cues and preconscious information which can often be spelled out in objective and public terms if one is willing to take the trouble. After considerable exposure to qualitative material, one is in a much better position to originate relevant components for quantification. By being forced to be explicit about what is important to score and to state written rules for the manner in which it should be scored, the critical thinking of the expert is honed to even greater sharpness, and the resultant objective formulations exist for others to share.

It is difficult to quantify the individual case. The implication of this statement is that one is either forced to use qualitative analysis or give up studying the individual case scientifically. Where the amount of material to be analyzed is small, a single dream, for instance, not much counting can be done and few categories will have any frequencies at all. Still, even for a single dream, the availability of a method of content analysis is not without value. A comprehensive classificatory system can serve as a guide or check list to the analyst of what to look for, even in a single dream. Quantitative analysis can also provide norms which may prove useful in evaluating the presence of a particular event in a single dream. For example, a young man dreams that he is being chased by a woman brandishing a knife. Our norms tell us that it is rare for young men to dream of being chased by women carrying weapons.

Of course, if one has considerable material on a single case, there is no reason why it cannot be quantified as readily as one quantifies material obtained from a number of cases. Three hundred dreams from a single individual can be scored in the same way as single dreams from 300 individuals. We have in our files several series of dreams from individuals which number in the hundreds and one that numbers in the thousands where just such a procedure has been followed.

Content analysis ignores associations between categories. This may have been true prior to 1950, except for the isolated example of Baldwin's (1942) personal structure analysis, but since the development of contingency analysis by Osgood and his associates (1959), the study of associations in verbal material has become widespread and is a characteristic feature of the content analysis that is being done currently.

Associations between components, i.e., contingencies, can also be built into the scoring system itself. This is what we have done in scoring social interactions in dreams. An aggressive interaction, for example, consists of four scores linked together. These are (1) the nature of the aggression, (2) the aggressor, (3) the victim, and (4) possible reciprocation by the victim. There is nothing in the methodology of content analysis which says categories have to be separate and "atomistic." They may be "holistic" or as "atomistic" as one desires, consisting either of broad interrelated units, or of single words.

Contingency, it should be noted, is not synonymous with relationship. Contingency analysis merely establishes that two items are found together more often or less often than would be expected by chance. It does not say that the items have a necessary or causal relationship. In view of this, contiguity is probably a more appropriate term than contingency.

The foregoing list of criticisms consist of those which may be leveled at any type of quantitative analysis and those which attempt to stigmatize content analysis specifically. There is no good way of answering criticisms of quantitative analysis except to point out that science has found classification and analysis to be useful operations. Criticisms of content analysis apply primarily to a misuse of the method and not to anything which is inherent in it. The misuse of the method may be minimized if one has a grasp of the relevant methodological issues.

METHODOLOGICAL ISSUES

There are only two methodological problems which must be considered in relation to the content analysis of verbal or other qualitative material (Guetzkow, 1950). These are (1) the formulation of a system of classification, and (2) the selection of a unit of analysis. A third problem, the measurement of intensity, is often raised in any discussion of content analysis and will be discussed here, but it is not central to content analysis.

FORMULATION OF A SYSTEM OF CLASSIFICATION

The formulation of a system of classification is the most crucial step in content analysis. Unfortunately, there are no cookbook recipes or even guidelines which tell the investigator how to do it. He must use his own imagination and judgment. There are, however, certain preliminary decisions which he must make, and to these we turn our attention.

Shall the system of classification be one that can be used generally or shall it be formulated for the individual case? Offhand it seems that it would always be preferable to formulate a set of categories of general applicability rather than a set which is going to be used only once and then discarded. Not only does the latter procedure seem wasteful but it is at variance with the principle of standardized units of measurement, a principle which is one of the foundations of science.

And yet some investigators deliberately choose to formulate an individualized set of categories (Baldwin, 1942; Eggan, 1952). Baldwin rejected the use of any universally applicable system of classification when he analyzed a group of letters written by an elderly woman because he believed it "destroys all possibility of discovering the unique characteristics of the individual case" (1942, p. 170).

This strikes us as being a fallacious argument for at least two reasons. How can one discover what is unique unless one knows what is not unique? The unique is known only by comparison with the general. And how does the use of a standard set of categories prevent the appearance of unique characteristics? Cannot an individual's pattern of scores differ from any other person's pattern of scores even though the scoring categories are the same? Have not standardized tests always been used to measure individual differences among people?

No set of categories is ever complete but if the investigator cannot find what he wants among those that have already been devised, he is free to formulate new ones which can then be added to the existing ones. In this way, the comprehensiveness of a classificatory system is continually being expanded.

Although there is usually no problem in deriving categories which generalize across different populations, it is more difficult to devise categories which generalize across different types of verbal material. A system that works well for psychotherapy interviews may not work well for dreams. Ideally, a system of classifying and scoring symbolic material should generalize across types of productions as well as across populations. There are those who believe that a truly universal classificatory system waits upon a universally accepted theory of personality. In our opinion, however, taxonomy and theory are so interdependent that each advance in one permits an advance in the other. The taxonomist and theorist both play a part in forwarding science, and both should therefore know what the other is doing.

Even if a comprehensive system of classification is available, it is not necessary for the investigator to use all of it. He may select from the system just those categories which will enable him to reach the objectives of his particular research project. If the categories need to be modified to suit his needs, they can be modified. The writers hope that the system presented in this book will be used in a selective and flexible manner. There is nothing sacrosanct about a classificatory system, and any slavish adherence to it is to be deplored.

Shall the system of classification be empirical or theoretical? By an empirical system, we mean one that is derived from the verbal material itself, and by a theoretical system, we mean one that is derived from a theory of personality and applied to the material. For example, the classification of verbal material into parts of speech is purely empirical whereas the classification of verbal material into Jung's archetypes is purely theoretical. When one exercises the empirical option, it might be said that he reads *out of* the material what is there; when one exercises the theoretical option he reads *into* the material what theory tells him he should find. If he finds what the theory has told him he should find, the theory is supported; if he does not find it, either he has not looked properly or the theory is incorrect.

Which alternative should be chosen—empirical or theoretical—will depend upon the objectives of the investigator. Naturally, if he is going to test propositions derived from a particular theory, he will formulate categories that have relevance for those propositions. But if he is interested in census-type studies for the purpose of establishing norms, or in the taxonomy of a particular type of symbolic behavior, or just in exercising his curiosity about phenomena, he can use empirical categories.

The formulation of empirical categories presents no real difficulties. One makes as many or as few categories as are necessary for his purposes. Nor does the formulation of theoretical categories present any special difficulties as long as one realizes that the categories must refer to something that can be identified in the material that is being investigated. That is, a theoreical category is at the same time an empirical one, since one cannot classify something that is not there. Empirical and theoretical categories draw their water from the same well. The difference between a theoretical category and an empirical one lies in the name that is given to the category. For example, in analyzing dreams one can have an empirical category which consists of injury to a part of the dreamer's body because such injuries are described in dream reports. But one can also label this category castration anxiety, because, according to Freudian theory, fear of injury to any part of the body, particularly to the extremities, is indicative of fear of castration.

Theoretical categories must always be validated. Calling something castration anxiety does not make it that, but if it can be shown that the rate for the category varies from condition to condition according to theoretical expectations, then one feels more entitled to label the category by its theoretical name. Nothing has changed, however, except the name. What has been read into the dream must actually be there. In that sense, reading *into* is equivalent to reading *out of*.

Although there are no rules for formulating theoretical variables, the investigator's success in devising meaningful ones will be enhanced by a thorough knowledge of the material which is to be analyzed. One should literally drench himself in the material he intends to analyze before starting to formulate theoretical categories. He should also be thoroughly conversant with the theory from which he is to derive his categories, for it is out of the dialogue between observation and hypothesis that a useful classificatory system will emerge.

What constitutes a good category? The initial criterion of a good category is that its limits shall be so clearly defined that there will be a high degree of agreement between scorers as to what should be included within the category and what should be excluded from it. For if scorers cannot agree, the category is useless and has to be discarded. The rules for excluding and including should be so carefully formulated that there will be few questions about the scoring.

This is not an easy task. It can only be accomplished by the most taxing sort of trial and error. One must refine and test, refine and test, refine and test until most of the ambiguities of scoring have been eliminated. Even so, there will always be an area of grayness at the boundary between what is to be included and what is to be excluded. It is in this area that many examples are required in order to guide the scorer. This is why content analysis appears to be, and is often, complicated and demanding and why some investigators prefer to use the quicker global rating systems or qualitative analysis.

After the scoring reliability of a category has been established, one can then determine its generalizability across subjects, time, or experimental manipulations, and its validity for measuring something that the investigator wishes to measure.

SELECTION OF UNITS

After the categories have been defined and a classificatory system developed, the next step is to decide upon the unit of analysis. An investigator is rarely interested in the absolute amount of something (frequency) but is interested instead in the amount of something in relation to units of something else (rates). He is interested, for example, in the number of whole responses relative to the total number of responses in a Rorschach record, or in the number of self-critical remarks per unit of 100 words spoken by a patient, or in the ratio of adjectives to verbs. This is the case because he usually wants to make comparisons of some sort, and comparisons of frequencies, if they are to have any meaning, must be for equal units of material. If we know, for example, only that two people give the same number of whole responses on the Rorschach, we really don't know anything about them relative to one another. For one person may have given a total of 15 responses and the other a total of 60 responses. We can only make meaningful comparisons when we know the total number of responses so we can compute the proportion of whole responses.

Just as there are no established ground rules for the formulation of categories, so there are none for the selection of suitable units of analysis. Both the formulation of categories and the selection of units are equally subjective. Each investigator must decide for himself what units are going to be appropriate for his particular study.

A variety of units have been used in content analysis—single words, phrases, sentences, lines, pages, or whole productions, for instance. Some of the problems that are encountered in selecting units may be illustrated by the analysis of dreams. The dream report itself may be used, in rare instances, as the unit of analysis. This would be the case if one were interested in comparing the length of dreams reported by males and females. The unit would be number of words per dream. But for most types of content analysis, the overall dream report is not an appropriate unit since it varies in length. Suppose one is interested in determining the number of misfortunes suffered personally by the dreamer. The number he experiences will depend, to some degree, upon the length of the dream. The longer the dream, the greater the probability that a misfortune will occur. Consequently, misfortunes to the dreamer should be computed for dreams of equal length or for frequencies per words of the dream texts (rates).

If one is counting misfortunes to characters other than the dreamer, the appropriate unit is not a fixed number of words of dream text but a rate based on the number of characters in the dreams. This is the correct procedure here, because the population of characters has more to do with determining the chances of a misfortune occurring to a character than the number of words do.

THE MEASUREMENT OF INTENSITY

The measure of intensity most widely used in content analysis is that of simple frequency. It is assumed that the more often something occurs, the more intense it is. If males have twice the number of aggressive encounters in their dreams that females do, the aggressive impulse of the average male is said to be stronger than that of the average female. How much stronger depends upon the kind of function that is assumed to exist between frequency and intensity. If one assumes that Frequency = Intensity, the average male, in the preceding example, would be twice as aggressive as the average female. But if the relationship is curvilinear, this means that the frequencies must be weighted in some manner by giving either more or less weight to increasing frequencies, depending upon whether there is positive or negative acceleration to the curve. Since there are no rules to guide one in weighting frequencies in order to transform them into intensities, any weighting that is done will be subjective and arbitrary.

Scales may also be used to obtain intensity measures. For example, an investigator may construct a scale to measure strength of aggression in dreams. Let us assume that in this scale, a hostile remark has been assigned a scale value of 1, and murder has been assigned a scale value of 8. This means that eight hostile remarks equal the intensity of one murder. Some people find this kind of calculus absurd, no matter how impeccable the scaling methods employed may have been.

It may be that, except for some simple sensory-motor measures, intensity cannot be defined operationally in psychology, and that any attempts to measure it in verbal material leads one into absurdities of the sort noted above. What would seem to be important is to define classes of a particular form of behavior—aggression, for instance—and to compare people with respect to the frequency within each class rather than to try to arrange the classes on a scale of intensity. The question of intensity is a recurrent problem in psychology, however, and one on which there is no consensus as yet.

REFERENCES

AULD, F. JR. and MURRAY, E. J. Content-analysis studies of psychotherapy. *Psychol. Bull.*, 1955, 52, 377-395.

BALDWIN, A. L. Personal structure analysis: a statistical method for investigating the single personality, *J. abnorm. soc. Psychol.*, 1942, 37, 163-183.

BERELSON, B. *Content analysis in communication research.* Glencoe, Ill.: Free Press, 1952.

BODER, D. P. The adjective-verb quotient. *Psychol. Rec.*, 1940, 3, 310-343.

CARTWRIGHT, D. P. Analysis of qualitative material. In L. Festinger and D. Katz (Eds.), *Research methods in the behavioral sciences*. New York: Holt, Rinehart, and Winston, 1953, 421-470.

COLBY, B. N., COLLIER, G. A., and POSTAL, SUSAN K. Comparison of themes in folktales by the General Inquirer System. *J. Amer. Folklore*, 1963, 76, 318-323.

DOLLARD, J. and MOWRER, O. H. A method of measuring tension in written documents. *J. abnorm. soc. Psychol.*, 1947, 42, 3-32.

EGGAN, DOROTHY. The manifest content of dreams: A challenge to social science. *Amer. Anthropologist*, 1952, 54, 469-485.

GEORGE, A. L. Quantitative and qualitative approaches to content analysis. In I. de Sola Pool (Ed.), *Trends in content analysis*, Urbana, Ill.: Univ. Illinois Press, 1959, 7-32.

GUETZKOW, H. Unitizing and categorizing problems in coding qualitative data. *J. clin. Psychol.*, 1950, 6, 47-58.

HARWAY, N. I. and IKER, H. P. Computer analysis of content in psychotherapy. *Psychol. Rep.*, 1964, 14, 720-722.

LASSWELL, H. D. *Propaganda technique in the world war*. New York: Knopf, 1927.

McCURDY, H. G. *The personal world*. New York: Harcourt, Brace, and World, 1961.

MURSTEIN, B. I. *Theory and research in projective techniques*. New York: Wiley, 1963.

NORTH, R. C., HOLSTI, O. R., ZANINOVICH, M. G., and ZINNES, D. A. *Content analysis: A handbook with applications for the study of international crisis*. Evanston, Ill.: Northwestern Univer. Press, 1963.

OSGOOD, C. E. The representation model and relevant research methods. In I. de Sola Pool (Ed.), *Trends in content analysis*, Urbana, Ill.: Univ. Illinois Press, 1959, 33-88.

POOL, I. DE SOLA. (Ed.), *Trends in content analysis*, Urbana, Ill.: Univer. Illinois Press, 1959.

SCHORER, M. Fiction and the "matrix of analogy." *Kenyon Rev.*, 1949, 11, 539-560.

SPURGEON, CAROLINE. *Shakespeare's imagery and what it tells us*. New York: Macmillan, 1935.

STEPHENSON, W. Critique of content analysis. *Psychol. Rec.*, 1963, 13, 155-162.

STONE, P. J., BALES, R. F., NAMENWIRTH, J. Z., and OGILVIE, D. M. The General Inquirer: A computer system for content analysis and retrieval based on the sentence as a unit of information. *Behav. Sci.*, 1962, 7, 1-15.

WHITE, R. K. Black Boy: A value analysis. *J. abnorm. soc. Psychol.*, 1947, *42*, 440-461.

WOLFENSTEIN, MARTHA and LEITES, N. *Movies, a psychological study.* Glencoe, Ill.: Free Press, 1950.

2

The
Content Analysis of Dreams

In the preceding chapter we discussed content analysis in general terms; in this chapter we propose to present some of the reasons why content analysis is applied to dreams. Before addressing ourselves to this question, however, several issues regarding dreams themselves must be investigated.

What is a dream? "A dream is something to look at while you are asleep" is a child's definition of a dream. It is not a bad definition, for it designates two important features of a dream: it occurs during sleep and is a visual experience. We can and do dream in other sensory modes, and people who have been blind from birth or from an early age dream entirely in other modalities, but most dreams are predominantly visual.

They are visual experiences even though the things we dream about are not being presented to our eyes at the time we are dreaming about them. Occasionally, a stimulus from the external world or from one's own body will be incorporated into a dream, but experiments in which the sleeping person is intentionally stimulated show that the stimulus rarely appears in the dream as it is. It is customarily altered in some way to fit into the context of an ongoing dream. The backfiring of a passing auto appears in the dream as the firing of a gun, and a pinched muscle is perceived as a snake that is squeezing one to death.

We have other experiences during sleep besides dreams. While we are falling asleep or waking up, fleeting images may pass before our eyes. The falling asleep imagery is called *hypnogogic;* the waking up imagery is called *hypnopompic.* These images are rarely confused with dreams, however, because a dream has continuity like a play or a movie. It usually tells a story. The sleeping person senses this story-like quality even if he remembers only a fragment or two of the whole dream when he awakens. He feels that the fragments were elements in a much longer experience. A person may remember nothing about a dream and still feel that he has been dreaming. Some dreams are extremely vivid and realistic: yet when a person awakens out of such a dream he knows it was a dream and not a "real" experience. Sometimes he is disappointed that it was not "real," but more often he is relieved.

A dream is like a play in other respects than that of having continuity. It has a setting or settings, props, characters, interactions among characters, and expressive behavior. It even has an audience—the dreamer himself. But the dreamer is also ordinarily a participant as well as an observer. He sees things happening, and at the same time he is in the midst of what is happening. Except for the hallucinations of waking life which are pathological in character, no other experience is like a dream. Not even a daydream bears much resemblance to a night dream. The unique quality of a dream accounts for the fact that everyone, including very young children, appears to know what a dream is. When asked to relate a dream, a person usually does so without question.

Although we have discussed several defining characteristics, we still have not provided a scientifically useful definition of a dream. A dream is a private experience, and private experiences, until they are objectified, cannot be studied scientifically. Dreams have to be reported before they can be studied. Therefore, a dream may be operationally defined as that which a person reports when he is asked to relate a dream, excluding statements which are comments upon or interpretations of the dream. This is the definition we shall follow throughout this book. When we speak of a dream we shall always mean a reported dream unless otherwise stated.

How does a reported dream differ from an experienced dream? About the only difference we can be sure of is that the reported dream consists of words, whereas the experienced dream consists primarily of pictures. The reported dream is a verbal description of a predominantly visual experience. It is like telling a friend about a play or a movie one saw last night. The accuracy of the dreamer's description cannot be estimated, however, because an independent record of the dream cannot be obtained at the present time. Conceivably, advances in instrumentation will eventually permit dreams to be "televized" as they are being dreamed. If this time ever comes, we will no longer have to ask people to tell us their dreams because we can record and study the dream exactly as it was experienced. Meanwhile, the only material that can be analyzed is verbal dream reports.

An investigator may add structure to the situation for reporting dreams by having the dreamer fill out a standard report form (such as the one which is reproduced in Appendix D), by having him answer questions about the dream, by asking the dreamer for his interpretation of the dream, or by asking him to free associate to elements of the dream. Answers to questions, interpretations, or free associations are not part of the dream report *per se,* and should not be confused with it. The dream report is restricted to descriptive statements of the experienced dream. This raises a controversial question regarding dreams, one that is usually traced back to Freud. We refer to the distinction between manifest and latent content of a dream.

Manifest versus latent content. By latent content, Freud meant the dream thoughts; by manifest content, he meant the consciously experienced and remembered dream. Dream thoughts are transformed into the manifest dream by the dream work, which consists of a number of operations such as condensation, displacement, and symbolization. The manifest dream is decomposed into its constituent dream thoughts by having the dreamer free associate to elements of the reported dream.

There are those who maintain that the manifest dream is without significance in its own right; that the "true" meaning of the dream resides in the dream thoughts. Without in any way intending to deny the usefulness of free association in the therapeutic situation or its potency for revealing unconscious material, we feel that the reported dream possesses great psychological significance and that the content analysis of reported dreams is an important tool in personality research. A detailed presentation of our views can be found elsewhere (Hall, 1947, 1953a, 1953b) and will not be reviewed here. Other contemporary dream investigators (Eggan, 1952; Beck and Hurvich, 1959; Jones, 1962; Sheppard and Saul, 1958) have also proceeded on the assumption that reported dreams constitute valuable research material.

As a matter of fact, it could be said that there is no such thing as the latent content of a dream. A dream is a manifest experience, and what is latent lies outside the dream and in the verbal material that the dreamer reports when he is asked to free associate to features of the reported dream. How the psychoanalyst arrives at the "true meaning" or interpretation of the dream from the verbalized associations is more of an art than a technique. This art may be of the utmost value in the therapeutic situation, but being a private, subjective type of activity it is of no direct value for research. Indirectly, of course, it may provide a seedbed of ideas for research which may be carried out when objective methods of verbal analysis have been devised. One can, of course, treat free associations as verbal material, which they are, and apply content analysis to them, just as one applies content analysis to reported dreams. The two records may then be analyzed for the presence of contingencies between them. This method may also be used for making objective, quantitative studies of symbols. One of us (Hall, 1963) has made a brief excursion into this promising area of research.

How does a dream report differ from other types of verbal material? Much of what is spoken or written, whether it be a cry for help, an editorial, or an encyclopedia, is done with the deliberate intention of influencing other people. Such verbal material may be said to be *instrumental* in character. Not all that is spoken or written, however, has as its conscious objective the altering of the behavior of others in some desired direction. Making entries into a diary, for instance, may be an impassioned act with no other intended aim than to portray the writer's feelings. This type of verbal product may be said to be *representational*.

Dream reports may be regarded as being primarily representational in character rather than instrumental. They are reports of something that has been represented in experience; they are not ordinarily contrived as instruments for the purpose of influencing another's behavior. (Parenthetically, it may be pointed out that a dream report is sometimes used for instrumental purposes as when a patient tries to influence his therapist by telling him a particular type of dream or when a wife communicates something to her husband by relating a dream.) Dream reports are not generally self-initiated as so many personal documents are, but are written or told at the specific request of another person. Had they not been asked, very few of our informants would probably have written down their dreams. Reported dreams are descriptive; they are accounts of something that happened to the dreamer, and not something he initiated, intended, influenced, or controlled. Consequently, the dreamer does not accept responsibility for his dreams as he would for something he said or wrote during waking life. In all these respects, reported dreams differ from other types of verbal material.

Since dreams are projections, their use for diagnostic or research purposes may be regarded as a projective method. Dream reports differ from other projective protocols in one important respect, however: they are not given in response to any specifiable stimulus material. They are pure projections, so that in analyzing them one does not face the problem of stimulus control or stimulus pull. In dreaming, a person is supposedly projecting something that is entirely within himself; he is not ordinarily responding to the external perceptual field. In the case of the Rorschach, for example, one can analyze the responses made by the subject in relation to the inkblots and ask such questions as how much of the inkblot was used, how accurate were the responses with respect to form, did the subject respond to color, and so forth. This cannot be done with dreams.

Although there are no identifiable stimuli to which a dream can be referred, one can compare a dream with the external reality represented in the dream and note any discrepancies. Several scales for measuring bizarreness, distortion, and irreality in dreams are described in Chapter 15. In a sense then, the dream's correspondence to the situations and events of waking life is analogous to the percept's similarity to a Rorschach inkblot or the story's correspondence to a TAT picture.

Various hypotheses regarding the differences in the kinds of information secured from dreams and other projective material have been advanced. A favorite hypothesis is that dreams tap deeper levels of personality dynamics than do other projective methods. Although there is some evidence that supports this hypothesis (see Chapter 15), it is probably premature to draw any hard-and-fast conclusions. Much research remains to be done on this and related questions.

Why is the behavioral scientist interested in dreams as research material? Until recently, dreams fell within the province of the healing arts and were not of much interest to researchers. They were considered too subjective and unsubstantial for serious scientific study. With the growth of personality theory and research, the emergence of psychoanalysis as a dominant force in psychology, the invention of projective techniques, the increasing use of personal documents as research material, the development of methods of content analysis of symbolic material, the concern for cognitive behavior, and particularly as a consequence of the discovery of dependable electroencephalographic indicators of dreaming, dreams, which were for so long "out" scientifically, are now suddenly "in." Hundreds of people throughout the world are doing dream research. There is even a professional society of sleep and dream researchers which meets annually and has a membership of several hundred at this writing.

Why are dreams of scientific interest? Probably for the simple reason that, like the Himalayas, they exist. They are a form of behavior to which every healthy adult devotes about an hour and a half each night. Behavior which occupies that much time deserves to be noticed, even if it should prove to have no significance beyond the sleep period.

Whatever status the dream had prior to the discovery of the objective EEG indicators is usually attributed to Freud. There can be no question of his influence in raising the dream to a preeminent position in the practice of psychoanalysis and psychotherapy. Yet it should be acknowledged, as Freud did, that the reason he began to pay attention to dreams was that his patients forced him to. Unbidden, they told him their dreams, and from them and from subsequent analysis of his own dreams, Freud learned to respect their significance and to use them in psychoanalysis.

People have always felt that dreams were important. It is estimated that the most popular book, after the Bible, in the century following the invention of the printing press was Artemidorus's *Oneirocritics*, the Adam of all dream books. Throughout recorded history, people have considered dreams as "different," mysterious, and paranormal; they thought that they were messages from gods, devils, ancestors, other planets, or the unconscious; that they foretold the future; and that they required decoding in order to be understood. "A dream that is not interpreted is like a letter that is not read."

No matter where one travels or whom one visits, an unfailing tie between visitor and host is the subject of dreams. Most primitive groups know about dreams and possess a rich lode of dream lore which they are usually willing to discuss. Dreams are not only a universal topic of conversation; they also seem to be a universal language. They may even cut across the boundaries that separate fetus from neonate, infant from adult, and humans from other animals.

And so what people everywhere have always regarded as being self-evident—namely, that the dream is a significant form of human behavior—is now being recognized by behavioral scientists. Dreams are considered by many to be expressions of the deepest levels and most remote recesses of the human mind. Some even believe that they contain traces of phylogenetic development. They are often regarded as the means by which the unlived lines of personality seek fulfillment. Dreams are said to be a record of a person's past or a portent of his future. They are proclaimed to be a "forgotten language," a "mirror of the conscience," or a reflection of the synthesizing capacity of the ego. They are thought to be as necessary to man's welfare as sleep itself.

However they may be regarded, the simple fact remains that dreams are there for man to be curious about. He needs no other justification for studying them. Their full significance will be determined by investigation and not by rhetoric or speculation. It is through the introduction of a comprehensive classification system for content analysis and the publication of normative material derived from its use that this book will make a contribution to the growth of a dependable body of knowledge about dreams.

Why does one make a content analysis of dreams? Content analysis is applied to dreams, as it is to other verbal or symbolic material, in order to obtain quantitative measures. This is achieved by devising a standard, comprehensive, and reliable classificatory system which yields scores, frequencies, rates, proportions, or other numerical expressions and indices.

These quantitative measures may then be employed in a variety of scientific enterprises. We will mention only a few. (1) The dreams of people differing in age, sex, ethnic group, pathology, or any other discriminable attribute may be compared for content classes and the significance of the obtained differences statistically evaluated. (2) The influence of natural or experimental variables upon dreams can be determined. For example, the investigator may wish to know whether the temperature of the sleeping quarters affects dreams. In order to show that it does, a significant change in some measurable feature of the dream must be demonstrated. Or if he wants to know whether some experience during the day can influence dreams that night, he will have to demonstrate its influence in quantitatively expressed variables. (3) What changes in dreams take place over a period of time or during the course of psychotherapy? In order to answer this question, some form of numerical index must be available for mirroring the changes, if any. (4) In what respects do dreams give the same, and in what respects do they give different, information from other devices used to assess personality? In order to determine the nature of the relationships between dreams and objective or projective personality tests, quantified measures of dream content are essential. (5) Does the behavior of the dreamer in his dreams correspond to his behavior in waking life? Does an aggressive person have aggressive dreams, and a depressed person depressed dreams? If he experiences much failure in his dreams, does he experience much failure in waking life? These and numerous other questions of a similar sort are best answered by having reliable measures of dream behavior and waking life behavior. (6) In order to test hypotheses derived from a particular personality theory, theoretical scales for analyzing dreams must be constructed which will measure the variables under investigation. (7) Finally, we would mention the tremendous scientific usefulness of appropriate norms for dreams expressed in numerical terms. Norms are almost a scientific *sine qua non* for any type of behavior research.

There is another imperative and immediate reason why methods of quantitative content analysis should be developed and applied to dreams. Since the discovery of the objective indicators of dreaming by Aserinsky and Kleitman (1953), research on dreams has become scientifically respectable. It is now known that every individual dreams; he actually spends approximately twenty percent of his sleeping time engaged in dreaming. The pattern of dreaming is a cyclical one throughout sleep. Dream periods occur with surprising regularity, their timing being such that approximately ninety minutes elapse between the onset of each successive dream period. Their duration may range from a few minutes to as long as an hour, and they tend to increase in length as sleep progresses.

This knowledge of dreaming behavior has been made possible by the revolutionary instrumentation break-through provided by the EEG. Tangible traces of the dream are inked out on the unfolding EEG record and constitute a permanent record of its periodic presence. The dream investigator can feel quite sure that he will obtain a dream if he awakens his sleeping subject when the EEG record indicates the joint appearance of rapid eye movements and stage 1 brain wave activity. Recent studies indicate that various physiological changes such as irregular breathing and variation in heartbeat (Snyder, 1963), and loss of muscle tonus in the throat region (Berger, 1961), also accompany dream periods.

These giant informational strides forward in the physiological domain have greatly outpaced the contributions forthcoming from psychological studies. Research efforts on the psychological aspects of dreaming have been hobbled because of a dearth of suitable measurement devices for dealing with the material of the dream in any objective or quantitative fashion. There have been only a few scattered attempts by others to construct scales for scoring dreams, and these have, for the most part, dealt with isolated dimensions. See Chapter 15 for a survey of these scales. What is needed is a comprehensive scoring system which will encompass within its purview all the main features of the dream. It has been our intent to provide such a system.

In bringing this chapter to a close we would like once more to reassure the reader that the application of objective, quantitative methods to qualitative productions need not misrepresent or distort them as long as the investigator respects the inherent properties of the material with which he is working—whether it be a dream, a story, or a painting—and does not try to impose an inappropriate system of content analysis upon it. The system of classification should grow out of the material and reflect its intrinsic nature. It is hoped that the scientist will try to analyze creative productions with the same amount of sensitivity used by their creator. If he does remain sensitive, intuitive, and empathic, then the scientist's effort to quantify qualitative material can be a rewarding exercise in disciplined, precise, critical thinking, and the outcome of the effort a contribution to knowledge.

REFERENCES

ASERINSKY, E. and KLEITMAN, N. Regularly occurring periods of eye motility, and concomitant phenomena during sleep. *Science,* 1953, *118,* 273-274.

BECK, A. T. and HURVICH, M. S. Psychological correlates of depression. I. Frequency of "masochistic" dream content in a private practice sample. *Psychosom. Med.,* 1959, *21,* 50-55.

BERGER, R. Tonus of extrinsic laryngeal muscles during sleep and dreaming. *Science,* 1961, *134,* 840.

EGGAN, DOROTHY. The manifest content of dreams: A challenge to social science. *Amer. Anthropologist,* 1952, *54,* 469-485.

HALL, C. S. Diagnosing personality by the analysis of dreams. *J. abnorm. soc. Psychol.,* 1947, *42,* 68-79.

HALL, C. S. A cognitive theory of dream symbols. *J. gen. Psychol.,* 1953a, *48,* 169-186.

HALL, C. S. A cognitive theory of dreams. *J. gen. Psychol.,* 1953b, *49,* 273-282.

HALL, C. S. Strangers in dreams: an empirical confirmation of the Oedipus complex. *J. Pers.,* 1963, *31,* 336-345.

JONES, R. M. *Ego synthesis in dreams.* Cambridge, Mass.: Schenkman, 1962.

SNYDER, F. The new biology of dreaming. *Arch. Gen. Psychiat.,* 1963, *8,* 381-391.

SHEPPARD, E. and SAUL, L. J. An approach to a systematic study of ego function. *Psychoanal. Quart.,* 1958, *27,* 237-245.

3

A Classification System
for the
Content Analysis of Dreams

The classification system that we are presenting in this book for the content analysis of dreams is primarily an empirical one, although we will also describe several theoretical scales. It has been our intention to make the system a comprehensive one so that it would be possible to score virtually all aspects of a dream. We wanted it to be empirical and comprehensive so that it could accommodate itself to many different kinds of research on dreams. Sixteen different empirical scales and three theoretical scales will be presented in subsequent chapters.

Formulation of Empirical Classes. The broad empirical classes are settings and objects; characters; their activities and interactions with each other and with the environment; their emotions, and the qualities and attributes which are used to describe people, things, and events. It was brought out in Chapter 1 that there are no established rules for the formulation of classes. It is pretty much the investigator's choice. Consequently, the system to be presented in this book represents our choice, although we suspect that anyone who started out to devise a set of empirical groups in dreams would come out with approximately the same broad headings we did. The formulation of classes was guided by the following considerations.

(1) We did not begin to formulate any classes within the broad headings until we were thoroughly conversant with dreams from having read and studied a large number of dream reports.

(2) No class of items which was represented fairly frequently in dreams was omitted. On the other hand, some classes which have low frequencies were included either because they were needed to fill out a total set of classes under a given rubric or because, in spite of their infrequency, they were regarded as having psychological significance.

(3) We attempted to select classes which would possess psychological significance. We tried to choose classes that would reflect dimensions or aspects of personality that would appear in almost any theoretical position and which we thought would be considered relevant by any theorist. This is a matter of judgment. Whether our judgment was good or bad will be revealed by the results obtained using the system.

(4) The classes should have a high degree of inter-scorer agreement. This is a necessary criterion because if two independent scorers cannot agree a good proportion of the time, the variance in scores is determined more by the scorer than by the conditions under investigation. We could not always tell beforehand what the reliability of a class would be. Many times we could improve the reliability of scoring by defining the class more carefully and by giving a larger number of scoring rules and examples. Sometimes we had to abandon the class when efforts to improve scorer reliability failed. (A presentation of inter-scorer reliability measures for our scales will be found in Chapter 13.)

Formulation of Theoretical Scales. In addition to the empirical scales, we have formulated and are presenting· some theoretical scales. A theoretical scale is one that purports to measure a theoretical concept such as regression, style of life, separation anxiety, archetype, needs, ego identity, and so forth. By contrast with the empirical scales, the number of possible theoretical scales is endless. Three theoretical scales which we have developed have been included in this book in order to illustrate the special problems of constructing such scales. Theoretical scales developed by other investigators are discussed in Chapter 15.

The most important initial step in constructing a theoretical scale is for the investigator to formulate as many classes of dream events as he can which presumably represent the concept under investigation. Unless he has considerable familiarity with dreams, he may formulate classes which just do not occur or occur so rarely in dreams that they will not serve his purpose. The investigator must also be thoroughly conversant with the theoretical framework underlying the particular concept he wishes to measure. There are no theoretical concepts in dream reports. There is no ego strength, no complex, no masculine protest, no N Ach, no valence, or no self. Concepts are in the mind of the investigator. In order to use dreams in investigations that pertain to theoretical concepts, the investigator has to find something in the dream report that represents the concept.

It is conceivable that reported dreams cannot be used as empirical material in the investigation of some theoretical concepts. This would be the case when the investigator cannot find any representation of the concept in the reported dreams. It may be that dreams are more useful for investigating the concepts of some theories than of others. Since so much of the theory of psychoanalysis grew out of the analysis of dreams, it is not surprising that psychoanalytic concepts seem to be prominently represented in dreams. In the same way, the TAT and Murray's theory of personality are *en rapport*. The difference between the TAT and dreams, however, is that Murray and Morgan selected the TAT picture in order to accommodate a theory of personality, whereas Freud did not invent the dream as a mirror for his theory of personality. Presumably, he wrenched his theory out of dreams and other material supplied by his patients, as well as from self-observation.

In constructing theoretical scales, the investigator is sometimes tempted to use global ratings in place of specific classes. We prefer the use of specific classes to global ratings. If a judge is asked to rate a dream for ego strength, he must have some idea of what the investigator means by ego strength. If the investigator is going to specifically define ego strength, as he must do, in terms of what is actually in the dream, he might just as well operationally define scoring categories and employ scorers instead of asking for global ratings from judges. We suspect that global ratings are used for "convenience," because the investigator is hesitant to undertake the disciplined work of formulating scoring categories. Although there are times when ratings are the only way by which one can obtain quantitative estimates of certain variables, viz., clarity of a dream, its degree of pleasantness, or other variables which the *dreamer* alone can estimate, we feel that for other types of variables it is more relevant to spell out the operational definitions of the concept and to score and tabulate the indicators of the concept according to precisely stated rules.

Types of reported dreams. In attempting validational work with content scales, an important consideration will be the type of dreams used for analysis. Some investigators have been satisfied to ask for a single dream from each subject. If such a procedure is followed, it has been our experience that a nightmare or an especially dramatic or unusual dream is much more likely to be reported. One would be given an erroneous impression of typical dream content if such a restricted sample of dreaming were examined. Another technique that is sometimes followed is to analyze dream records from clinician's files. Biased sampling may occur in such a situation because all the reported dreams may not have been recorded, those that were recorded may not have been done so in their entirety, and selective theoretical biases may have influenced the manner in which they were recorded by the therapist.

With the advent of the objective EEG indicators of dreaming, many investigators are obtaining their dream samples by continually awakening subjects throughout the night and tape recording their dream reports following each REM awakening. Although additional studies are needed, preliminary work by ourselves and by Domhoff (1962) suggests that dream reports obtained in this fashion do not differ in any important respects from those written to describe dreams that are recalled sometime after arising in the morning. However, since some differences in aggressive and oral content have been noted between these two types of dream report, normative material based upon one type of report may not be appropriate to use for other types of dream reports.

In order to secure normative material for the scales described in this book, we selected folders—each of which contained a series of 12-16 dreams—that had been obtained from college students between the ages of 19-25. All the dreams were written on a standard form. The students had turned in these dreams as part of an optional class assignment. Five dream reports which met the criterion of being between 50-300 words in length were randomly selected from the dream series folders of 100 male students and 100 female students. These 1000 dreams were then analyzed by means of the various content scales which appear in the subsequent chapters. The normative material based upon these analyses is reported in Chapter 14. We strongly urge that the characteristics of our subject population and the manner of collecting reports be kept in mind when utilizing these normative figures.

The limits of a dream. Regardless of what constitutes the form of dream report—clinician's notes, tape-recorded account following a REM awakening, or a self-written report—one problem that remains for the content analyst is that of disentangling the description of the dream itself from the general comments that the dreamer makes about his reactions to the dream. Our procedure is to score only those statements which refer to the dream itself. Thus, if a dream report contains the introductory remark, "I was mad at my boyfriend and thinking about him before I fell asleep," we do not score this as part of the dream proper. Neither do we score explanatory comments appearing in the body or at the conclusion of the dream report, if they refer to events outside of the dream. The Negative Scale provides the only exception to not scoring such comments. This is so because we think that the use of negating words is important in any communication provided by the reporter, and such stylistic preferences in descriptive material should be scored regardless of what is being described.

On the basis of our experience in working with the particular scales presented in this book and with dreams in general, we will offer several suggestions as to how one might proceed to score dreams using our classification system.

Procedure for scoring dreams. If possible, the dreams should be typed on 5″ by 8″ cards with explanatory comments about the dream indicated by enclosure within parentheses. This size card is easy to handle and can be readily stored. The convenience and saving of time involved in working with a typed report will be quickly appreciated when the investigator is required to read the dream repeatedly as the different scales are taken up in turn. A 5″ by 8″ scoring card is also helpful to use and can be filed next to the dream report card. The type of scoring card we have developed for this purpose is illustrated in Appendix B.

In scoring dreams, we generally prefer to score a unit of 50 dreams on each scale. After having experimented with various approaches, we have decided that it is better to score across all 50 dreams for a particular scale than it is to score across all scales for a single dream. In this way, a scoring "set" for the particular scale can be acquired, and the various scoring rules or scoring exceptions can be kept in mind as one goes through an extensive series of dreams. We would advocate that the sequence of scoring follow the same sequence of scale presentation found in the subsequent chapters. Some scales are closely enough related so that the scorer may read the report with a set for two or more related scales simultaneously.

Our suggestion would be that scoring follow the scale grouping and sequence printed below:

1. Setting and Objects
2. Characters
3. Aggressive, Friendly, and Sexual Interactions
4. Activities
5. Success, Failure, Misfortune, and Good Fortune
6. Emotions
7. Modifiers
8. Temporal, Negative, and Oral
9. Castration

Before beginning to score for a particular scale, the description of the scale, the illustrative examples, and special rules for that scale should be thoroughly studied. After some familiarity with the scale has been developed in this fashion, the scorer should next attempt to score the dreams appearing in Appendix B. By doing so, he can compare his scoring with that listed for the dreams. Hopefully, any uncertainties he experiences as to why the dream was scored in that particular way will be resolved by reading the description of the scoring rationale which accompanies each dream. An additional advantage of scoring the dreams in Appendix B is that practice is provided with an actual set of dreams before embarking on the final scoring of the investigator's dreams. It may also be helpful to survey the normative figures contained in Chapter 14 so that an approximate idea of the frequency with which different subclasses appear can be gained. This will enable the investigator to gauge whether he appears to be over or under scoring any of the dream elements.

Following these various "warm-up" exercises, the investigator should now be in a position to proceed with the actual scoring of his dream sample. After scoring a unit of 50 dreams, the careful researcher will rescore the first ten or so dreams of the unit to insure that the scoring set he evolved toward the completion of the unit did not differ from the one he had when he started the unit.

Probably the initial reaction of the prospective scorer as he thumbs through the pages of the scoring manuals presented in Chapters 4-12 is one of dismay. At first glance, the scales may appear complicated and elusive to grasp. It is true that they are rather comprehensive and detailed, because they are intended to reflect the multifaceted material that makes up the fabric of a dream. However, our experience has been that a new scorer can learn to use the scales with surprising ease. One factor contributing to this is that there is considerable overlap between the scales. Once the scoring of characters has been learned, for example, this knowledge is used on nine other scales. The method of scoring interactions is identical whether aggressive, friendly, sexual, physical, or verbal interactions are involved. In the same way, the scoring paradigm is similar for emotions, misfortunes, good fortunes, success, failure, and most of the classes in activities. Duplication of scoring format is also present for most of the remaining scales.

There will be infrequent occasions when a scorer will be confronted with a scoring problem that does not seem to be handled by the manuals. Since dreams are vehicles for the expression of such an infinite variety of plots and the elements within them are not required to conform to the usual logical requirements of time and space, it is not possible to anticipate every scoring mutation which might appear within a dream report. Even if it were, the cataloguing of sufficient scoring rules to handle all these situations would require a book many times the size of this present one. We have sought to include enough information in each scale to provide for ready scoring of the fairly obvious and frequently represented elements. We have also tried to strike a reasonable balance between including so many rules that the system becomes cumbersome and yet trying to provide sufficient material so that a "feel" for the scale would be developed which could be generalized to situations not specifically covered in the manual.

It will be noted in looking through the scoring manuals that all of the scoring symbols consist of capital letters or marks that are found on a regular typewriter. Although over 100 scoring symbols exist, exclusive of the several hundred character combinations possible, no duplication of a scoring symbol appears within or between any scale. Due to these features, it is possible to have the entire classification system punched on IBM cards and thereby take advantage of mechanical data processing procedures.

REFERENCES

DOMHOFF, G. W. A quantitative study of dream content using an objective indicator of dreaming. Ph.D. dissertation, University of Miami, 1962.

4

The Classification and Scoring of Physical Surroundings

SETTINGS

In the second chapter, an analogy between a dream and a stage production was suggested. If we were to view a play, the first thing we would notice when the curtain goes up is the setting of the play. The back-drops may be painted and arranged to suggest the interior of a home or a garden scene. In rare cases, the stage may be bare. Almost all dreams take place in some form of recognizable setting, and the dreamer frequently begins the description of his dream by saying something about the setting. In the same way that there are often several acts and scenes to a play, so, too, is it common for the setting to change during the course of a dream, although this shift in dream background may be an abrupt one.

In initial efforts to classify settings, our breakdown included a rather extensive number of possible settings. Since it was difficult to obtain adequate inter-scorer agreement when such a large number were involved, we eventually collapsed all settings into two broad groupings—indoor and outdoor settings.

Indoor settings consist of those in which the dreamer is within a building. The building may be a house, hotel, church, factory, barracks, or some other structure. Any room such as a living room, cellar, or attic is therefore an indoor setting, as are offices, elevators, hallways, stairs, or other regions within buildings. Also considered indoor settings are those areas attached to or part of the exterior of a building. Examples of the latter which would be scored as indoor settings are instances where the dreamer is located on a porch, roof, fire escape, or ledge of a building. Open-air buildings such as amphitheaters or stadiums are also scored as indoor settings. The scoring symbol for indoor settings is I.

Outdoor settings are those where the dreamer is described as being out-of-doors or outside a building. Settings occurring in nature, such as when the dreamer is at the beach, in the woods, or on a mountain, are included, as well as urban settings, such as streets, sidewalks, yards, parking lots, and cemeteries. The setting is considered an outside one if the dreamer is in a car, train, boat or airplane, unless the car is in a garage or the airplane is in a hangar. Being in a tunnel or cave is scored as an outdoor setting. The scoring symbol for outdoor settings is O.

The decision as to whether a setting should be scored I or O is generally not a difficult one, and a high level of scoring agreement can be readily achieved for the distinction between them.

In a few cases, it appears that a setting is definitely present, but it cannot be determined whether it should be scored I or O because the dreamer has not supplied sufficient information. For instance, he might say, "We went to the country club," and it is not clear whether the dreamer is referring to some sort of building or whether he means the golf course, tennis area, or swimming pool. We handle these infrequent cases by scoring such settings as ambiguous and indicate this by the scoring symbol A.

An even more infrequent situation is the one in which no setting is described. Short dreams or those which seem to be only some fragment of a longer dream are the ones most likely not to contain any setting. These dreams are scored with the symbol NS which stands for no setting. The presence of any object or description of any surroundings, no matter how vague, is sufficient to warrant some type of setting score, other than NS.

Having determined the locale of the dream, the next phase of scoring settings involves determining the degree of familiarity that the dreamer reports for the setting. Five levels of familiarity are distinguished in our scoring system.

Familiar settings (Scoring symbol: F) are those in which it appears quite clear that the dreamer recognizes the setting as being a personally familiar one, such as his own or a friend's home, place of employment, or worship. If the setting is a well-known or famous one which the dreamer can identify, such as the Empire State Building, Mt. Everest, or Arlington Cemetery, it is scored as being a familiar setting, even though the dreamer may never have been there. Thus, if the dreamer is able specifically to identify a setting or indicates that he has prior acquaintance with it, an F score is given.

Distorted settings (Scoring symbol: D) are familiar settings which the dreamer indicates involve an element of peculiarity or incongruity because they differ in some respect from the way the dreamer knows the setting to be in waking life. Scoring is fairly liberal for this category so that a setting containing any distortion, even of a minor nature, is scored D. The distortion, however, must involve the physical surroundings rather than the appearance of any character. *The D score takes precedence over any other setting score.*

Geographical settings (Scoring symbol: G) are those in which the dreamer identifies the settings according to their geographical location, such as Europe, Illinois, or San Francisco. If the dreamer also indicates that the setting is a personally familiar one, the F scoring is given precedence over the G scoring.

Unfamiliar settings (Scoring symbol: U) are those which are not known to the dreamer. Sometimes the dreamer will be very explicit and state that the setting is a place he has never seen or visited before, or sometimes the adjective "strange" will be used to indicate that the setting is not recognized as a familiar one. In other instances, the vague description of the setting will often reveal the lack of familiarity. Statements showing this vague quality are: "I was in some house," "I was driving down the street of a large city," "We went to what looked like a hotel," "The furniture suggested this was a kitchen where we were talking." If the scorer can answer yes to the question, "Does the description of the setting strongly suggest that the dreamer has not actually been in this setting in his waking life," the setting is scored U. It should be kept in mind that the scoring will not always be U if the dreamer has never been in the setting in waking life for if the setting is a famous one it is scored F, if it is referred to as some specific geographical location it is scored G, and if there is something incongruous about the arrangement of the setting it is scored D.

Questionable settings (Scoring symbol: Q) are scored when it cannot be determined whether the setting is a familiar or unfamiliar one. The description provided in the dream report is often insufficient to establish the familiarity or unfamiliarity of a setting with any degree of assurance, so Q is a frequently employed score.

Scoring settings is generally fairly easy. Deciding whether a setting should be scored U or Q and determining the total number of settings are the scoring problems which pose the greatest difficulty. In order to illustrate the various combinations of scores which may occur, a list of examples is provided below.

Examples

IF	"I was in MY ROOM getting dressed."
ID	"It looked like my HISTORY CLASSROOM EXCEPT THE DESKS WERE OF KINDERGARTEN SIZE."
IG	"I looked out the hotel window and saw NEW YORK CITY below."
IU	"We were in what seemed to be A CELLAR."
IQ	"I was IN A STORE buying a pair of shoes."
OF	"I was yelling from OUR NEIGHBOR'S DRIVEWAY."
OD	"I was in OUR BACKYARD BUT THE BIG OAK TREE WAS MISSING."

OG	"We were swimming AT SOME HAWAIIAN BEACH."
OU	"The path THROUGH THESE UNFAMILIAR LOOKING WOODS was a very crooked one."
OQ	"THE FOOTBALL FIELD we were playing on was muddy."
AF	"THE VIEW OF THE EIFFEL TOWER was magnificent."
AD	"I WAS BACK AT COLLEGE BUT IT LOOKED MORE LIKE MY HIGH SCHOOL."
AG	"I WAS BACK SOMEWHERE IN VERMONT again."
AU	"I COULDN'T TELL MUCH ABOUT MY SURROUNDINGS BUT I KNEW I HAD NEVER BEEN THERE BEFORE."
AQ	"I was sitting ON TOP OF A FLAG POLE."
NS	"ALL I COULD SEE WAS THIS OLD LADY WHO KEPT SCOWLING AT ME. THAT WAS THE WHOLE DREAM."

DETERMINING THE NUMBER OF SETTINGS

The rules for determining the number of settings are given below along with scoring examples. Consistent with the format to appear throughout the following chapters, items to be scored will appear in capital letters while items which may seem relevant, but which should not be scored, are italicized.

1. In order for a setting to be scored, the dreamer must appear as an observer in the setting. Do not score settings in which other characters are located unless the dreamer appears as an observer in the same place.

Examples

"I was walking through what I thought were THE STREETS OF NEW ORLEANS (OG)."
"He said that he and my other fraternity brothers had gone for a drive through *the streets of New Orleans.*"

2. All changes in location within a single building are scored as a single indoor setting. Changes in location from one building to a different building are scored as separate indoor settings.

Examples

"I stopped IN THE TODDLE HOUSE (IF) for a cup of coffee and
   then went to A BEAUTY PARLOR (IQ) to get my hair done."
"We hunted for it IN THE ATTIC (IQ) then went downstairs and
   continued the search in the *rooms on the second floor* and finally
   wound up looking *in the cellar* but without any success."

3. If any type of scorable intervening setting occurs, the same indoor location may be scored more than once.

Examples

"We quickly packed a lunch AT DOROTHY'S HOUSE (IF), then
   drove for a while IN THE COUNTRY (OQ) and returned to
   DOROTHY'S HOUSE (IF) and listened to records."
"I left the LIVING ROOM OF THIS OLD GLOOMY HOUSE
   (IU), walked THROUGH THE STRANGE GARDEN OUT-
   SIDE (OU), and then for some reason returned again to THE
   HOUSE (IU) and walked through the back door."

4. Outdoor settings are scored separately if they involve clearly differentiated and separate regions. If the dreamer is describing different areas of a larger region, a single overall outdoor setting is scored.

Examples

"We attended the burial at THE CATHOLIC CEMETERY (OF),
   then drove off to SOME NEARBY SMALL TOWN (OQ) to
   talk."
"As I was walking THROUGH SOME FOREST (OU) I came across

a *group of pine trees,* then I walked through a *grove of aspen* and further on through a small *stand of junipers.*"

5. If any type of scorable intervening setting occurs, the same outdoor location may be scored more than once.

Example

"We were surfing at SOME BEACH THAT I COULDN'T RECOG-NIZE (OU) when the scene shifted to some STRANGE ROOM THAT HAD PAINTINGS ALL OVER THE WALLS (IU), and then I was back surfing at the SAME BEACH (OU) again."

6. In order for an additional setting to be scored, some action should take place within the new setting or the dreamer must describe himself as actually being located in the new setting.

Examples

"AFTER WALKING IN THE RAIN (OQ) for what seemed a long time, I ARRIVED AT MY FRIEND'S HOME AND WENT INSIDE TO GET DRY (IF)."

"AFTER WALKING IN THE RAIN (OQ) for what seemed a long time, *I arrived at my friend's home.*"

OBJECTS

The settings of the dream provide the general background against which the various dream activities are viewed. In order to provide a more detailed picture of the physical surroundings which the dreamer creates for the enactment of his nightly dramatic productions, attention must also be paid to the various "props" that remain on the stage or are introduced as the play proceeds. These "props" are classified under the heading of objects.

An object is a thing. It has tangibility, palpability, and dimensionality. It also has definite physical boundaries or limits. Intangibles such as air, wind, fog, and sky are excluded by such considerations as are songs or sounds which have temporal boundaries but not physical ones. Locations such as cities, streets, rooms, and lakes have physical boundaries and are consequently classified as objects. In some cases, a thing such as a building which is always scored as an object may also be scored as a setting if the dreamer indicates he was engaged in some activity within the building. Persons and animals are not scored as objects because they are handled separately under the classification of characters, but parts of persons and animals are treated as objects.

Since any object we encounter in waking life can be represented in dreams, and some items may also show up in dreams that we would be startled to see with our eyes open, the problem of formulating a system for the classification of objects is a difficult one. The number of possible groupings could be very large if one chose to categorize by reference to size, shape, color, weight, age, composition, ownership, location, function, and other qualities that could readily be suggested. After several arrangements had been tried, we finally settled on a system which includes twelve broad classes, three of which are further subdivided, plus a miscellaneous class. All objects that appear in dreams are therefore classifiable under one of these headings. These classes are presented below.

ARCHITECTURE

Architecture refers to buildings or structures and their component parts. Seven different subclasses of architecture are scored. The first letter of the scoring symbol for architecture is A which is followed by a second letter to indicate the class. The first four classes deal with entire buildings or units within buildings while the next two deal with small component parts of buildings. Any architectural object not included in these six classes is scored in the subclass of miscellaneous architecture.

Residential (Scoring symbol: AR). This subclass is composed of all buildings and units of buildings (rooms) that are used for residential purposes. It includes house, mansion, castle, palace, cabin, shack, hut, tent, and other type of private dwelling place. It also includes apartment house, dormitory, hotel, motel, inn, and other types of multiple dwelling places in which people reside temporarily or permanently. In addition to obvious residential rooms such as bedrooms and living rooms, AR also includes hallways and stairways as well as levels within a residential building such as the second floor, downstairs, and basement.

Vocational (Scoring symbol: AV). This subclass includes buildings and rooms in buildings devoted mainly to business transactions, manufacturing, employment, or education. What such buildings share in common is that they are primarily concerned with work or vocational activities. Included is any type of store, factory, and office. Classroom buildings and classrooms are also scored as vocational because of their implied work emphasis; other educational buildings such as school dormitories, cafeterias, and chapels are classified under other headings. Banks are included in the money class. Home workshops and study rooms are not included here. They are scored AR.

Entertainment (Scoring symbol: AE). This subclass covers buildings and rooms that are used for recreation, entertainment, sports, or other pleasurable activities. Included are restaurant, cafeteria, diner, bar, nightclub, casino, dance hall, theater, museum, art gallery, bowling alley, stadium, gymnasium, and indoor swimming pool. Recreation or hobby rooms in a home are not included in this subclass; they are scored AR.

Institutional (Scoring symbol: AI). This subclass is composed of buildings or units within them that society maintains for collective action in dealing with social or governmental problems. Such buildings are therefore generally supported by taxes or subscription. Included are hospital, infirmary, jail, penitentiary, court house, government building, military building, and church, as well as the units within them such as surgery room, cell, court room, tax collector's office, and choir loft.

Details (Scoring symbol: AD). This subclass consists of all parts of a room or smaller units of a building not usually regarded as separate rooms. Included are door, window, wall, ceiling, fireplace, aisle, steps, and floor. In the last example, floor refers to the walked-on surface of a room, not to a level within a building. It does not matter what type of building is involved; a house door, restaurant door, or church door are all scored as AD. In addition to internal components, architectural details also include those structures viewed from outside a building such as roof, chimney, spire, belfry, ledge, balcony, railing, fire escape, shutters, arch, and column.

Building Materials (Scoring symbol: AB). Included in this subclass are those objects used to construct buildings such as boards, lumber, bricks, concrete blocks, and cement.

Miscellaneous (Scoring symbol: AM). Any building or part of a building which cannot be classified within the preceding architectural groupings would be included here. Some examples are tower, dam, and fountain.

HOUSEHOLD

(Scoring symbol: HH). Contained within this class are all objects frequently encountered in a household setting. Included are furniture such as table, chair, and bed; appliances such as stove, refrigerator, and vacuum cleaner; furnishings such as rug, drapes, and lamp; and supplies such as sheet, lightbulb, and soap. Silverware, dinner ware, and cooking utensils are scored HH. Examples of other objects scored HH are broom, clock, scissors, needle, safety pin, thermometer, medicines, cosmetics, bottle, mirror, faucet, rope, garbage can, and hose. Office furniture and furnishings are also considered HH.

FOOD

(Scoring symbol: FO). Both food and drink are scored in this class. Included are all forms of food or drink whether on the shelf of a store, in a refrigerator, in a container, on a plate, or on the table. It does not include food that is growing. Growing food is scored in the nature class. It does include general terms such as groceries, drinks, and things to eat, but not a reference to a meal or to eating without any specification as to what the meal consisted of or what was eaten. Grocery store and meat market are scored as AV, restaurant and cafeteria are scored as AE, dining room as AR, and dining room table as HH.

IMPLEMENTS

Three subclasses of implements are scored. The first letter of the scoring symbol for implements is I to which a second letter is attached to indicate the subclass.

Tools (Scoring symbol: IT). This subclass includes tools, machinery, and machinery parts. Objects that are used in vocational activities are generally included here, although some such as typewriter are scored in the communication class. Examples of the IT subclass are hammer, nail, saw, screwdriver, wrench, pliers, shovel, rake, lawn mower, lathe, X-ray machine, jack, lever, and starting button of a machine. Household appliances are scored in the household class and parts of conveyances are scored in the travel class.

Weapons (Scoring symbol: IW). This subclass consists of such weapons as gun, club, sword, grenade, missiles, or bomb. Tanks and bombers are scored here rather than in the travel class.

Recreation (Scoring symbol: IR). This subclass incorporates sporting goods such as baseball bat, tennis racquet, balls, ice skates, and fishing pole; objects used in playing games such as cards, checkers, and dice; and toys such as dolls, miniature trucks, and blocks. This subclass also includes musical instruments.

TRAVEL

(Scoring symbol: TR). Encompassed within this class are all forms of conveyance such as car, truck, bus, streetcar, subway, train, boat, airplane, bicycle, elevator, and escalator. Parts of a conveyance such as wheel, brakes, motor, windshield, and propeller are also included. In addition, objects associated with travel such as bus depot, train station, airport, license plate, passenger ticket, and luggage are scored TR.

STREETS

(Scoring symbol: ST). Covered within this class are all types of roadways by which a person can go from one place to another. Included are street, highway, road, path, trail, alley, sidewalk, driveway, intersection, bridge, and train tracks.

REGIONS

(Scoring symbol: RG). This class primarily takes in all land areas that are limited by some form of boundaries. It includes city, village, block, square, parking lot, yard, park, playing field, lot, cemetery, farm, college campus, and military camp. Also considered as regions are water areas whose boundaries have been established by man, such as outdoor swimming pools and reservoirs.

NATURE

(Scoring symbol: NA). This class consists of all outdoor objects that exist in nature. Included are all forms of plant life such as tree, flower, and grass; terrain such as mountain, plateau, cliff, cave, valley, field, meadow, swamp, and forest; natural bodies of water such as ocean, lake, pond, river, and waterfall; weather elements such as rain, snow, hail, and ice; heavenly bodies such as sun, moon, star, and planet; earth and its mineral products such as ground, soil, dirt, clay, mud, sand, pebbles, rocks, iron ore, gold ore, crude diamonds, rubies, or other gems. Growing fruits or vegetables are NA, but fruits or vegetables prepared for eating are FO. Similarly, water or ice as it appears in nature is NA, but a glass of water intended for drinking is scored FO.

BODY PARTS

Both human and animal parts are included under this heading. Five subclasses of body parts are scored. The first letter of the scoring symbol is B which is followed by a second letter to indicate the subclass.

Head (Scoring symbol: BH). This subclass is composed of all visible body parts in the head region. It includes head, neck, throat, face, hair, horns, eyes, beak, nose, mouth, lips, tongue, real and false teeth, jaw, ears, and beard.

Extremities (Scoring symbol: BE). All extremities of the body such as leg, arm, tail, and fin as well as parts of extremities such as finger, hand, elbow, toe, foot, knee, and claw are included in this subclass.

Torso (Scoring symbol: BT). All visible parts of the torso such as shoulders, chest, abdomen, hips, side, and back are included in this subclass. Terms such as body, build, and physique are scored BT.

Anatomy (Scoring symbol: BA). This subclass contains internal body parts, both bony and visceral, and includes such parts as skull, ribs, leg bone, tonsils, heart, lungs, and intestines. Terms such as insides or guts are scored BA. Also included are body secretions such as blood, perspiration, saliva, and pus. Note should be made of the following grouping before scoring BA.

Sex (Scoring symbol: BS). This subclass embraces all body parts and organs related to reproduction and excretion such as penis, testicles, vagina, clitoris, uterus, pelvis, pubic hair, breasts, nipples, buttocks, and anus. Also included are secretions or products from these organs such as semen, menstrual blood, urine, and feces. Embryo and fetus are scored BS.

CLOTHING

(Scoring symbol: CL). Covered within this class are clothing and parts of clothing. Included are outer garments, underwear, headgear, and footwear, as well as such items as pocket, collar, and button. Accessories that are carried or worn by a person such as handbag, cane, wristwatch, and eyeglasses, and jewelry such as ring, necklace, and ornamental pin are scored CL.

COMMUNICATION

(Scoring symbol: CM). This class is composed of all forms of visual, auditory, and written communications and the means for transmitting them. Included are TV set, movie, photograph, drawing, painting, picture, sculpture, telephone, radio, tape recorder, phonograph, book, magazine, newspaper, letter, telegram, postcard, advertisement, map, and test. Objects used to produce communications such as camera, film, microphone, typewriter, pen, pencil, and paper are also scored CM.

MONEY

(Scoring symbol: MO). This class incorporates money and objects closely associated with money. Included is any type of money in the form of currency and coins; objects that can easily be exchanged for money such as checks, gambling chips, and subway tokens; negotiable objects such as stocks and bonds; records referring to monetary values such as check stubs, bills, receipts, and price tags, and containers for money such as piggy banks, wallets, and change purses. Unless a purse is mentioned as a coin or change purse, it is scored CL because a purse is considered a stylistic accessory that is a receptacle for a wide variety of objects beside money. Bank buildings are scored MO.

MISCELLANEOUS

(Scoring symbol: MS). An object that cannot be included in any of the preceding classes is scored MS.

Scoring Rules   Some objects raise problems as to whether they should be scored in one class or another. Their placement must be decided on the basis of context, usage of the object, and the manner in which it is described. For example, a knife can be used as an aggressive implement (IW) or as cutlery (HH). A key may open a home (HH) or it may start a car (TR). To use rags for household cleaning (HH) is quite different from wearing them for clothing (CL). Thus, objects such as knives, keys, and rags cannot be mechanically assigned to the household class in every instance.

1. Each object is to be assigned to only one class. A knife, for example, cannot be both a household object (HH) and a weapon (IW).

Examples

"My mother said to put the KNIVES (HH) and FORKS (HH) on the TABLE (HH)."
"He kept coming after me with a KNIFE (IW) in his HAND (BE)."

2. Any object that is mentioned in the dream is scored. An object need not be physically present to be scored.

Examples

"I was planning to buy a CAR (TR)."
"We were reading about how they made CHEESE (FO)."

3. If the same object is mentioned several times in a dream, it is only scored once. If two or more similar but different objects of the same type are mentioned, each is scored.

Examples

"I looked at the NECKLACE (CL), passed it along to Jim, and he handed the *necklace* to Walt."
"There was a red BOOK (CM), a blue BOOK (CM), and a yellow BOOK (CM) lying on the FLOOR (AD)."

4. If an object is a part or subunit of a larger unit, each of the subunits as well as the larger unit is scored.

Examples

"His NOSE (BH) was very large for his FACE (BH)."
"The LIVING ROOM (AR) of this HOUSE (AR) was all decorated
in blue."
"The DOOR (AD) to the LIVING ROOM (AR) was made of oak."

5. An object is not scored if it is referred to in a generic
sense, or if the dreamer mentions an object in order to exclude it.

Examples

"I told her that I was eager to finish *school*."
"I got cold *feet* and couldn't go through with it."
"He said it was not a *flower* but a TREE (NA)."

5

The Classification
and Scoring of Characters

The correspondence between a dream and a dramatic production becomes very pronounced when it comes to a consideration of characters. They may be few or many, young or old, male or female, but they are the principal means whereby the plot is developed. It is through their behavior that the story is told or communicated.

The chief character in almost every dream is the dreamer himself. He is an active participant in many of the events that take place, and when he is not participating he is observing what others are doing. Since the dreamer is such a constant factor in almost every dream, we do not list him as a character nor score him among the classes of characters described below. It should be pointed out, however, that in subsequent chapters the dreamer's emotions and his interactions with other characters and with the environment are always classified and scored. Consequently, in those situations he does have his own scoring symbol which is D.

DEFINITION OF A CHARACTER

Characters consist of people, animals, or mythical figures. They are scored as characters when any one of the conditions set forth below can be satisfied. It should be kept in mind that the term character is used to refer both to an individual person or animal and also to a group of such individuals. A couple or a crowd is therefore called a character.

It will be recalled that capital letters are used to indicate scorable items, while italics are used for nonscorable items. In the examples given in this chapter, neither capitals nor italics will be used to designate the dreamer.

1. The character is described as being physically present in the dream.

Examples

"I met a GIRL FRIEND for lunch."
"My FATHER drove me and my BROTHER to school."
"A GIRL was being chased by a GANG OF MEN."
"I saw a DEER and raised my gun to fire."
"A GIANT walked out of the woods."

2. The character is heard or seen by some form of communication but he is not physically present in the dream.

Examples

"I spoke with my WIFE on the telephone."
"LOWELL THOMAS was giving the news on radio."
"I was watching DANNY KAYE on television."
"A telegram arrived from UNCLE FRANK."
"I saw a movie. LASSIE was in it."
"There was a picture of CHRIST on the wall."
"The painting had a LOT OF ANIMALS in it."

3. The character is mentioned in the dream report.

Examples

"The POLICE were supposed to come."

"My FRIENDS were going to meet me at the station."
"My HUSBAND was in New York."
"VAN GOGH is my favorite painter."
"I was saving my money to buy a HORSE."
"I expected to see a GHOST in the old house."

4. A character is referred to in order to establish the ownership of an object or the relationship of the character to another character.

Examples

"I went into my BROTHER'S room."
"My FAMILY'S car is a blue Ford."
"I was wearing my SISTER'S dress."
"I saw GRANT'S tomb."
"The BOYFRIEND of my best FRIEND came to visit me."
"MR. SMITH'S DOG began to bark."

5. A part of the character appears in the dream.

Examples

"I just saw the legs of the BAND MEMBERS marching down the street."
"The head of DONALD DUCK was sticking out of the bag."
"I held my BOYFRIEND'S hand."

Do not score any of the following cases as characters.

1. A character is referred to in a generic sense.

Examples

"*Everyone* has a right to happiness."
"I wonder if *people* believe in *ghosts* anymore."

"*Anyone* can do that."
"*No one* seemed to be reacting but me."
"*Dogs* are friendly *animals.*"

2. A character is referred to in order to establish that it is not that character but another character.

Examples

"I was with another BOY, not my *boyfriend.*"
"It was my OLDER SISTER, not my *younger one.*"
"They were OLD WOMEN, not *witches.*"

3. A character is not mentioned in the dream report but his presence is implied by the action that is described.

Examples

"I heard guns being fired."
"My car was run into by another car."
"The airplane took off and suddenly burst into flames before crashing."

CLASSES OF CHARACTERS

After the characters of a dream have been determined using the foregoing criteria, each scorable character, except animal characters, is classified under each of the four following headings:

1. Number
2. Sex
3. Identity
4. Age

The order of these headings is from the more general to the more specific, and the scoring system for characters used throughout this book always appears in the sequence of: Number, Sex, Identity, and Age.

NUMBER

Number refers to whether a single individual or a group of characters is involved. There may be any number from two to a very large number in a group, but no distinction is made in this scoring system between groups of different sizes.

1. An individual character is one who is described in the dream report as being a separate and distinct entity. This ordinarily means that he is described as doing something or being somebody or having certain characteristics which sets him apart from others.

Examples

"The CLERK showed me a pair of shoes."
"I asked my TEACHER if I could speak to my GIRL FRIEND."
"I was being chased by a WITCH riding a black HORSE."
"ONE DOG was a collie, and the OTHER DOG was a poodle."

2. A group consists of two or more individuals who are not individually identified or distinguished.

Examples

"I went home to visit my PARENTS."
"THREE BOYS whistled at me."
"A HERD OF BUFFALO was running across the field."
"A big CROWD gathered around the wreck."
"I was attending a meeting of the BOARD OF DIRECTORS."
"The SEVEN DWARFS marched across the stage."

The scoring symbol for an individual character is 1; for a group, the scoring symbol is 2.

Animals are classified as individuals or groups but they are not classified by Sex, Identity, or Age. (Scoring symbol: 1ANI for a single animal; 2ANI for a group of animals.)

SEX

In addition to the two sex subclasses of male and female, there has to be a subclass for groups made up of both sexes and a subclass for characters whose sex is not known by the dreamer or whose sex is not clearly identified in the dream report.

1. Male (Scoring symbol: M). Classify as Male any character identified as being male, or for whom the masculine pronoun is used, or whose role is typically a male one.

Examples

"The MAN spoke to me."
"HE was coming closer and closer and then I awoke."
"The POLICEMAN stopped me."
"The two FOOTBALL TEAMS lined up on the field."

2. Female (Scoring symbol: F). Classify as Female any character identified as being female, or for whom the feminine pronoun is used, or whose role is typically a female one.

Examples

"This GIRL threw me a towel."
"My teacher gave me an angry look and then SHE asked me to leave the room."
"The TELEPHONE OPERATOR asked what number I wanted."

If a character changes sex in the course of a dream, classify the character as both male and female. See below under Metamorphoses for a description of such changes and how to treat them.

3. Joint Sex Group (Scoring symbol: J). Classify a group as a Joint Sex Group when the group is described as being made up

of both males and females or when the group is known by its nature to consist of both sexes, or when the group is a large one so that it might be expected to include members of both sexes.

Examples

"There were both MEN AND WOMEN in the audience."
"My PARENTS asked me where I was going."
"There was a large CROWD in the street."

4. Indefinite Sex (Scoring symbol: I). Classify as Indefinite Sex any character or small group whose sex is not identified in the dream report. Classify also as Indefinite Sex any character who is identified by occupational role alone, when that occupational role may be either a masculine or feminine one.

Examples

"SOMEONE hurried by me."
"There were a FEW OTHER PEOPLE in the room."
"The TEACHER wrote something on the blackboard."

IDENTITY

There are eight subclasses of identity. These subclasses are arranged below in a hierarchical order of decreasing familiarity to the dreamer. If a character can be assigned to more than one identity subclass, he should always be scored for the subclass indicating the greater familiarity, e.g., "my family doctor" is scored as Known (subclass 3) rather than Occupational (subclass 5).

1. *Immediate family members of the dreamer.* The following list containing relevant scoring symbols is inclusive.

Father (F)	Husband (H)	Child (C)
Mother (M)	Wife (W)	Infant or Baby (I)
Parents (X)	Son (A)	Family member (Y)
Brother (B)	Daughter (D)	
Sister (T)		

2. *Relatives of the dreamer* (Scoring symbol: R). These are characters other than immediate family members who are related to the dreamer by blood, marriage, or adoption. The following list is illustrative and not exhaustive:

Grandmother	Nephew	Stepmother
Grandfather	Niece	Foster father
Aunt	Cousin	Ex-husband
Uncle	Brother-in-law	Half-brother

3. *Known characters* (Scoring symbol: K). If it seems clear that the dreamer is currently, or was formerly, personally acquainted with a character or the probability seems very high that the dreamer could, if requested to do so, identify by name a character in his dream, the character is scored as Known. If a large majority of a group consist of familiar characters, score the group as Known.

Examples

"My ROOMMATE cut her hand."
"The BOY who lives next door came over."
"Our POSTMAN handed me a letter."
"My BOSS gave me a lot of work to do."
"My CLASSMATES were all wearing class rings."
"My FRIEND'S BOYFRIEND bought a new car."
"Some BUDDIES of my FRATERNITY BROTHER drove by the house."

4. *Prominent persons* (Scoring symbol: P). Score as Prominent any character who is well known by his general reputation but who is not known personally by the dreamer. Fictional, dramatic, imaginary, and supernatural figures are also scored under this heading as they are usually familiar because of their reputation. (See additional scoring rule 7 for the scoring of fictional, dramatic, imaginary, and supernatural characters.)

Examples

"I saw WINSTON CHURCHILL sitting at the end of the table."

"It was like I was seeing a cartoon strip with ORPHAN ANNIE in it."
"HAMLET walked out on the stage holding his sword in front of him."
"Then GOD appeared and said everything would be all right."

5. *Occupational identification* (Scoring symbol: O). Any character whose occupation is designated but who is not otherwise identified by the dreamer as being more familiar is scored as Occupational. Occupation includes not only vocations and professions and other forms of gainful employment, but also avocations such as stamp collector, golfer, and hunter, as well as illegal or nonsanctioned pursuits such as gangster and prostitute. A student at any educational level who is not otherwise identified as being more familiar is scored O.

Examples

"The WAITRESS asked me what I wanted to eat."
"The ARMY OFFICER pointed his gun at the SOLDIER."
"The JUDGE said I was guilty and sentenced me to death."
"The CHOIR sang a hymn."
"The man turned out to be a COUNTERFEITER."

6. *Ethnic, nationality, and regional identifications* (Scoring symbol: E). These are characters whose race, nationality, or regional identification is designated but who are not otherwise identified as being more familiar by the dreamer.

Examples

"I was being tortured by INDIANS."
"I dreamed I was living with a GERMAN FAMILY."
"This man who was a SOUTHERNER said he knew all about growing cotton."

7. *Strangers* (Scoring symbol: S). A character is considered a stranger if the dreamer specifically indicates the character is

unknown or unfamiliar or his identity remains hidden because the character is faceless or wearing a mask. If, from the language used in the dream report, the probability seems very high that this is the first time that the dreamer has become acquainted with the character, the character is scored as a Stranger. A crowd, unless otherwise being identified as more familiar, is scored as a group of Strangers.

Examples

"There was a little BOY I had never seen before."
"I was being chased by some mean-looking MEN."
"I was lost in the CROWD."

8. *Uncertain identity* (Scoring symbol: U). The dream report frequently does not contain sufficient information as to whether a character is known or a stranger to the dreamer. When degree of familiarity cannot be established, the character is scored as Uncertain. In addition to scoring vague character descriptions as Uncertain, this scoring is also used when the character is described as known in the dream but this character cannot be identified later by the dreamer when he is reporting his dream.

Examples

"I was with a bunch of KIDS my age."
"SOMEONE asked me if I were going to the meeting."
"I showed this GIRL my engagement ring."
"I was mad because THEY wouldn't let me out of the cellar."
"Several BOYS asked me to dance."
"A MAN had called me while I was at the store."
"I wasn't sure that I knew HIM."
"I was with a GIRL FRIEND but I didn't know who she was."
"This FELLOW . . . I knew him in the dream but I can't remember him now . . . took me for a ride in his car."

AGE

There are four age groups. These are arranged below in order of decreasing chronological age grouping.

1. *Adult* (Scoring symbol: A). All characters are scored as Adults unless they meet the requirements for inclusion in one of the other three age groups.

2. *Teenager* (Scoring symbol: T). Any character whose age is indicated as being from 13 through 17 or whom from the context of the dream report appears to be an adolescent should be included in this age group. All high school students, whether of junior or senior level, are scored as Teenagers. All college students are scored as Adults. The use of such terms as kid, youth, boy or girl does not in itself identify a character as a teenager since these terms are also used in referring to other age groups. The decision as to how to classify characters referred to by these terms has to depend upon the context in which they are used. Friends and acquaintances of teenage dreamers are presumed to be teenagers unless otherwise stated.

3. *Child* (Scoring symbol: C). Any character whose age is from one through 12 or who is referred to as a child is included in this age group. Any elementary school pupil is scored as a Child.

4. *Baby* (Scoring symbol: B). A character who is less than one year old or who is referred to as an infant or baby is scored Baby, except when the word baby is used as a term of endearment or one of reproach for a character who is older than one year.

Scoring the Characters The procedure for scoring characters is illustrated in this section. In actual practice, the characters in a dream report are classified and scored at the same time. The order of scoring is Number, Sex, Identity, and Age. It will be recalled that italics are used below for all individuals except the dreamer who should not be scored as characters.

Examples

"My FATHER (1MFA) and MOTHER (1FMA) were in the AUDI-
ENCE (2JUA) when I sang one of COLE PORTER'S (1MPA)
songs."

"My TEENAGE BROTHER (1MBT) got the measles so I couldn't
go out with my BOYFRIEND (1MKA)."

"My SISTER-IN-LAW (1FRA) invited me to come over and see the
INFANT TWINS (2IRB) she had just adopted from *Children's*
Hospital."

"Three of my CLASSMATES (2IKA) and several of my FRATER-
NITY BROTHERS (2MKA) were standing around at the party
with a lot of older PEOPLE (2JUA)."

"I dreamed I had a date with SOPHIA LOREN (1FPA), and she
told me how difficult the life of a *movie star* is."

"A parade of SOLDIERS (2MOA) marched by and ONE OF THEM
(1MOA) was riding a HORSE (1ANI) and ANOTHER
(1MOA) was leading a pair of HORSES (2ANI)."

"A group of my FRIENDS (2IUA) . . . well, anyway I think they
were my friends, but I can't be sure now . . . came over to the
house and said my BROTHER'S (1MBA) car had been stolen
by an ORIENTAL MAN (1MEA) and that I should call the
POLICE (2MOA)."

"When I finally walked past the last GUARD (1MOA) and into the
PRESIDENT'S (1MPA) office, there were all these FAMOUS
PEOPLE (2JPA) and they were looking at a picture of the *Wash-
ington* monument. Some MAN (1MSA) I didn't know began to
slash at the picture with a knife until the White House GUARDS
(2MOA) came running and took him off to jail. *No one* seemed
to notice that I was there. The next thing I remember I was
home with my MOTHER (1FMA) and STEPFATHER (1MRA)
and they were asking me whether I wanted to be a *doctor* or
lawyer. There was SOMEONE (1IUA) else in the room, too, and
I heard some DOG (1ANI) barking outside, and that's all I can
remember of that dream."

"I was in a room with TWO PEOPLE (2ISA) who were *strangers*
to me and a CHILD (1IUC) and a BABY (1IUB). The RUS-
SIANS (2MEA) began to break down the door, and I hid in a
secret room that my GRANDFATHER (1MRA) had built for
just such an emergency. The room was full of SPIDERS (2ANI)

that were covered with little green ANTS (2ANI). Three BOYS
(2MUA) discovered my hiding place, and *they* were going to
tell on me. ONE OF THE BOYS (1MKA) turned out to be my
BROTHER'S (1MBA) *friend* and then I remember I had seen
him around the house. *He* asked me if my *brother* had got out
of the *Army* yet and I said he might go to OTS and become an
officer."

METAMORPHOSES

It sometimes happens in a dream that a character changes
his sex, identity, or age in the course of the dream. It is also possible for a human being to change into an animal or *vice versa*.
When this occurs, the character is scored for his original form
and for his metamorphosis as well. The numeral 7 is the scoring
symbol used for the original form and the numeral 8 is used
for his changed form. These numerals precede the character's
scoring symbol and appear in the same number column used
to indicate whether an individual (1) or group (2) character
is involved. If a character dies or a dead character comes to life,
this is not scored as a metamorphosis.

Examples

"My GIRL FRIEND (7FKA) suddenly changed into my BOY-
　　FRIEND (8MKA)."
"When I turned around the DOCTOR (7MOA) had turned into my
　　FATHER (8MFA)."
"The MAN (7MUA) grew smaller and smaller until he was a CHILD
　　(8MUC)."
"A BEAR (7ANI) was chasing me, and then it was no longer a bear
　　but a strange NEGRO MAN (8MEA)."

Additional Scoring Rules

1. A character who makes several appearances in the same
dream should be scored only once in each dream.

2. If several characters are simply enumerated and the dreamer does not further describe the appearance or activities of any of these individual characters at any point in the dream, the enumerated characters are scored as a single group.

Examples

"My *mother, father, brother,* and *sister* (2JYA) came to my graduation."
"I was being chased by a *lion,* a *tiger,* and two *snakes* (2ANI)."
"First, *one* man, then *another,* and *another* (2MUA) climbed the ladder and entered my room."

3. If some, but not all, of the members of a group are distinguished with regard to appearance or activities as individuals, score as an individual character each of them who is so distinguished and score the remainder as a group.

Examples

"My whole FAMILY (2JYA), all ten of us, were sitting around talking in the living room. My FATHER (1MFA) got up to fix the fire and then started to talk to my oldest BROTHER (1MBA), who began to laugh."
"A GROUP OF FIREMEN (2MOA) marched by. ONE (1MOA) was very tall and ONE OF THEM (1MOA) waved at me."

4. If one or more small groups are differentiated out of a large group because of their appearance or activities, score both the small groups and the large group.

Example

"There was a big CROWD (2JUA) at the party. THREE SOLDIERS (2MOA) were fooling around and began a fight with THREE SAILORS (2MOA)."

5. If the dreamer says that a character might be either one person or another person, score for the first mentioned character unless the dreamer later resolves his uncertainty.

Example

"I wasn't sure whether it was my MOTHER (1FMA) or my *wife*."

6. The numeral 3 is the scoring symbol used to indicate individual dead characters; numeral 4 is the symbol for a group of dead characters. These numerals appear in place of the numerals 1 or 2 which would have been employed if the characters were not dead. The numerals 3 or 4 are not used if a character dies during the dream.

Examples

"I cried as I saw my FATHER'S (3MFA) body in the coffin."
"There were the corpses of SEVERAL YOUNG WOMEN (4FSA) whom I didn't know."
"These STRANGERS (2MSA) were laughing when suddenly they dropped dead with a horrible look on their faces."

7. The numeral 5 is the scoring symbol used to indicate a single imaginary character or one that is a fictional or dramatic portrayal; the numeral 6 is used to indicate group characters of this type. These numerals precede the character's scoring symbol and appear in the same number column ordinarily used to indicate individual or group status. These numerals, therefore, appear in place of the numerals 1 or 2 which would have been employed if the characters were not imaginary.

Examples

"I was so surprised because in my dream I was going to a dance with STEVE CANYON (5MPA)."
"She was playing the part of QUEEN VICTORIA (5FPA)."

"I dreamed I gave birth to TWINS (6IIB), but I'm not even pregnant."

8. Very infrequently, a character cannot be identified as either human or animal, or is referred to as a creature. In either case, score it as a Creature (Scoring symbol: CZZ).

Examples

"SOMETHING (1CZZ) was chasing me. I couldn't tell what it was."
"Then these ROBOT-LIKE CREATURES (2CZZ) climbed on my bed and I was terrified."

Summary of Scoring Symbols   In order to be able to obtain an overall view of the various scoring symbols employed for characters, the following summary table should prove useful.

SUMMARY OF SCORING SYMBOLS FOR CHARACTERS

NUMBER	SEX	IDENTITY		AGE
1 individual	M male	F father	I infant	A adult
2 group	F female	M mother	Y family	T teenager
3 individual	J joint	X parents	member	C child
dead	I indefinite	B brother	R relative	B baby
4 group dead		T sister	K known	
5 individual		H husband	P prominent	
imaginary		W wife	O occupational	
6 group		A son	E ethnic	
imaginary		D daughter	S stranger	
7 original form		C child	U uncertain	
8 changed form				

MISCELLANEOUS

ANI animal
CZZ creature

6

The Classification
and Scoring
of Social Interactions

With the cast of characters introduced and listed on the dream program, attention can now be devoted to the unfolding of the play. Lines will be spoken, characters will move about the stage, and the plot will develop. The relative emphasis given to dialogue as contrasted with actions will depend upon the author of the dream and the message he wishes to express. A character's remarks may serve to insult, flatter, or "proposition" another character, or a character may act by assaulting, supporting, or seducing another character. These social interactions may occur between individual characters or sometimes groups of characters may be involved.

In treating the social interactions present in dreams, we score three classes: aggressive, friendly and sexual interactions. Scoring procedures are identical for these three classes and the same notational system is also followed for some of the classes in the Activities classification that will be discussed in the next chapter. This chapter will deal only with social interactions.

AGGRESSIVE INTERACTIONS

The first class of social interaction to be described is that of aggression. We score eight subclasses of aggression, which are numbered from 1 to 8. Those numbered from 1 to 4 involve various forms of nonphysical aggression. Verbal remarks comprise the most frequent form of nonphysical aggression, although on occasion, expressive behavior may be used for the same purpose. Feelings of aggression which the character experiences but which do not reach any overt level of expression are also included within this grouping. The subclasses numbered from 5 to 8 involve various forms of physical aggression. Included are those acts where a character kills, hits, chases, or robs another character.

Although we have referred to these eight subclasses as units of an aggression "scale," it should be pointed out that it is not a scale in the usual psychometric sense. In order to qualify as an equal interval scale, the difference in intensities between adjacent subclasses should be of equal magnitude. To be considered an ordinal scale, each subclass should possess greater intensity than that expressed in any lower ranked subclass, although the differences between ranks need not be of equal intensity. Consideration of a concrete example may illustrate this more clearly. Locking someone in a closet would be scored A6, while calling someone a "lousy, rotten, no-good S.O.B." would be scored A2 in our system. To qualify as an equal interval scale, A6 should express three times as much aggressive intensity as A2; to qualify as an ordinal scale, A6 should express more intensity than any act scored as A5, A4, A3, or A2. It seems evident that neither condition is met when the preceding example is considered.

The term scale will be used throughout the following chapters to mean a nominal scale. In a nominal scale, numbers or other means of identification are assigned to various subclasses without any implication of ordering or magnitude being involved in making the assignment of numbers to the subclasses. Therefore we treat any aggressive act, regardless of subclass number, as a single aggressive score. No weighting system of any type is employed.

It should be noted that in all the subclasses that follow, except for A1, the situations involve a *deliberate, intentional* act on the part of one character to harm or annoy some other character. The classification of Misfortunes, which will be discussed in a later chapter, is used to handle those situations where injury, mishap, or adversity occurs to a character through chance or environmental circumstances over which it is impossible to exert personal control.

Subclasses of Aggressions

A8 An aggressive act which results in the death of a character.

Examples

"This dark stranger sprang at the blonde woman and HACKED HER TO PIECES with a big knife."
"I SQUASHED the bug with my foot."

A7 An aggressive act which involves an attempt to physically harm a character. The attempt may be carried out through personal assault or through use of a weapon. Threatening a character with a weapon is also included in this subclass.

Examples

"I SLAPPED him in the face."
"These two boys were THROWING STONES at each other."
"He POINTED A GUN at me and told me to hurry up."

A6 An aggressive act which involves a character being chased, captured, confined, or physically coerced into performing some act.

Examples

"I kept trying to run faster but the gorilla was CATCHING UP with me."
"The little baby had been KIDNAPPED by someone."
"The police PUT the suspect IN JAIL."
"HE HELD MY WRIST AND HE PULLED ME ALONG the street with him."

A5   An aggressive act which involves the theft or destruction of possessions belonging to a character.

Examples

"My room was all messed up and the TV WAS MISSING."
"He SET FIRE to the farmer's barn."
"She THREW her father's spectacles INTO THE LAKE."

A4   An aggressive act in which a serious accusation or verbal threat of harm is made against a character.

Examples

"This old lady kept SHOUTING THAT I WAS THE MAN THE POLICE WERE LOOKING FOR."
"Jim told his boss that if he didn't stop, he was GOING TO PUNCH HIM ON THE NOSE."

A3   This subclass covers all situations where there is an attempt by one character to reject, exploit, control, or verbally coerce another character. Such activity may be expressed through dismissals, demands, refusals, disobedience, or any other type of negativistic or deceitful behavior.

Examples

"My boyfriend from back home sent me a letter saying that HE WASN'T GOING TO WRITE ME ANYMORE."
"She TURNED HER BACK on her husband and WALKED OUT OF THE ROOM."
"This fat lady INSISTED that the crying child finish all his supper."
"My roommate's parents WOULDN'T ALLOW her to go to New York."
"I found out that my brother HAD LIED ABOUT ME to my teacher."

A2   Aggression displayed through verbal or expressive activity.

Included are such activities as one character yelling or swearing at another or when a character criticizes or scowls at another.

Examples

"I could hear the couple next door ARGUING."
"My father SAID I WAS A LOUSY DRIVER."

A1   Covert feeling of hostility or anger without any overt expression of aggression.

Examples

"I KEPT GETTING MADDER AND MADDER at him BUT NEVER
     SAID ANYTHING."
"I FELT LIKE SPANKING my son BUT I DIDN'T."

Terminology Employed for Aggressive Interactions   In order for an aggressive act to occur, some character usually initiates the activity and some character has this aggressive activity directed against him. The character who initiates the aggression is called the *aggressor,* and the person who is the recipient of the aggression is called the *victim*. If the victim responds with any type of counteraggression, it is called a *reciprocated aggression*. In those cases where no aggressor or victim can be clearly identified because the characters are engaging in the same aggressive activity at the same time, the interaction is called a *mutual aggression.*

It will be recalled that in the preceding chapter, the dreamer was not listed as a character because he is virtually a constant factor in every dream. The dreamer is scored (scoring symbol: D), however, for interactions because he is a participant in many of them. Aggressions in which the dreamer is not a participant are called *witnessed aggressions*. When a character aggresses against himself, this is called a *self-directed aggression*.

Procedure for Scoring Aggressive Interactions   In the examples given below, it will be seen that the scoring symbol for the aggressor is written first. The type of aggression displayed by the aggressor is then indicated by placing the number of the appropriate subclass after the scoring symbol for the aggressor. This is followed by a "sideward V" (>) pointing toward the scoring symbol for the character who is the victim. Reciprocated aggressions are designated by placing the letter R after the aggressive subclass number rather than a sideward V. Mutual aggressions are indicated by an "equals" (=) sign. If more than one character is involved, either as aggressor or victim, the scoring symbols for the characters are joined by plus (+) signs. Self-directed aggressions are denoted by placing an asterisk (*) after the number of the aggressive subclass and scoring the character as both aggressor and victim.

Examples

"I HIT my brother with all my might on the head."

D 7> 1MBA

"My girl friend SAID I WAS A TIGHTWAD."

1FKA 2> D

"This fellow and I started to TRADE PUNCHES."

D 7= 1MUA

"This tough-looking guy started to TIE UP the policeman."

1MSA 6> 1MOA

"The two boys . . . I should judge they were about 15 . . . were CALLING EACH OTHER BAD NAMES."

1MST 2= 1MST

"As I entered my bedroom, my mother who had been sweeping the floor and my sister who had been cleaning the woodwork suddenly took all my clothes out of the closet and began THROWING ALL MY CLOTHES OUT the window."

1FMA + 1FTA 5> D

"This sinister-looking man LUNGED AT ME with a club in his hand so I KICKED HIM in the groin."

1MSA 7> D
D 7R 1MSA

"I CALLED HER A SIMPLETON, and she GRABBED MY BLOUSE AND TORE IT."

D 2> 1FUA
1FUA 5R D

"She told her husband she WAS GOING TO GET A DIVORCE. Then he grabbed a gun from the drawer and KILLED HER."

1FUA 3> 1MUA
1MUA 8R 1FUA

"I SAID that I WAS A LOUSY DANCER."

D 2° D

"The old man started to SLASH HIS OWN WRISTS."

1MUA 7° 1MUA

Scoring Rules

1. It is considered an aggressive act even though the aggressor may be a sanctioned agent of punishment or professionally employed for such a purpose.

Examples

"My nine-year-old cousin Tommy was BEING SPANKED BY HIS MOTHER."

1FRA 7> 1MRC

"The POLICEMAN CAPTURED THE ITALIAN MOB LEADER."

1MOA 6> 1MOA

2. Criticism of a character's possessions is treated as criticism of the character himself.

Examples

"My sorority sister said that MY NEW FORMAL LOOKED VERY UNATTRACTIVE."

1FKA 2> D

"My 16-year-old brother Jack said MY CAR SHOULD BE IN A JUNK YARD."

1MBT 2> D

3. If the aggressor or the victim is unknown use a Q to indicate this lack of identification.

Examples

"The miners REFUSED to go to work."

2MOA 3> Q

"The company FIRED me."

Q 3> D

4. If there is a continued sequence of aggressive acts between the same aggressor and victim and these acts are identical as to the subclass of aggression involved, only one aggression is scored.

Example

"This big sailor PUSHED the little sailor, then *began hitting* him, and after he *had knocked him down,* he began to *kick* him."

1MOA 7> 1MOA

5. If more than one aggressive act takes place between the same aggressor and victim, score each aggression where a differ-

ent subclass of aggressions occurs and indicate this linkage by placing a { mark in front of the linked aggressive interactions.

Example

"This wild-looking fellow came out of the alley and approached my boyfriend Sam and me. He CALLED SAM YELLOW, then he said he WAS GOING TO CALL HIS GANG TO TAKE CARE OF SAM. We didn't say or do anything, and then he TOOK A KNIFE AND STARTED TOWARD Sam."

$$\begin{cases} 1MSA\ 2> 1MKA \\ 1MSA\ 4> 1MKA \\ 1MSA\ 7> 1MKA \end{cases}$$

6. When aggressive acts are separated in time through intervening events, score each aggression even if the same subclass of aggression is involved between the same aggressor and victim.

Example

"I RIPPED UP some of my husband's love letters from an old girl friend that were up in the attic but then thought about it and quit. I went downstairs and started to sew. After awhile I turned on TV but I kept thinking about the other letters so I went back up to the attic and RIPPED UP all the rest of them."

$$D\ 5> 1MHA$$
$$D\ 5> 1MHA$$

7. Reciprocated aggressions are scored according to the same rules that are applied to initiated aggressions.

FRIENDLY INTERACTIONS

The second type of social interaction that we score is friendliness. Seven subclasses of friendliness are distinguished below. These subclasses cannot be grouped as easily as the aggressive ones into physical versus nonphysical or verbal forms of expression. Once again, we urge that the numbers associated with the subclasses not be treated as if they represented some measure of intensity or strength of response. The various subclasses discussed below all involve a *deliberate, purposeful* attempt on the part of one character to express friendliness toward another. This may eventuate in some pleasant outcome for the person receiving the friendliness. The classification of Good Fortunes, to be discussed in a later chapter, is used to handle those situations where some pleasant outcome (e.g., finding money) occurs as the result of environmental circumstances rather than as a result of personal interaction with another character.

Subclasses of Friendliness

F7 Friendliness expressed through a desire for a long-term close relationship with a character. Included in this subclass are getting married, becoming engaged, and falling in love.

Examples

"I dreamed my boyfriend and I WERE GETTING MARRIED in this unusual-looking church."
"I was so happy because my boyfriend had just GIVEN ME A BEAUTIFUL ENGAGEMENT RING."

F6 Friendliness expressed through socially acceptable forms of physical contact. Included in this subclass are such acts as shaking hands, cuddling a baby, and dancing. Kissing and embracing are also included when they are clearly nonsexual in intent. Sexual activity is not included here but is treated later in this chapter as a separate interaction.

Examples

"My son began TO PET the new puppy."
"I was so glad to see Mom that I GAVE HER A BIG KISS."
"My brother gave me A PAT ON THE SHOULDER."

F5   Friendliness expressed by taking the initiative in requesting a character to share in a pleasant social activity. Included are situations where one character requests another to accompany him to some event, asks for a date, and visits someone. In the latter case, friendliness is scored because visiting implies someone is taking the initiative or an active role in furthering a relationship with another character. Simply associating with a character or jointly participating in an activity is not scored as a friendly act.

Examples

"My roommate ASKED ME TO SPEND THE WEEKEND at her
      home."
"I phoned Judy to ASK FOR A DATE."
"The boy I *had a date with* and I *went bowling.*"

F4   Friendliness expressed through extending assistance to a character or offering to do so. Included in this subclass are helping, protecting, and rescuing acts.

Examples

"When we received the news, our family BEGAN TO PRAY FOR
      HIS RECOVERY."
"I found out where the poor child lived and TOOK HER HOME."

F3   Friendliness expressed by offering a gift or loaning a possession to a character.

Examples

"John GAVE ME A LOVELY BLANKET for our anniversary."
"I let my brother BORROW MY CAR for the trip."

F2   This subclass covers a wide variety of expressions of friendliness that may be conveyed through either verbal or gestural means. Included are such activities as welcoming, greeting, waving hello or goodby, introducing one person to another person, smiling at someone, phoning or writing someone for a friendly purpose, and sympathizing with or praising someone.

Examples

"He TOOTED THE CAR HORN IN RECOGNITION as he passed me on the street."
"I CALLED my father TO TELL HIM THE GOOD NEWS."
"I COMPLIMENTED Jean on her new dress."

F1 Friendliness is felt toward a character but it is not expressed overtly.

Examples

"I FELT SO GOOD INSIDE just to be with Tom."
"I FELT VERY SORRY when I heard what happened to Mrs. Smith."
"I THOUGHT that the new girl LOOKED VERY ATTRACTIVE."

Terminology Employed for Friendly Interactions   The initiator of a friendly act is called the *befriender,* and the recipient of a friendly act is called the *befriended.* If the befriended responds with any type of friendliness, it is called a *reciprocated friendliness.* In those cases where no befriender or befriended can be clearly identified because the characters are engaging in the same friendly exchange at the same time, the interaction is called a *mutual friendliness.* If the dreamer does not participate in the friendly interaction, it is called a *witnessed friendliness.* When a character may express friendliness to himself it is called *self-directed friendliness.*

Procedure for Scoring Friendly Interactions   The procedures are exactly the same as those for scoring aggressive interactions. The scoring symbol for the befriender is written first, followed by the number of the appropriate subclass. Next the "sideward V" (>) appears and points toward the scoring symbol for the befriended character. Reciprocated friendliness is denoted by placing the letter R after the friendly subclass number rather than a sideward V. Mutual friendliness is indicated by an "equals" (=) sign. If more than one character is involved, either as befriender or befriended, the scoring symbols for the characters are joined by a plus (+) sign. Self-directed friendliness is indicated by placing an asterisk after the number of the friendly subclass and scoring the character as both befriender and befriended.

Examples

"I noticed this little kitten meowing high in the tree. I CLIMBED UP AND BROUGHT IT DOWN."

D 4> 1ANI

"Mother had sent some kind of CONGRATULATORY CARD to the Browns on the birth of their new son."

1FMA 2> 2JKA

"Jim and I rushed toward each other, then STARTED TO SHAKE HANDS AND SLAP EACH OTHER ON THE BACK."

D 6= 1MKA

"The principal came from the burning school building CARRYING a little girl. Just before he put her down, SHE GAVE HIM A BIG HUG."

1MOA 4> 1FUC
1FUC 6R 1MOA

"My cousin ASKED ME TO GO TO THE FAIR with him, and I SAID I WOULD BE GLAD TO GO."

1MRA 5> D
D 5R 1MRA

"I SMILED AT MYSELF IN A PLEASED WAY in the mirror."

D 2* D

Scoring Rules

1. It is considered to be a friendly act even though the befriender may be acting in a societal or professional role.

Examples

"I dreamed our house caught on fire and a FIREMAN HELPED ME CLIMB DOWN A LADDER from the second floor."

1MOA 4> D

"The DOCTOR .SET my baby's broken leg."

1MOA 4> 1IIB

2. If a character treats another character's possessions in a friendly manner, it is scored as a friendly treatment of the character himself.

Example

"My girl friend ADMIRED MY NEW CAR."

1FKA 2> D

3. If the befriender or the befriended is not specified in the dream report, use Q to indicate this lack of identification.

Examples

"The WELCOME WAGON left some gifts for me."

Q 3> D

"I gave the CHURCH a hundred dollars."

D 3> Q

4. If there is a continued sequence of friendly acts between the same befriender and befriended characters and these acts involve the same subclass of friendliness, only one friendly act is scored.

Example

"After class, she SMILED, *said 'Hello,'* and then began to *tell the professor how much she enjoyed his lecture.*"

1FUA 2> 1MOA

5. If more than one friendly act takes place between the same befriender and befriended characters, score each different subclass of friendly acts separately and indicate their linkage by placing a { mark in front of the linked interactions.

Example

"The truck driver gave me a BIG SMILE and then he HELPED me change the tire."

{ 1 MOA 2> D
1 MOA 4> D

6. When friendly acts are separated in time through intervening events, score each friendly act even if the same subclass of friendliness is involved between the same befriender and befriended characters.

Example

"I WAVED HELLO to Sally as I walked into Grants. I bought some records, watched part of a TV show, and ate lunch at the snack bar there. As I walked out the door I saw Sally again and WAVED HELLO a second time."

D 2> 1FKA
D 2> 1FKA

7. Reciprocated friendliness is scored according to the same rules that are applied for initiated friendliness.

SEXUAL INTERACTIONS

The remaining class of social interactions is the sexual one. Five subclasses of sexual interaction are described below. The most frequent form of sexual expression involves some type of physical contact, although we have one subclass to handle sexual fantasies.

Subclasses of Sexual Interactions

S5 A character has or attempts to have sexual intercourse with another character.

Example

"My girl was willing and I was just getting ready to INSERT MY PENIS when I woke up. It was a wet dream."

S4 This subclass involves the various types of fore-play activities generally preceding intercourse. Included are handling another character's sex organs and related fondling and petting activities.

Example

"I dreamed I looked in the window across the street and I saw this man I didn't recognize FONDLING THE NEIGHBOR LADY'S BREASTS."

S3 This subclass covers necking and "nonplatonic" kissing. Kissing as a form of greeting, e.g., between family members, is scored under friendliness.

Example

"And then my boyfriend KISSED me long and hard.

S2   A character makes sexual overtures to or "propositions" another character.

Example

"This good-looking woman who was a stranger to me SUGGESTED
   WE GO TO HER APARTMENT AND MAKE LOVE."

S1   A character has sexual thoughts or fantasies about another character.

Example

"I IMAGINED what it would be like to SLEEP WITH Elizabeth
   Taylor."

Terminology Employed for Sexual Interactions   The character who takes the initiative in starting a sexual interaction is called the *initiator;* the character who is the object of the sexual interaction is called the *recipient.* If the recipient responds with any type of sexual activity, it is called *reciprocated sexuality.* When no initiator or recipient can be clearly identified, the interaction is called a *mutual* one. If the dreamer does not participate in the sexual interaction, it is called a *witnessed sexuality.* When a character indulges in solitary sexual activity, it is called *self-directed sexuality.*

Procedure for Scoring Sexual Interactions   The procedure is exactly the same as that for scoring the other social interactions. The scoring symbol of the initiator is written first, followed by the subclass number and a > pointing toward the scoring symbol for the recipient. Reciprocated sexuality is designated by placing the letter R after the sexual subclass number rather than a sideward V. Mutual sexual interactions are indicated by an equals sign. If more than one character is involved, either as initiator or as recipient, the scoring symbols for the characters are joined by a plus sign. Self-directed sexuality is denoted by placing an asterisk after the number of the sexual subclass and scoring the character as both initiator and recipient.

Scoring Rules

1. It is considered a sexual act even though the initiator is acting in a professional role.

Example

"A red-headed PROSTITUTE walked up and ASKED ME if it were worth five dollars for a little fun up in her room."

$$1 \text{ FOA } 2> \text{ D}$$

2. If there is a continued sequence of sexual activities between the same initiator and recipient and these activities involve the same subclass, only one sexual activity is scored.

Example

"I dreamed that J. R. and I were married and it was our wedding night. WE WERE MAKING LOVE and trying out different positions. First J. R. *lay on top of me*, then we had relations *lying on our side,* and then finally I got *on top of him*."

$$\text{D } 5= \text{ 1MKA}$$

3. If more than one sexual activity takes place between the same initiator and recipient, score each different subclass involved and indicate their linkage by placing a { mark in front of the linked interactions.

Example

"I was in a hotel room with some gorgeous-looking blond wearing a flimsy nightgown. I walked over to the bed where she was and started to KISS HER. I got into bed and began to RUN MY HANDS OVER HER BODY. Just as I started to ENTER HER, I woke up and had to change my pajamas."

$$\begin{cases} \text{D } 3> \text{ 1FSA} \\ \text{D } 4> \text{ 1FSA} \\ \text{D } 5> \text{ 1FSA} \end{cases}$$

4. When sexual activities are separated in time through intervening events, score each sexual activity even if the same subclass of sex is involved between the same initiator and recipient.

Example

"My boyfriend and I WERE NECKING on my living room couch. My parents came home and we all watched TV for a while and had some coffee later. After they went upstairs to bed, we BEGAN TO NECK AGAIN."

$$\text{D } 3= \text{ 1FKA}$$
$$\text{D } 3= \text{ 1FKA}$$

5. Reciprocated sexual acts are scored according to the same rules applied to initiated sexual acts.

7

The Classification
and Scoring of Activities

In this chapter a system of classifying what characters *do* in dreams is presented. It includes activities that may be done by a character acting alone or in conjunction with other characters, as well as interactions between characters. We have already taken up some social interactions in the preceding chapters. These social interactions and the interactions described in this chapter are not mutually exclusive. For example, a hostile act of one character hitting another which would be scored A7 on the aggression scale is also scored as a physical activity on the activities scale. In the same way, a friendly remark made by one character to another which would be scored F2 on the friendliness scale of the preceding chapter is also scored as a verbal activity on the activities scale of this chapter.

Eight classes of activities are included in our scoring system. They are described below.

CLASSES OF ACTIVITIES

PHYSICAL

(Scoring symbol: P). Any voluntary movement of the whole body or of part of the body while the character remains more or less in one place is scored as a physical activity. Physical activity in a limited spatial area is emphasized, because physical activity such as walking or running which results in the character moving into a different location is scored in the subsequent class of movement. In order for a physical activity to be scored, the nature of the physical activity should be clearly recognizable from the dream report. Reference to a character shopping, for example, is too vague to be scored because the description does not explain the precise activities of the character. It is possible that it might have referred primarily to visual activities, as in window shopping; or to verbal activities, as in telephone shopping or haggling with a merchant; or to movement activities, in walking from store to store; or to physical activities, in handling various objects.

A rough criterion that may be employed for judging whether or not a physical activity should be scored is: can the scorer, with the information provided in the dream report, pantomime the activity successfully enough so that an observer could correctly identify the activity? If the answer is yes, a physical activity is scored. A few examples of scorable physical activities are: dressing, combing one's hair, brushing one's teeth, sitting down, getting up, bending, writing, picking up an object, and chopping wood.

MOVEMENT

(Scoring symbol: M). When a character changes his physical location by self-propelled movements of his body, a score is given for movement. Change in location through various means of transportation is scored in the subsequent class. Walking and running are the most frequent forms of movement activity but a number of other possibilities such as crawling, sliding, swimming, and climbing are also reported. Terms such as entering or leaving are also scorable if they refer to a character voluntarily carrying out these activities under his own muscular power. Entering a house would be scorable as movement if it seems clear that the character walked into the house, but entering a hospital on a stretcher would not be scorable in this class. Involuntary movements such as falling, slipping, or being thrown through space are not scored as movement.

LOCATION CHANGE

(Scoring symbol: L). Whenever a character moves in a spatial dimension and arrives at a different location through any means other than self-propelled muscular activity, a location change score is given. The change in location may occur because the character uses some means of transportation such as a car, plane, or boat, or the character may fall through space, be carried, or dragged by someone else. Any verbs which suggest a change in location, even though they are somewhat vague as to just how the change was effected, are grounds for scoring a location change. A few examples of such verbs are went, came, arrived, departed, journeyed, and traveled. If a character suddenly finds himself in a new location because there has been an abrupt shift in setting, a location change score should not be entered. In order for a location change score to be given, there must be an indication that the new surroundings have appeared after some intervening travel by the character, even though the means of travel have not been specified. Movement activities such as walking and running which were described in the immediately preceding class are not included in the location change class.

VERBAL

(Scoring symbol: V). Any type of vocalization, whether it be a breakfast conversational grunt, a thundering speech, a whispered affectionate term, an abusive curse, a recited poem, or a dramatic soliloquy, is scored as verbal activity. Singing is also scored as verbal activity.

EXPRESSIVE COMMUNICATION

(Scoring symbol: E). Included in this class are those non-verbal activities associated with emotional states which are sometimes not under voluntary control. Numerically, it is a very infrequently used class. Laughing and crying are the most common forms of expressive communication, although smiling, scowling, baring one's teeth, drooling, and gasping all belong to this class.

VISUAL

(Scoring symbol: S). All types of seeing activities are included here. Among the large number of words denoting visual activities are those such as see, notice, read, watch, peek, glance, view, inspect, and distinguish.

AUDITORY

(Scoring symbol: A). Whenever a character is described as being engaged in any type of hearing or listening behavior, a score for auditory activity is given.

THINKING

(Scoring symbol: C). The remaining class consists of the most *covert* form of activity—thinking activity. In order to be scored as a thinking activity, the description should indicate that deliberate continued mental effort was involved. This thinking should possess a goal-directed or problem-solving quality. Some verbs reflecting this quality of thinking are: concentrate, puzzle over, contemplate, ponder, brood, ruminate, preoccupy, engross, study, weigh, speculate, deliberate, and think about. Attempts to decide, figure out, understand, grasp, and plan are also reflective of the kind of sustained ideation that is included in this class. Brief, transient mental activities are not scored. For example, such reports as "I think it was blue," "I remember the room was familiar," "I forgot my coat," and "I couldn't recognize him" do not convey any sense of prolonged or intentional thinking activity. Wishes, feelings, and sensations represented in such reports as "I wished I were home," "I felt sorry for him," or "I was thrilled by the view" are not included in the thinking class.

Procedure for Scoring Activities   For two of the activity classes the scoring procedure may be identical with that followed for social interactions. These two classes are physical and verbal activities. If a physical or verbal interaction occurs between two or more characters, the scoring symbol for the character beginning the interaction is shown, followed by the letter P or

V depending on the class involved, then a sideward V (>), and finally the scoring symbol for the character toward whom the activity is directed. A character who is the recipient of a physical activity may return a physical activity to the initiator, or the recipient of a verbal activity may reply with a verbal activity to the initiator. These are called reciprocated physical or verbal activities and are scored by placing the letter R after P or V, in place of a > mark. When the physical or verbal interactions do not have a clearly defined initiator and recipient they are called mutual interactions and are scored by placing an equals (=) sign after the P or V.

In the case of interactions at least two characters are always involved because one character is doing something to another character. As indicated above, physical and verbal activities may sometimes involve an interactional pattern, and so the scoring is the same in these situations as it is for the social interactions. However, there are quite a large number of physical activities and some occasional verbal activities where only a single character is involved, or where two or more characters are engaged in a parallel physical or verbal activity at the same time. The scoring procedure in such cases is simply to list a P or V if only the dreamer is involved. If other characters or the dreamer and another character are involved, they are scored and appear after a comma following the P or V. If two or more characters are involved in a parallel activity, they are joined by plus signs.

Interactions and reciprocated activities are not scored for any of the other six classes of activities. The scoring procedure for these six classes is the same as that explained above for noninteractions. If the dreamer alone engages in these activities, the class letter alone is listed. If other characters or the dreamer and another character engage in an activity together, the scoring symbols for these characters appear after the comma which follows the scoring symbol for the activity class. Joint activity by more than one character is indicated by a plus sign.

Examples

"I PUNCHED this guy in the stomach and then he CONNECTED WITH AN UPPERCUT to my jaw."

D P> 1MUA

1MUA PR D

"The doctor and I HAD A LONG TALK TOGETHER about my mother's condition."

D V= 1MOA

"I SLICED A PIECE OF BREAD from the loaf on the table."

P

"When Roger and I finally REACHED THE TOP OF THE MOUN-TAIN we rested, and then HE PILED A GROUP OF ROCKS on top of each other to make a marker."

M, D + 1MKA

P, 1MKA

"We LOOKED AT EACH OTHER for awhile and then we both SMILED."

S, D + 1IUA

E, D + 1IUA

Scoring Rules   In order to be scored, an activity must be described as a current or completed activity. Do not score contemplated or anticipated activities. The latter are indicated by such terms as would, could, should, and might. An activity is indicated by the use of a verb. Since a dream report will often contain a large number of verbs, the following rules are intended to serve as a guide with regard to the number of activities that should be scored.

1. A continuous sequence of similar actions performed by the same character is scored as one activity.

Examples

"I was TALKING to my young son. I *asked* him what he did in second grade that day. When he didn't answer, I *asked* him again. Finally I *asked* in a very loud voice and he REPLIED, 'Nothing much.'"

D V> 1MAC
1MAC VR D

"The pitcher THREW the ball and the umpire YELLED, 'Ball one.'
The pitcher *threw* again and the umpire called it a strike. The
pitcher *threw* three more times and the count was three and two.
Then the pitcher *threw* once more and the umpire *yelled*, 'Strike
three.' "

P, 1MOA
V, 1MOA

2. A sequence of activities performed by the same character
and belonging to the same class are scored as separate activities
if they involve different activities.

Example

"I WALKED into the bathroom, TURNED ON the light, TOOK A
SHOWER, SHAVED, BRUSHED my teeth, and then COMBED
my hair."

M
P
P
P
P
P

3. If activities belonging to the same class are separately engaged in by different characters, they are scored as separate
activities.

Example

"I was WALKING down one side of the street and Mary was WALK-
ING down the other side of the street."

M
M, 1FKA

4. If activities belonging to the same class are jointly engaged in by different characters, they are scored as a single activity.

Example

"Mary and I were WALKING down the street TOGETHER."

$$M, D + 1FKA$$

5. If the same character engages in interactional activities with different characters, separate activities are scored.

Examples

"I was TALKING to my mother and then my father CAME HOME and I began TALKING to him."

$$D \ V> \ 1FMA$$
$$L, \ 1MFA$$
$$D \ V> \ 1MFA$$

"I SHOOK HANDS WITH my uncle John, then WITH my uncle Henry and then WITH my cousin Jim."

$$D \ P= \ 1MRA$$
$$D \ P= \ 1MRA$$
$$D \ P= \ 1MRA$$

6. If intervening events occur, separate activities are scored even though they involve identical activities, identical characters or identical interactional patterns.

Example

"My sister and I WENT FOR A WALK in the woods. As we *turned* down one trail, we SAW two squirrels. One squirrel was RUN-NING along a branch and the other WAS CRACKING a nut. I HEARD a bluejay and CALLED to my sister to listen. We both LAUGHED at the sound. We then CONTINUED OUR WALK."

M, D + 1FTA
S, D + 1FTA
M, 1ANI
P, 1ANI
A
D V> 1FTA
E, D + 1FTA
M, D + 1FTA

8

The Classification
and Scoring
of Achievement Outcomes

In dealing with the interactions and activities engaged in by characters, scoring attention has been paid, so far, only to whether reciprocal acts follow some initial act. Left out has been an important consideration—does a character succeed or fail in carrying these activities through to some desired outcome? In order to take account of possible results, we have developed a classification of Achievement Outcomes. Included within this classification are the two classes of Success and Failure.

In our efforts to fashion a workable achievement outcome scale, our greatest difficulty was encountered in attempting to decide how much latitude should be allowed for the criteria governing success and failure. We eventually settled on a rather stringent and rigorous standard. First, it must be reasonably clear from the dream report that a character has formulated some definite task to accomplish or goal to achieve and sets out in a deliberate attempt to realize this ambition. If he is then successful in pursuing his objective to a satisfactory conclusion, a success is scored; if he is unsuccessful, a failure is scored. Scoring examples are provided below.

SUCCESS

In order for a success to be scored, the character must be described as expending some energy and perseverance in pursuit of his goal. The objective need not be of epic significance; a successful handling of some difficulty encountered in a character's daily life is sufficient to qualify. What is important is that the character is confronted by some problem, decides to deal with it, and then works at its solution before eventually managing to succeed. Any type of magical solution would be scored as a good fortune, which will be discussed in the next chapter.

Examples

"I discovered I had a flat tire so I got my tools and began to change it. It turned out to be a rather difficult job, but I KEPT AT IT AND FINALLY MANAGED TO FIX IT."

"A man was chasing me with a gun. By running down some narrow dark alleys and climbing some high fences, I FINALLY WAS ABLE TO GET AWAY."

"The exam was a tough one but I was determined to get a good grade. I wrote as fast as I could and put down all the examples I had memorized. I FELT SURE THAT I HAD DONE WELL ON IT."

"I had asked this beautiful blond for a date earlier but she said no. I sent her flowers, a box of candy, and a singing telegram. When I called again SHE SAID THAT SHE WOULD GO OUT WITH ME NEXT SATURDAY."

FAILURE

The same prerequisites described for success—willingness to deal with an existing problem and continuing efforts to master it—must also be met before failure can be scored. The difference is only in the matter of outcome. When a character is not able to achieve his desired goal because of personal limitations and inadequacies, a failure is scored. If a character is thwarted in his achievement efforts because of some adverse environmental intervention such as a storm or sudden illness, a misfortune is scored.

Examples

"I wanted to board this boat and kept trying to climb the ladder but every time I got near the top I SLIPPED BACK INTO THE OCEAN AGAIN."

"When I saw all the parts to the TV lying on the table top, I decided to repair the set. I kept trying to put the parts together but I NEVER WAS ABLE TO ASSEMBLE THEM CORRECTLY."

"My father COULDN'T FIND HIS GLASSES although he looked high and low for them all over the house."

"My sister kept trying to sell a raffle ticket to my uncle. She asked, pleaded, and begged him but no matter what she tried, she still WASN'T ABLE TO SELL HIM ONE."

Scoring Procedure for Success and Failure   The scoring symbol for the type of achievement is listed first, followed by a comma. The scoring symbol for success is SU, for failure it is FL. After the comma, the scoring symbols for the relevant characters are recorded. Multiple characters are joined by a plus sign.

Examples

"I wanted to hit a home run. After two consecutive strikes, I decided that it would be the next one that I would belt out of the park. I swung real hard and heard the ump yell, 'STRIKE THREE, YOU'RE OUT.'"

FL, D

"Betty, my roommate, and I came up with the idea to redecorate our room. We painted, wallpapered, and moved everything around. When IT WAS FINALLY COMPLETED, we were very pleased with the results, and everyone who saw it complimented us on how well done it was."

SU, D + 1FKA

"My brother, teenage sister, and cousin announced that they were going to climb this nearby mountain. They all came 'back later and said that it had been hard going but THEY HAD FINALLY MADE IT TO THE TOP."

SU, 1MBA + 1FTT + 1IRA

Scoring for Consequences of Success and Failure   Sometimes after achieving a success or failure, something else will occur which will change the outcome for a character. Fate, or some other character, may step in to alter what a character has just achieved. The character himself may push his efforts harder which again may result in a reversal of the previous outcome. To handle such situations, three subclasses of consequences which may modify the original outcome are scored for each of the achievement outcomes. These consequences are represented by placing the scoring symbols for them in parentheses after the scoring that appears for the achievement outcome unit. Since these consequences are classifications that appear in other chapters, these scores also appear separately and independently of their consequence status. The rationale for scoring such consequences is that of preserving the sequence of dream events in order to answer certain dynamic questions which might be raised. Such questions might take the form of "How often does a character succeed only to have his efforts nullified by the environment?" or "In what percentage of failures does some other character intervene and attempt to help the failing character?" The three consequences of success are illustrated below.

1. A character achieves success but it is nullified by a misfortune. The scoring symbol for misfortunes is M. This class of events is discussed in the following chapter on environmental press.

Example

"I had worked very hard to make the cheerleading squad. After finally receiving word that I had made it, I BROKE MY LEG AND COULDN'T BE A CHEERLEADER."

> SU, D (M)
> M5, D

2. A character achieves success but subsequently overextends himself and failure occurs.

Example

"I was making a great deal of money by skillful maneuvering on the
stock market. Then I began to speculate and LOST ALL MY
MONEY."

SU, D (FL)
FL, D

3. Another character intervenes in an aggressive fashion and
intentionally nullifies the success.

Example

"My brother and I had been struggling to build this fancy model
house out of wooden match sticks. After we finally glued the last
one in place, my 11-year-old brother came along and INTEN-
TIONALLY DROPPED A BRICK ON IT WHICH DEMOL-
ISHED IT."

SU, D + 1MBA (A)
1MBC 5> D + 1MBA

The three consequences of failure are:

1. A failure is reversed by a good fortune. The scoring symbol for good fortune is GF. This class of events is discussed in
the following chapter on environmental press.

Example

"I was really sweating over a chemistry problem and couldn't come
up with the answer when, as if by magic, THE ANSWER AP-
PEARED WRITTEN DOWN ON THE PAPER. I could hardly
believe what I saw."

FL, D (GF)
GF, D

2. A failure is overcome when the character through unusual effort or new approach manages to succeed.

Example

"My father kept trying to get a job but was always getting turned down. In desperation, he ran a newspaper ad and MANAGED TO GET ONE AT LAST."

FL, 1MFA (SU)
SU, 1MFA

3. A failure is overcome through the friendly intervention of another character.

Example

"My teenage brother had his car apart and couldn't get it together. I GAVE HIM A DIAGRAM OF THE ENGINE and then he was able to complete the job."

FL, 1MBT (F)
D 4> 1MBT

9

The Classification
and Scoring
of Environmental Press

In the preceding three chapters emphasis has been placed upon the various interactions and activities of the characters. They may fight, dance, make love, converse, walk around, look, listen, or struggle to accomplish something. All of these acts involve some deliberate, voluntary choice on the part of the character engaging in them. As the result of these acts, characters may be killed, hurt, or defeated, or they may become engaged, popular, or prosperous. These bad and good outcomes are, therefore, the consequences of what the characters have done or attempted to do.

It sometimes happens that bad or good outcomes occur to a character independent of anything he may have done. Fate, in a sense, has stepped in and produced certain results over which no character has any control. We have labelled this impersonal "fatalistic" event as an *environmental press*. The word press is taken from the scoring system used by Murray for the TAT, where press is the term for an environmental force which affects a character. We do not differentiate the large number of press forces contained within Murray's system; instead we distinguish only two types of environmental press: misfortunes where bad things happen to a character and good fortunes where good things happen to a character.

MISFORTUNE

We shall first deal with misfortune (Scoring symbol: M). A misfortune is any mishap, adversity, harm, danger, or threat which happens to a character as a result of circumstances over which he has no control; it happens to him through no fault of his own. A misfortune differs from the consequence of an aggressive act, since in an aggression there is an intent by one character to harm another character. There is no such intent in a misfortune. A misfortune also differs from a failure, as was pointed out in the last chapter. In a misfortune a person is not trying to do anything; rather, something "bad" happens to him "out of the blue." The six subclasses of misfortune are listed below.

M6   A character is dead or dies as a result of accident or illness or some unknown cause. Death because of murder is categorically excluded because it is scored as an aggression.

Examples

"I went up to the coffins and opened them. Lying in one box was my mother, in the other my sister, and in the third my brother. They all appeared TO BE DEAD."
"I was attending my FATHER'S FUNERAL."

M5   A character is injured or ill. This class includes pain, operations, any bodily or mental defects, insanity, amnesia, blindness, etc.

Examples

"Her baby boy had a serious congenital HEART DEFECT."
"My mother LOST HER MEMORY."
"A TOOTH BROKE OFF in my mouth."

"He had a CLUBFOOT."
"My boyfriend had a STOMACHACHE."

M4   A character is involved in an accident without suffering physical or mental injury; a character loses a possession or has one destroyed or damaged; a character has a defective possession.

Examples

"As I was driving down the mountain, my car CRASHED BECAUSE OF THE ICY ROAD."
"The DIAMOND CAME OUT of my engagement ring."
"The LIGHTNING DAMAGED our house."
"My boyfriend's car had a FLAT TIRE."

M3   A character is threatened by something in the environment. A threat of falling is classified under the next heading.

Examples

"The wall began to crack and bulge out and I thought it was GOING TO FALL ON ME."
"The waves were very high and I was afraid the boat we were in WAS GOING TO CAPSIZE."

M2   A character is falling or is in danger of falling.

Examples

"I dreamed that I WAS FALLING AND FALLING and never hit bottom."
"As I stood on the edge of the cliff, the rocks began to move and I WAS AFRAID I MIGHT FALL."

M1   A character encounters an environmental barrier or obstacle; a character is unable to move; a character is lost; a character is late or is in danger of being late. This class of misfortunes includes situations which produce frustration for the character who confronts them. In some cases, the frustrating agent is clearly environmental in origin as when a road is washed out; in other cases, where the character is lost or late, it is possible that the character himself has made a contribution to the difficulty he encounters. However, since the character has not consciously or intentionally produced the difficulty and he views the problem as external to himself, it seems more appropriate to treat it as an environmental press that bears upon the character, rather than as a failure in achievement or as an intropunitive aggression. Having encountered the obstacle which warrants the M1 scoring, it is possible for success or failure to be scored if the character makes an effort to overcome the barrier and the outcome is described in the dream report.

Examples

"When we reached the river, we discovered that the BRIDGE HAD COLLAPSED so we couldn't get to the picnic grounds."
"As the truck bore down on me, I tried to run but found that MY LEGS WOULDN'T MOVE."
"I started toward home but the streets became more and more unfamiliar until I finally realized that I WAS LOST."
"As I entered the office, I saw that I WAS LATE FOR WORK."

GOOD FORTUNE

Good fortune is the opposite of misfortune. A misfortune is scored when "something bad" happens to a character; a good fortune is scored when "something good" happens to a character. The "something good" is not the result of an *intentional* beneficial act by another character. That would be scored as friendliness. Neither is the "something good" the result of any purposeful striving by the character. That would be scored as success. A good fortune is scored when there is an acquisition of goods or something beneficial happens to a character that is completely adventitious or the result of a circumstance over which no one has control. A good fortune is also scored if the dreamer finds himself in a bountiful environment. In a word, it might be said that a good fortune is scored whenever a character becomes "lucky." Good fortunes are rather rare in dreams. As the result of their paucity, we have not attempted to subclassify them and score for only one class of good fortune. The scoring symbol is GF.

Examples

"I dreamed I FOUND A LOT OF MONEY."
"My girl friend WON ONE OF THE DOOR PRIZES."
"I was out hunting when a LARGE HERD OF DEER JUST SEEMED TO APPEAR from out of nowhere."
"I dreamed I WAS LIVING IN A MANSION, HAD CLOSETS FULL OF NEW CLOTHES, AND WAS DRIVING A NEW ROLLS-ROYCE."

Scoring Procedures The scoring procedure is the same as that followed in the last chapter. A comma is placed after the scoring symbol for the environmental press and then the scoring symbols for the characters are shown. Multiple characters are joined by a plus sign.

Examples

"I LOST MY WATCH over the side of the boat."

M4, D

"My buddy and I FOUND A BRAND-NEW BOAT that had drifted up on the beach."

GF, D + 1MKA

"My teenage brother and my new baby sister both CAME DOWN WITH THE MUMPS."

M5, 1MBT + 1FTB

CONSEQUENCES

In the last chapter, it was indicated that consequences can occur which would modify the initial achievement outcomes. In a similar fashion, the scoring system for environmental press includes provisions for consequences which alter the initial fate bestowed on a character. Three subclasses of consequences have been developed for each of the environmental press classes. These consequences are either a form of social interaction, an achievement outcome, or the opposite type of environmental press. They are also scored independently of their scoring as a consequence. Their scoring as a consequence is indicated by enclosing the relevant scoring symbol in parentheses following the scoring unit. The purpose of scoring as a consequence is to preserve the sequence of events in order to answer certain dynamic questions which might be raised. Such questions might ask, "How often does a character struggle to overcome a misfortune and succeed?" or "In what percentage of good fortunes does fate intervene and turn an initial blessing into some misfortune?" The three consequences of misfortune are illustrated below.

1. The misfortune is transformed into a good fortune.

Example

"My mother was very sick but ALL OF A SUDDEN SHE APPEARED WELL AND HEALTHY."

M5, 1FMA (GF)
GF, 1FMA

2. The character suffering the misfortune tries to cope with the misfortune and succeeds.

Example

"The door was locked and wouldn't open. After trying several times, I finally used a bent hairpin and MANAGED TO GET IT OPEN."

M1, D (SU)
SU, D

3. Another character intervenes in a friendly fashion and dispels the misfortune.

Example

"I was hopelessly lost in the woods and wandering around in circles. Suddenly a man I had never seen before appeared and SHOWED ME THE WAY OUT OF THE WOODS."

M1, D (F)

1MSA 4> D

The three consequences of good fortune are as follows:

1. The good fortune is transformed into a misfortune.

Example

"I found a lot of money but on my way home IT DISAPPEARED."

GF, D (M)

M4, D

2. The character to whom the good fortune occurs tries to press his luck and fails.

Example

"I dreamed I had found a lot of money. I invested it in order to make more money but THEN I LOST IT ALL."

GF, D (FL)

FL, D

3. Another character intervenes in an aggressive fashion and intentionally destroys the good fortune.

Example

"My teenage sister found this real cute puppy but my father said
  SHE COULDN'T KEEP IT."

GF, 1FTT (A)

1MFA 3> 1FTT

1. Score each misfortune that happens to the same character
when the misfortunes belong to different subclasses.

Example

"My brother's car WAS WRECKED and HE GOT CUTS ON HIS
  FACE and *broke his arm* in the accident."

M4, 1MBA

M5, 1MBA

2. Score each environmental press, even those that belong to
the same subclass, if they happen to the same character at different times in the dream.

Examples

"I was hungry and began to scratch my nose. All of a sudden A
  STEAK SUPPER APPEARED in front of me. I ate this and
  after awhile I scratched my nose again. Suddenly I WAS
  DRESSED IN THE FINEST OF CLOTHES. I began to wonder if my nose were magic."

GF, D

GF, D

"I was skiing when I ran into a tree and CUT MY LIP. I went back
  to the lodge and put a Band-Aid on it. Then I started out again.
  This time I SPRAINED MY ANKLE when one of my skis came
  off."

M5, D

M5, D

10

The Classification
and Scoring of Emotions

The classification of emotions was one of our most difficult tasks. The problem of reducing the hundreds of words in the English language that represent affective states to a fairly small number of classes that seemed to be fairly comprehensive, yet discrete in coverage, was a formidable one. Another stumbling block involved the question of extensity of scoring e.g., should we try to classify the types of situations that caused the emotion as well as consequences following the emotion? After experimenting with a large number of scoring schemes, we eventually arrived at the answer to this question and several others by limiting our emotional states to five in number and simply indicating which characters experienced these emotions.

When a scorer goes over dream reports he is generally surprised at how few emotions are actually reported, unless the dreamer is specifically and strongly urged to state what emotions he experienced during the dream. Situations that would undoubtedly be terrifying or depressing for the average individual may be reported in some detail, but a description of their emotional impact upon the dreamer is often curiously lacking.

The five classes of emotion are presented below.

110

ANGER

(Scoring symbol: AN). This class of emotions is generally easy to identify. Representative of some of the terms scored under anger are: annoyed, irritated, mad, provoked, furious, enraged, belligerent, incensed, and indignant. As with the following emotional classes, all degrees of intensity are included within each class, and no scoring distinction is made between weak expressions of anger such as being peeved or strong expressions such as being infuriated.

APPREHENSION

(Scoring symbol: AP). The emotions included in this class can be considered related to fear, anxiety, guilt, and embarrassment. Although differences are recognizable among them, all these conditions lead to conscious concern on the part of the person experiencing them. The person feels apprehensive about the possibility of physical injury or punishment, or the possibility of social ridicule or rejection. Thus the common denominator underlying these emotions is that the person is uncomfortable because the threat of some potential danger exists for him. The following terms, which are not meant to be all inclusive, refer to various degrees of apprehension: terrified, horrified, frightened, scared, worried, nervous, concerned, panicky, alarmed, uneasy, upset, remorseful, sorry, apologetic, regretful, and ashamed.

HAPPINESS

(Scoring symbol: HA). All the words that describe a general state of pleasant feeling tone are included in this class. Some of the terms that would be scored as happiness are: contented, pleased, relieved, amused, cheerful, glad, relaxed, gratified, gay, wonderful, elated, joyful, and exhilarated.

SADNESS

(Scoring symbol: SD). All the words that describe an unhappy emotional state are scored in the sadness class. References to physical pain or physical distress are not included in any of the emotional classes. Some examples of terms that would be scored as sadness are: disappointed, distressed, hurt, depressed, lonely, lost, miserable, hopeless, crushed, and heartbroken.

CONFUSION

(Scoring symbol: CO). Although it may be debatable as to whether confusion is a condition possessing the same degree of autonomic involvement as the preceding emotions, we have chosen to place it in the classification of emotions. It is true that confusion resides more in the head as a state of cognitive ambiguity than it does in the viscera as a gut-type reaction. However, the feeling state accompanying uncertainty may begin to shade toward a type of free-floating anxiety, toward frustration, or toward depression. Since confusion is therefore "emotionlike," and also because it is reported fairly frequently in dreams, mention of it seems to belong most appropriately in the classification of emotions. Confusion is generally produced either through confrontation with some unexpected event or else through inability to choose between available alternatives. Some words that may indicate confusion are: surprised, astonished, amazed, awestruck, mystified, puzzled, perplexed, strange, bewildered, doubtful, conflicted, undecided, and uncertain.

Scoring Procedures   Since emotions are often not described, the scorer may be tempted to infer emotions on the basis of the physical surroundings or activities mentioned in the dream report. This temptation should be resisted. If a dreamer says that he was in a torture chamber or being chased, the scorer should not assume that apprehension was being experienced unless the dreamer himself says that such an emotion was being experienced. We make only one exception to this. If the dreamer describes definite autonomic activity accompanying an event, and it is clear from the combination of context and the autonomic description that the dreamer was experiencing an emotion that could be clearly classified as one of the five scorable emotions, we will score an emotion. For example, if the dreamer says, "Tears began running down my face when I received word of my mother's death," we would score an SD for that description. We would score AP if the dreamer said, "As the monster approached, I began to sweat and tremble and tried to cry out but no sound would come." The above situations appear infrequently, however, and restraint is urged as the general rule in attributing any emotion to a character unless the dream report provides ample material to do so.

The scorer should not attempt to automatically assign an emotion on the basis of its listing in the preceding groups. In some cases, the same word may take on quite different meanings in different contexts. For example, the statement "I was shocked" might possibly indicate any one of the five emotional classes, depending upon how the dreamer goes on to describe his reaction.

The scoring procedure followed in the last two chapters is also employed for emotions. A comma is placed after the scoring symbol for the emotion and then the scoring symbols for the characters are presented. As usual, multiple characters are joined by plus signs.

Examples

"I became FURIOUS when I saw my boyfriend holding this girl's hand."

AN, D

"Suddenly, I realized that I was walking down the street with no clothes on. I became terribly EMBARRASSED."

AP, D

"My buddy and I were OVERJOYED when we finally found the treasure."

HA, D + 1MKA

"My sister was very DISAPPOINTED when she didn't get the job."

SD, 1FTA

"My aunt and uncle were SURPRISED to see this half-dog and half-cat creature walk across the floor."

CO, 1FRA + 1MRA

Additional Scoring Rules

1. If the terms used to describe a reaction to a particular event all belong to the same class, that class of emotions is only scored once for that event.

Example

"I was so PLEASED and *happy* to hear the news."

HA, D

2. The same class of emotion may be scored more than once if it appears as a reaction to different events.

Example

"I was MAD at my wife for not fixing coffee. Then I got MAD at the bus driver because he wouldn't give me change for a ten-dollar bill. When I arrived at work, I became MAD at my boss because he asked me to do someone else's work besides my own."

AN, D
AN, D
AN, D

3. If more than one class of emotion is described as a reaction to the same event, each class is scored separately.

Example

"I was SAD when I saw the damage to the roof but was GLAD that the rest of the house had not been damaged."

SD, D
HA, D

11

The Classification
and Scoring
of Descriptive Elements

The preceding chapters have contained information about scoring the physical surroundings in which the dream takes place, the characters in the dream, the various activities they engage in, what environmental events befall the characters, and how they felt about what happened to them. In addition to noting that objects and people appeared in a dream and that certain events took place, a dreamer may also describe some attributes and qualities of objects, people, actions, and emotional states. He says it was "a red car," "a large house," "an old lady," "a crowded church," "a cold day," "a crooked stick," "an intense fear," or "an ugly dog." In dream reports, a person may be characterized as "running rapidly," "working very hard," or "dancing beautifully." The dreamer may also note the passage of time—"we seemed to be riding for about an hour"—or refer to a particular time—"it was midnight." He may also describe things, people, and happenings not in terms of what they were but in terms of what they were *not*—"It was not my mother." We call all of these *descriptive elements*.

In scoring descriptive elements, three different scales are involved—the modifier scale, the temporal scale, and the negative scale. Each of these will be discussed below and illustrated by scoring examples.

MODIFIERS

A modifier is any adjective, adverb, or phrase that is used for descriptive elaboration. Since any object can be classified with regard to an extremely large number of attributes, the number of modifier classes could be a large one. We have limited the number of classes to nine. These nine represent those upon which satisfactory reliability could be obtained and for which psychological significance probably exists. Each of the nine classes can be considered to represent bipolar qualities, and each class of modifiers is therefore scored with a plus or minus sign to indicate which pole of the modifier is represented.

COLOR

(Scoring symbol: C). Any mention of color or a color name is scored unless the term is used to describe an emotional state. Chromatic colors are scored C+ and achromatic colors (black, white, and grey) are scored C—. The same color can be scored more than once if it refers to separate things. In the following examples, the reader is reminded that italics represent nonscorable elements.

Examples

"She was wearing a BLACK (C—) and YELLOW (C+) striped dress and was carrying a BLACK (C—) purse."

"The rainbow contained a great many COLORS (C+)."

"The WHITE-haired (C—) gentleman rose when I entered the room."

"Her cheeks turned RED (C+) with embarrassment."

"It was a *dark night*."

"I felt sad and *blue*."

"I called him a *yellow* coward."

"She *blushed* as the cheap *silver* utensils were put on the table."
"The *dark*-haired stranger was with a *blond* woman."

SIZE

(Scoring symbol: S). This class contains all references to the largeness or smallness of things. Descriptive terms indicating a large size such as big, huge, thick, tall, high, broad, and deep are scored S+. The antonyms of these terms such as small, tiny, thin, short, low, narrow, and shallow are scored S−. The concept of size is ordinarily thought of as being appropriate only for objects which have height, width, and length—that is, for three dimensional objects. As is evident from the above list of terms, we score a reference to any one of these three physical dimensions as a size term. References to the temporal dimension as when an interval of time is described as short or long are not scored as size modifiers. It should be remembered that although many nouns such as midget or giant could be classified as indicating size differences, it is only the modifying terms that are included in the modifier scale.

Examples

"I climbed a HIGH (S+) wall and ran down a NARROW (S−) street between TALL (S+) buildings."
"This boy, who was SHORT (S−), had on a shirt that was too SMALL (S−) for him and a LONG (S+) tie with TINY (S−) polka dots."
"A FAT (S+) lady with a MINIATURE (S−) poodle was walking down a WIDE (S+) street."
"I waited a *long* time for the train to arrive."
"We had a *narrow* escape."
"The baby was sitting on a ledge of the *skyscraper*."

AGE

(Scoring symbol: A). References to a person being old or to an object being old are scored A+. References to a person being young or to an object being new are scored A−. Synonymous terms for old, young, and new are also scorable as are comparative age terms such as older and younger. Only these bipolar distinctions in age are included in this class and mention of a character's specific age is therefore not scored.

Examples

"The YOUNG (A—) man was driving a NEW (A—) car."
"I walked up to this ANCIENT (A+) mansion and an ELDERLY (A+) man greeted me."
"My OLD (A+) boyfriend laughed at my YOUNGER (A—) brother."
"All of the rooms in this MODERN (A—) hotel had furniture of the LATEST (A—) style."
"I cuddled and sang to this *baby*."
"My grandfather is *80 years old*."

DENSITY

(Scoring symbol: D). Modifiers included in this class must refer to a bounded area or to some type of container. References to such areas or containers as being full, bulging, or crowded are scored D+. If such areas or containers are described as empty they are scored as D—.

Examples

"The church was CROWDED (D+) with people."
"I felt STUFFED (D+) after the large meal."
"The elevator was JAM-PACKED (D+) with passengers."
"His wallet was BULGING (D+) with dollar bills."
"The suitcase was EMPTY (D—)."
"The tree trunk was HOLLOW (D—)."
"I was unable to move in the *crowd*."
"*No one* was at home."
"I was all *alone* in the big house."

THERMAL

(Scoring symbol: T). References to contrasting temperatures are included in this class. Things that are described as warm or hot are scored T+; things that are described as cool or cold, are scored T−. Other descriptive terms that refer to measurable qualities of temperature are also scorable. Objects that are inferentially known to be hot or cold or descriptions of verbal interactions as heated, etc., are not scored.

Examples

"I suddenly felt WARM (T+)."
"The water seemed FRIGID (T−) when I stepped into it."
"The wind was CHILLY (T−)."
"The cowboy was cooking something over a *fire*."
"The *ice* on the lake was covered with *snowy* slush."
"He spoke *coldly* to me when I said that he wasn't such *hot* stuff."

VELOCITY

(Scoring symbol: V). This class contains references to the speed with which objects or people move. Fast movement is scored V+ and slow movement is scored V−. Speed of mental activity is scorable if described in such terms as quickly or slowly but the word suddenly is not scored.

Examples

"I walked FAST (V+) down the street."
"I drove the car SLOWLY (V−) through the RAPIDLY (V+) flowing stream."
"I QUICKLY (V+) calculated the answer and wrote it down."
"*All of a sudden,* I realized that this man who had *stopped* the truck was some sort of spy."
"She *ran* to meet her father who was *limping* toward her."
"The train was *suddenly* going about *70 miles an hour* down the tracks."

LINEARITY

(Scoring symbol: L). References to whether an object possesses linear or nonlinear qualities are included in this class. Objects that are described as straight or flat are scored L+ and objects that are described as curved, crooked, or in synonymous terms are scored L−. Knowledge that an object is straight or curved is not sufficient grounds for scoring; the dreamer himself must indicate that attention was paid to these qualities of linearity.

Examples

"Ahead, the road across the FLAT (L+) prairie rose and TWISTED (L−) around the mountain."
"The girl with the STRAIGHT (L+) hair asked the CURLY-haired (L−) girl for a match."
"The floor was WARPED (L−) and the walks were very BUMPY (L−)."
"She drew a *line* with the *ruler*."
"He wanted a *straight* answer as to whether the deal was *on the level* or *crooked*."

INTENSITY

(Scoring symbol: I). Contained within this class are modifiers that are used to describe force or expenditure of energy. Modifiers indicating a strong intensity are scored I+; modifiers indicating a weak intensity are scored I−. Intensity modifiers may refer to either physical or mental energy or to emotions and sensations. Simple mention of an emotion generally associated with a strong affect is not sufficient for scoring; the dreamer must use some intensity modifier such as very, or greatly, in order to be considered scorable.

Examples

"There was a LOUD (I+) clap of thunder followed by a BRIGHT (I+) flash of lightning and a STRONG (I+), VERY (I+) cold wind."
"I worked VERY HARD (I+) on solving the physics problem."
"I felt TERRIBLY (I+) happy for the winner and SLIGHTLY (I−) sad for the loser."
"It was a QUIET (I−), DIMLY-lit (I−) room and as my boyfriend held me GENTLY (I−) in his STRONG (I+) arms, I became A LITTLE BIT (I−) aroused."
"The husband became *furious* because his wife kept *screaming*."

EVALUATION

(Scoring symbol: E). This class covers evaluative remarks that are made about people or objects. Since so many terms could be considered to represent a judgment, opinion, or evaluation of some sort, we found it difficult to obtain any appreciable degree of scoring reliability until we finally limited our scoring to only two areas. These two areas are those of aesthetic and moral evaluation. Descriptions indicating that something is considered aesthetically pleasing or morally correct are scored E+; descriptions indicating the aesthetically unpleasant or morally incorrect are scored E−. Reference to any type of stimulus considered to be pleasant or unpleasant to the senses is included in the aesthetic class. Included in the moral class are references to personal conduct as being right, correct, appropriate, or approved, and references indicating the opposite kind of evaluation.

Examples

"The sunset was BEAUTIFUL (E+)."
"This HANDSOME (E+) boy asked me to dance while the band played a LOVELY (E+) tune."
"A DIRTY LOOKING (E−) man came out of a SHABBY (E−) hut."
"I thought that was a TERRIBLE (E−) thing for him to say to his mother because she had always been GOOD (E+) to him.
"She made a *wrong* turn and caused a *bad* accident."
"None of my answers were *right* on the quiz and I felt *terrible*."

TEMPORAL SCALE

Within the dream report, references may occur to various time intervals or to particular points in time. Such temporal references are indicated by the scoring symbol T. No distinction is made between long and short units of time; thus, unlike the bipolar modifier scales, + and − differentiations are not included as part of the scoring symbols. The thermal class is also indicated by the scoring symbol T, but the + or − sign is always included in the thermal scoring. Examples of the two subclasses of temporal references which are scored are included below as well as examples of situations which are not scored.

1. References to a specific unit of time such as a minute, hour, day, week, or year and references to a nonspecific interval of elapsed time.

Examples

"My girl friend spent the DAY with me."
"He worked on the NIGHT SHIFT."
"My roommate went home for the WEEKEND."
"My mother had had the ring for MANY YEARS."
"A FEW MINUTES later I got up and went outside."
"He kept me waiting for a LONG TIME."
"We talked for A WHILE and then he asked me to dance."

2. Reference to a particular time for the purpose of dating an event.

Examples

"It was EARLY IN THE MORNING when we started out."
"I said I would met him about 10 O'CLOCK."
"AT THAT MOMENT, I saw a snake cross the road."
"I thought to myself that the examination is TODAY."
"We were planning to go on a picnic TOMORROW."
"It was the FOURTH OF JULY."

Do not score the age of a person.

Examples

"She was *ten years old.*"
"My father is *middle-aged.*"

Do not score the use of the word "time" when it refers to an occasion.

Examples

"I had a good *time*."
"I had a real hard *time* starting the car."

Do not score sequence of events.

Examples

"*After* the parade, we went to get something to eat."
"*Then* the *next* thing that happened, we were in a car."
"*After* struggling hard, I *finally* got free."

Do not score salutations in which there is a reference to the time of day.

Examples

"He said *good-night* and left."
"I yelled *good-morning* to the mailman."

NEGATIVE SCALE

The remaining scale that appears in the classification of descriptive elements is the negative scale. Some dreamers use direct, straightforward language in describing just what happened in their dreams, while other dreamers take a much more devious approach and describe what was not happening or what something did not resemble. Since these differences in descriptive approach can be discerned in reading dream reports, we decided that a negative scale should be constructed that would reflect these stylistic differences. This is the only scale in which comments by the dreamer on his dream such as "It was not a long dream" are scored. Scoring examples for the two types of negative words are given below. The scoring symbol for negative words is N.

1. Use of any of the common negative words such as no, not, none, never, neither, and nor.

Examples

"There was NO one at the door when I opened it."
"It was NOT a gun but a bottle that the man had in his hand."
"When I asked him for some candy, he said he had NONE."
"My brother NEVER wears a tie."
"It was NEITHER my mother NOR my father, but some strange couple that was living in our house."
"I recognized the person in my dream but I can NOT remember who it was now."
"There were NO other people in the dream."

2. Use of negative words that are created by adding certain prefixes to adjectives or adverbs. When these prefixes are added and used in such a way that the word *not* could be substituted for the prefix without changing the meaning, the word is counted as a negative. These prefixes are un, im, in, il, ir, and non.

Examples

"I was UNSURE of my ability and thought I would be INCAPABLE of doing it."
"His behavior was INEXCUSABLE and he broke an IRREPLACE-ABLE vase."
"We were UNAWARE that what we had done was IMPROPER but the policeman said it was ILLEGAL."
"The mechanic said it was a NONESSENTIAL part that was missing."
"It seemed *imminent* that he would be *imprisoned*."
"I thought I was *infatuated* with this boy *until* I saw him *inebriated*."
"After the bomb exploded, the sky was *illuminated* and I knew the *irradiation* had begun."

12

Theoretical Scales

A theoretical scale presumes to measure a construct or group of constructs which are associated with a particular personality theory. Instances of constructs which have been operationally or ostensively defined in terms of dream contents are castration anxiety, masochism, ego strength, orality, regression, and ego identity. Of necessity, a theoretical scale consists of selected items of dream contents; it points, so to speak, to certain things in dream reports and says, in effect, "That's castration and that's orality and that's masochism." That which is pointed to sometimes is a direct representation of the construct. People do dream of eating (orality) and they do dream of the past (regression). More often, however, that which is pointed to in the dream is an indirect or symbolic representation of the construct. People rarely dream of being castrated but they often dream of injuring some part of the body or of damaging a car. What gives one the right to say that cutting a finger or crumpling a fender symbolizes castration? Such symbol-referent associations are in the nature of hypotheses which in turn are derived from a theory of symbolism.

Although this is not the place to discuss the complex question of symbolism (see, for example, Hall, 1953), it may be pointed out that hypotheses regarding dream symbols are often based upon a psychoanalytic theory whose conceptual ingredients include displacement, identification, anxiety, and sleep protection.

The cutting of the penis is displaced to the cutting of a finger because (1) finger is identified with penis through similarity of form and function, and (2) to dream of castration would produce so much anxiety that (3) it would awaken the dreamer. One may dismiss the theory as absurd or one may utilize it for formulating testable hypotheses.

In this chapter we will discuss three theoretical scales that we devised. Two of the scales have already shown their usefulness in empirical investigations. We look forward to seeing their validity, as well as that of the third scale, more fully investigated in future studies.

THE CLASSIFICATION AND SCORING OF CASTRATION ANXIETY, CASTRATION WISH, AND PENIS ENVY

The first scales to be discussed are those that purport to measure the three components of the castration complex—namely, castration anxiety, castration wish, and penis envy. Using these scales, Hall and Van de Castle (1965) scored a large number of male and female dream series and found, as had been predicted on the basis of psychoanalytic theory, that significantly more males than females displayed castration anxiety, whereas significantly more females than males expressed castration wish and penis envy in their dreams.

CASTRATION ANXIETY

Four subclasses of castration anxiety are included in our scoring system. Descriptions of situations which should and should not be scored are presented below along with illustrative examples. The scoring symbol for Castration Anxiety is CA.

CA1   This subclass involves injury or threat to the dreamer's body. In four of the five conditions listed below, emphasis is

placed upon a part of the dreamer's body being involved; in only
one of the conditions is emphasis placed upon the dreamer's body
as a whole.

1. Actual or threatened loss of a part of the dreamer's body.

Examples

"MY FINGER was CUT OFF."
"I got a HAIRCUT."
"The nurse said they were going to REMOVE MY TONSILS."

2. Actual or threatened injury to or pain in a part of the
dreamer's body.

Examples

"I CUT MY FOOT."
"He tried to PUNCH ME ON THE JAW."
"I had a HEADACHE."

3. Defect in a part of the dreamer's body.

Examples

"MY LEGS BECAME PARALYZED."
"MY HAND was all CRIPPLED UP."
"I COULDN'T SEE out of one eye."

4. Some part of the dreamer's body is juvenile, infantile, or
undersized.

Examples

"The dentist said I still HAD BABY TEETH."
"In the mirror MY FACE LOOKED LIKE AN INFANT'S."
"I was amazed to see that I HAD NO PUBIC HAIR."

5. Actual or threatened cutting, clawing, biting, or stabbing of the dreamer's body as a whole.

Examples

"He JABBED AT ME WTH A SWITCHBLADE."
"An eagle CAME AT ME WITH HIS CLAWS OPEN."
"The crocodiles TRIED TO BITE ME."

Do not score as CA1.

1. No specific part of the dreamer's body is mentioned as being injured, threatened, defective, diseased, or infantile.

Examples

"I was hurt in the accident."
"I fell off this high cliff."
"I was trapped in a burning building."
"I ached all over."
"I was paralyzed."
"I had the measles."
"I looked like a little child."

2. A blemish or swelling is mentioned on a part of the dreamer's body.

Examples

"I had a pimple on my face."
"I had a scar on my arm."
"A ball hit me and my ankle swelled up."

CA2   Actual or threatened injury, loss, defect, disease, or damage occurring to an animal or object belonging to the dreamer or that is in his possession in the dream.

Examples

"My dog had his TAIL INJURED."
"I LOST MY BOOKS."
"MY RADIO WOULDN'T WORK."
"I had a FLAT TIRE on my car."
"The AIRPLANE I was in CRASHED."
"The CHAIR I was sitting on HAD A BROKEN LEG."

Do not score as CA2.

Nonspecific losses to the dreamer or damage, defect, or loss of objects in the dreamer's possession which are primarily symbolic of female genitals.

Examples

"*I was robbed* during the night."
"The *stone fell out of my ring.*"
"*I lost my purse.*"
"*My suitcase was broken.*"
"The *box* I was carrying *split open.*"

CA3 The dreamer reports inability or difficulty in using a gun, airplane, automobile, piece of machinery, or other symbolic phallic objects that are in his possession; difficulty in using a penis; or difficulty in placing an object in a receptacle.

Examples

"I COULDN'T START THE CAR."
"I COULDN'T SHOOT STRAIGHT WITH THE RIFLE."
"When I came up to bat, I STRUCK OUT."
"I WASN'T ABLE TO GET AN ERECTION."
"I COULDN'T GET MY KEY IN THE LOCK."

Do not score as CA3.

The dreamer's difficulty in using a phallic object is caused by an environmental event rather than his own inadequacy.

Examples

"I couldn't steer straight because of the icy road."
"I couldn't sink the putt because the wind blew my ball off course."

CA4   A male dreamer reports that he is a woman or changes into a woman during the dream, or that he has acquired female secondary sex characteristics, or that he is wearing women's clothes or accessories.

Examples

"Suddenly at that point, I TURNED INTO A GIRL."
"When I looked down, I saw that I HAD BREASTS."
"For some reason, I WAS WEARING A DRESS AND HIGH HEELS."

CASTRATION WISH

There is only one subclass of Castration Wish. The scoring symbol is CW.

CW   The criteria for castration wish are the same as those for castration anxiety except that they do not occur to the dreamer but to another specified person in the dream.

Examples

"My brother HURT HIS LEG."
"My mother CUT HER FINGER."

"My friend WRECKED HIS CAR."
"HE HAD THE FACE OF A FIVE-YEAR-OLD."
"MY SISTER'S DOG WAS STOLEN."
"HE COULDN'T GET HIS GUN TO WORK."
"My buddy BROKE HIS BAT."
"My best FRIEND CHANGED INTO A GIRL."
"HE DIDN'T HAVE ANY PENIS."

Note: Occasionally one finds instances of wish for self-castration in dreams. Although we have not used these in scoring CW, it is conceivable that there may be times when an investigator would want to take them into account. In any event, they are quite rare. The following are examples:

"I gave my car away."
"I gave my buddy my gun."
"I gave my girl my fountain pen."

PENIS ENVY

There are three subclasses of Penis Envy. The scoring symbol is PE.

PE1 Acquisition within the dream by the dreamer, or by a group of which the dreamer is a member, of an object that has phallic characteristics. In addition to some of the specific objects mentioned in CA3, include any object that is elongated (ruler, pencil, banana), intrusive (knife, key, needle), or capable of discharging its contents in a squirting fashion (syringe, fountain pen, toothpaste tube). Acquisition of money is also included.

Examples

"I BOUGHT A RIFLE."
"My boyfriend LOANED ME HIS CAR."
"The old-style plane I was riding in BECAME A JET PLANE."
"HE GAVE ME A CIGARETTE."
"I FOUND A SCREWDRIVER."

"Suddenly there was a SWORD IN MY HAND."
"The stranger HANDED ME A BAG OF COINS."

Do not score as PE1

Situations where the dreamer is in possession of an object but did not acquire it *within* the dream.

Examples

"I was hunting *with my rifle*."
"I was driving *my boyfriend's car*."
"I was riding *in a jet plane*."
"I was *smoking a cigarette*."
"I *used a screwdriver* to fix it."
"I was dueling *with a sword*."
"I was rich and *had bags of money*."

PE2   The dreamer envies or admires a man's physical characteristics, his prowess, or his possessions that have phallic characteristics.

Examples

"I ADMIRED HIS BROAD SHOULDERS."
"HE WAS A MUCH BETTER SHOT than I was."
"I wished that I OWNED A FANCY CAR LIKE HIS."
"HIS GOLF CLUBS WERE IN MUCH BETTER CONDITION than mine."

PE3   A female dreamer reports that she is a man or changes into a man during the dream, or that she has acquired male secondary sex characteristics, or that she is wearing men's clothes or accessories. Since women frequently wear men's clothes, it must be an article of clothing not commonly worn by women.

Examples

"Then I BECAME A MAN."
"I felt my face and discovered I HAD GROWN A BEARD."
"I was WEARING AN IVY LEAGUE SUIT."

Additional Scoring Rules

1. If more than one possession is lost or acquired, one point is given for each different type of possession involved.

Examples

"I LOST MY RIFLE and MY FISHING POLE." Two points on CA
"I LOST MY REMINGTON and *my Winchester rifle.*" One point on CA
"George had a FLAT TIRE ON HIS CAR and a SMASHED FENDER ON HIS MOTORCYCLE." Two points on CW
"I FOUND A KNIFE and a HAMMER." Two points on PE

2. If a joint possession is lost or acquired by more than one character, a score is given for each character involved.

Examples

"The CAR, which belonged to my fraternity brother and me, WAS DAMAGED by the storm." One point CW and one point CA
"My father GAVE A BASEBALL BAT to my brother and me." Two points PE

3. If more than one body part is involved in castration, one point is given for each different type of body part that is mentioned.

Examples

"MY ARM and MY LEG WERE CUT from the accident." Two points
  CA

"*Two of* MY FINGERS WERE CUT from the accident." One point
  CA

"Jack received a BLOODY NOSE and a BROKEN LEG in the football game." Two points CW

THE CLASSIFICATION AND SCORING
OF ORAL ACTIVITIES AND
ORAL REFERENCES

We have constructed two scales of orality; one that deals with oral activities and one that deals with oral references. They are not to be construed as complete measures of orality as that term is usually defined by psychoanalysis. They do not include any derivatives of the oral period, such as dependency and nurturance needs. Nor do they include any reaction formations against the oral mode. These scales do have the virtue, however, of possessing face validity since the subclasses which make up the scales are quite directly oral or oral-related in nature. The use of these scales in empirical investigations will show whether they have construct validity and whether the presence of orality in dreams is correlated with the character traits often assumed to be derived from the oral period.

THE ORAL INCORPORATION SCALE

This scale consists of the consummatory activities of eating and drinking and of preparatory activities that precede and lead up to these consummatory activities. The five subclasses listed below are arranged in order of increasing distance from the consummatory responses which constitute the first subclass. The scoring symbol for Oral Incorporation is OI.

OI1   A character is reported as actually eating, drinking, nursing, swallowing, etc., or these activities are referred to although they do not actually occur during the dream.

Examples

"My boyfriend and I ATE hamburgers after the movies."
"I was reminded of the fish we ATE on our last camping trip."
"They say he DRINKS a quart of liquor a day."
"I SWALLOWED the nasty stuff in spite of its bitterness."

OI2   A character is actually in an eating place such as a restaurant, bar, dining room, picnic grounds, or cafeteria, or an eating place is referred to in the dream report. *Do not score* if it is explicitly stated that the character is in the eating place for a reason other than that of eating or drinking.

Examples

"I went into the DINING ROOM to set the table."
"He said he had been at THE PUMP ROOM in Chicago."
"There was a small band playing in the TAVERN."
"We were in the *dining room* playing cards."
"I went into the *bar* to use the telephone."

OI3   A character is preparing food, cooking it, or seeing or using utensils associated with food, or these activities or objects are mentioned in the dream report.

Examples

"My mother was MIXING SOME CAKE BATTER."
"There was a set of COPPER FRYING PANS hanging on the wall."
"My girlfriend got an ELECTRIC TOASTER for her birthday."
"My sister said I had better attend COOKING SCHOOL if I wanted to catch a husband."

OI4   A character secures food by buying it, picking it, or some other means, or a character is in a food store, or these are mentioned in the dream report. *Do not score* if it is explicitly stated that the character is in the food store for a reason other than that of buying food.

Examples

"My mother sent me to BUY BREAD AND BUTTER."
"I told her I was going to PICK STRAWBERRIES."
"I saw the old man STEAL AN APPLE from the stand."
"I dreamed that a new SUPERMARKET was being built across the street from our house."
"I went into the *grocery store* to get change for a dollar."

OI5   Food is seen or mentioned in the dream report but not in connection with any of the foregoing activities; that is, it is not being eaten, served, prepared, or bought. If food is seen or mentioned in connection with one of the foregoing subclasses 1-4, do not give food an additional scoring.

Examples

"There were GRAPES hanging from a vine."
"She asked me if I liked APPLES and I said yes."
"A still life painting of VEGETABLES hung on the wall."
"She was carrying a huge HAMBURGER in her hand."
"I BOUGHT *two candy bars*."

Additional Scoring Rules

1. Score one point for each different subclass that is contained in the dream report.

Examples

"We BOUGHT *marshmallows,* TOASTED them over the campfire, and ATE THEM." Three points

"We PICKED *blackberries* and MADE WINE." Two points

2. Score one point for each repetition of the same subclass in a dream report when the subclass repetitions take place in different locations or involve different characters.

Examples

"My mother BOUGHT *bread* while I was PICKING OUT the *meat.*" Two points

"First we went to a BAR for a *martini* and then we went to the CAFETERIA for *roast beef.*" Two points

"The neighbor's TOMATOES were larger than our TOMATOES." Two points

3. Score one point for each repetition of the same subclass when the subclass repetitions are separated by intervening events in the dream report.

Example

"I ATE A QUICK BREAKFAST and dashed off to school because I was late. After class, I studied for awhile and then had A SECOND BREAKFAST." Two points

4. *Do not score* mention of a food or food utensil if they are used as some standard of comparison.

Examples

"It was a rock the size of a *grapefruit.*"

"The dress had the same color as a *plum.*"

"His eyes got as big as *saucers.*"

THE ORAL EMPHASIS SCALE

This scale contains two subclasses which deal with oral activities other than eating and drinking, and with references to the oral zone or cavity. It does not include any verbal activities. The latter are covered by the Activities scale which contains a class explicitly devoted to verbal activities. The scoring symbol for Oral Emphasis is OE.

OE1   A character engages in an activity involving the mouth such as smoking, kissing, playing an instrument requiring the use of the mouth or lips, grinning, blowing up a balloon, smiling, whistling, chewing gum, biting, laughing, and singing; it also includes any mention of these activities even if the activity does not actually occur in the dream. Count also any reference to an object, other than the mouth or part of the mouth, which is used primarily for an oral activity. Score only when there appears to be an intent on the part of a character to use it for oral activities. *Do not score* when the object is being used, or there is an intent to use it, for nonoral purposes.

Examples

"The dog was LICKING its hurt paw."
"My brother PLAYS THE TUBA in the high school band."
"I broke my FLUTE, and I was very unhappy."
"These children were all BLOWING BUBBLES."
"My boy friend went in the store to buy a CIGAR."
"He SMACKED HIS LIPS with pleasure."
"My father SMOKES A PIPE."
"The lifeguard was using MOUTH-TO-MOUTH ARTIFICIAL RESPIRATION on the unconscious swimmer."
"I used a *toothpick* to clean my ears."

OE2   Reference is made to the oral zone or parts of the oral zone such as the mouth, lips, teeth, and tongue. Do not include throat or any region below the throat. If the mouth or a part of it is mentioned in connection with an oral activity under OE1, do not give the mouth or mouth part an additional scoring.

Examples

"He had big, thick LIPS and beady eyes."
"My GUMS were swollen and they were very painful."
"I dreamed all of my TEETH fell out."
"She was APPLYING LIPSTICK (OE1) to her *lips*."

Additional Scoring Rules

1. Score one point for each reference to a different oral activity in a dream report.

Examples

"I said I would KISS her as soon as I finished SMOKING." Two points
"First he WHISTLED the tune, and then he SANG the words." Two
points

2. Score one point for each reference to a different part of the mouth in a dream report.

Example

"His TEETH and GUMS were a mess. His TONGUE was heavily
coated and his LIPS were almost bloodless. He looked like a
very sick little boy to me." Four points

3. Score one point for each repetition of the same oral activity when it is performed by different characters.

Example

"My sister PLAYS THE TRUMPET and I also PLAY THE TRUM-
PET." Two points

4. Score one point for each repetition of the same oral activity when the repeated occurrences are separated by intervening
events in the dream.

Example

"I was BRUSHING MY TEETH when the phone rang. I answered it
and discovered it was my girl friend. We talked for so long that
my father got angry. Finally, I hung up and went back to finish
BRUSHING MY TEETH." Two points

5. Score one point for each repetition of the same part of the
oral zone when it belongs to different characters.

Example

"He put his LIPS to my LIPS and they felt warm and wonderful."
Two points

THE CLASSIFICATION AND SCORING
OF REGRESSION

It is commonly believed that as a person grows older he
lives more and more in the past. In technical parlance, he is said
to regress with age. Smith and Hall (1964) made a study of regression in the dreams of a person who had recorded her dreams
for fifty years. The incidence of regression in her dreams did not
change significantly over a period of fifty years. Seven subclasses
of events in dreams are scored as being regressive. They are listed
below. The scoring symbol for Regression is RE.

RE1   The dreamer dreams of being in a setting or locale in which he has not been for over a year.

Example

"I was teaching in a school that I taught in WHEN I WAS A YOUNG WOMAN."

RE2   The dreamer dreams of being younger by at least a year.

Example

"In this dream, I SAW MYSELF AS A CHILD with long pigtails."

RE3   The dreamer dreams of someone he has not seen or heard from within a year.

Example

"I was at a party when in walked Nancy Jones. I HAVE NOT SEEN HER OR THOUGHT ABOUT HER FOR YEARS."

RE4   The dreamer dreams of doing something he has not done for at least a year.

Example

"My brother and I were climbing a mountain. I HAVE NOT BEEN ABLE TO DO ANY CLIMBING FOR THE LAST FIVE YEARS, although I used to do a lot when I was younger."

RE5   The dreamer dreams of someone who has been dead for at least a year.

Example

"I SAW MY FATHER come into the room and kiss my mother. I knew
    he was my father ALTHOUGH HE'S BEEN DEAD FOR OVER
    FIFTY YEARS because he had a black beard which he used to
    let me pull when I was a child."

RE6   The dreamer dreams of another person as being younger,
by at least a year, than he currently is.

Example

"My sister appeared to be about 18 YEARS OLD in the dream al-
    though she is actually over 40."

RE7   The dreamer dreams of an object which he has not had for
at least a year.

Example

"I was wearing a dress THAT I GAVE AWAY YEARS AGO."

Do not score the following as being regressive.

1. The dreamer or another character is talking in the dream
about something that happened in the past.

Example

"My cousin recalled the time when *we were children* and had got lost
    in the woods."

2. The dreamer or another character is reminded in the dream of something that happened in the past.

Example

"We were all on this large boat which was pitching and tossing. I felt seasick. It reminded me of *the time I had been seasick on our first voyage to Japan.*"

3. Something in the dream is like something in the past but it is recognized as being different.

Example

"*He looked like an old beau of mine* except he was much taller."

4. After the dreamer has awakened and recalls a dream, he associates something in the dream with something in the past.

Example

"The car we were riding in—well, now that I think about it—*it was like one we had when I was in college.*"

REFERENCES

HALL, C. S. A cognitive theory of dream symbols. *J. gen. Psychol.*, 1953, *48*, 169-186.

HALL, C. S. and VAN DE CASTLE, R. L. An empirical investigation of the castration complex in dreams. *J. Pers.*, 1965, *33*, 20-29.

SMITH, MADORAH E. and HALL, C. S. An investigation of regression in a long dream series. *J. Gerontol.*, 1964, *19*, 66-71.

13

Reliability of Scoring

When the term reliability is used in connection with a measurement device, it refers to consistency of measurement. This consistency is generally investigated by comparing scores from one half of a test to those from the other half of the same test, by comparing scores from one form of a test to those from a parallel form of the test, or by comparing scores obtained from a test at one point in time with scores from the same test at a later point in time. When utilizing these indices of consistency, the emphasis in interpreting the errors of measurement is placed upon subject variables, such as fatigue, and test variables, such as uneven sampling of items. This emphasis is appropriate when dealing with simple tests, such as those of the multiple choice variety, where consistency of scoring can be assured by means of a template or scoring key containing the acceptable answers. However, when dealing with more complex measurement devices such as projective techniques, a more fundamental source of error must first be considered—that of scoring reliability—because if judges cannot agree as to the scores assigned to a measurement device, it is pointless to consider any other types of reliability indices.

Scoring reliability has been a sadly neglected topic among researchers of projective techniques. It is a rare study that reports any figures for scoring agreement, and those that do are generally quite vague in describing the methods that were used to obtain their figures. Since we are considering the dream report to be a type of projective protocol, the problems and the approaches to the solutions of these problems will coincide for both types of productions.

Scoring reliability can be assessed in several ways. The answer as to which procedure is the correct one for a particular study will depend upon the type of final score that the investigator wishes to extract from his material and the unit of analysis that he intends to employ. Once these have been decided, the investigator then determines how successfully his judges can agree on the occurrence of these selected scores. Perhaps this will become clearer by considering some of the possible measures which could be computed from the data shown in Table 13-1.

Table 13-1
Hypothetical Aggressive Scores

Series				I				II		
Dream No.	1	2	3	4	5	6	7	8	9	10
Judge A	8	0	7	3,4	0	3,7	6	2	2	4,7
Judge B	7	5	8	0	2	0	3	6,6	2,3	1

The figures shown in Table 13-1 represent some hypothetical ones which might have been obtained if two judges had scored two dream series, each containing five dreams, for the number and types of aggressive incidents present in each dream. The numerals in the table refer to the subclasses of aggression that are differentiated in our classification system. It will be recalled that subclasses 5-8 consist of various forms of physical aggression, while subclasses 1-4 consist of nonphysical forms of aggression.

If the unit of analysis were to consist of a dream series, and the judges asked to place these series into two aggressive groups —a low group containing four or less aggressive incidents and a high group containing five or more aggressive incidents—the judges would have obtained 100% agreement. Judge A and Judge B both scored four aggressive incidents for the first series and five or more for the second series, so both would classify the first series in the low aggressive group and the second series in the high aggressive group.

An investigator might make the individual dream the unit of analysis and ask whether judges could agree on how many dreams contained an aggressive incident. Since both judges scored a total of eight dreams for the presence of some aggressive incident, they again obtain 100% scoring agreement.

If an investigator were interested only in the number of aggressions, he might ask whether the judges would report similar totals for the number of aggressive incidents. When the total number of aggressions for Judge A (11) is divided into the number for Judge B (10), a figure of 91% agreement is obtained. Focusing interest only on the number of nonphysical aggressions, Judge A scored six and Judge B scored five incidents, which would represent 83% agreement.

If an investigator asked whether judges could agree on which individual dreams contained some aggressive incident, a different reliability figure would be obtained. Both judges agreed that some aggression was present in Dreams 1, 3, 7, 8, 9, and 10, and they disagreed on whether aggression was present or absent in the other four dreams. In this case, their agreement on six of the ten dreams would represent 60% scoring agreement.

Generally, the type of question most meaningful for an investigator to ask is whether the judges can agree on the number and types of aggressive incidents which occur in each dream. Examination of Table 13-1 indicates that the judges agreed in only one instance; both had scored a subclass 2 for Dream 9. The number one therefore appears in the numerator, but what number should appear in the denominator when computing the percentage of agreement? If the number of dreams is used, the percentage of agreement is 10%. A more appropriate denominator would consist of the number of agreements plus the number of disagreements. Thus Judge A scored an 8 for Dream 1 but since Judge B did not, this is a disagreement. Similarly, Judge B scored a 7 for Dream 1 but Judge A did not, so another failure to agree appears. If this is done for all the dreams, 1 agreement and 19 disagreements are tallied and the percentage of agreement becomes 5%. If the question were phrased, "In what percentage of dreams did the judges agree exactly on both the number and type of aggressions," the percentage figure becomes 0%, because the judges did not agree on the number of aggressions present in Dream 9.

The preceding examples have shown that at least eight different reliability figures could have been reported for the data of Table 13-1. It is possible for the percentage of agreement figures to range from values of 100% to 0%, depending upon the type of score used and the unit of analysis that is employed. These examples have all involved reliability computations based upon whether judges agreed that a certain index of aggression was present. It would also be possible to compute reliability figures based upon agreement that a certain type of aggressive index was absent.

Referring again to Table 13-1, it can be seen that a subclass 1 score was given by Judge B for Dream 10. If agreement as to absence of this subclass were tallied, the judges agreed that nine of the ten dreams did not contain a subclass 1 score, thereby obtaining 90% scoring agreement. Particularly when dealing with some infrequently appearing category, we can expect that there will be a high level of agreement that the category was not present. Thus a very inflated reliability figure can be obtained, if it is based upon agreement as to whether a scoring element is present or absent. Percentage of agreement should be based only upon those cases where at least one scorer has rated the particular element to be present. If this more appropriate measure is used, the judges attain 0% agreement rather than the 90% figure reported for presence or absence of subclass 1 aggressions.

The preceding illustrations have not been intended to discourage the use of percentage agreement figures in reporting reliability measures. These figures can be relevant and very informative in many situations. What we are discouraging are such vague statements as "The judges agreed 78% in their scoring of aggression" or "The incidence of aggression was agreed upon in 85% of the cases." These statements are almost completely lacking in communication value. If one wishes to use percentage of agreement measures, he must assume the responsibility of being very explicit and detailed in describing how the figures were obtained.

Some have felt that the correlation coefficient is a more meaningful measure for evaluating consistency of judges' scores. A correlation coefficient is the standard statistic to report split-half, parallel form, and test-retest reliabilities. An inherent property of this statistic is that statements about "true" scores and standard errors of measurement can be provided. Use of this statistic, however, involves certain assumptions which frequently cannot be met in treating some types of data. If scores must be assigned to a small number of categories or are limited in the magnitude they can reach, a correlation coefficient will not provide a meaningful measure of scoring reliability. Moreover, it is possible that scoring disagreements may be effectively masked through the use of this statistic. To take an extreme example, two judges might obtain a perfect correlation coefficient of 1.00 between them, yet one of them could have scored 45 aggressive incidents and the other 110 incidents. This could occur if for ten dream samples, Judge A gave scores of 1, 2, 3, 4, 5, 6, 7, 8, 9, and 10 while Judge B gave scores of 2, 4, 6, 8, 10, 12, 14, 16, 18, and 20. Thus, if one judge is consistently more or less lenient than another judge, the consistent relationship between their scores may result in a statistically significant correlation coefficient even though the total number of scores for each judge is dissimilar.

The norms reported in the following chapter are concerned with the frequency of occurrence for various dream elements in two sample sizes, each containing 500 dreams. We must therefore be concerned with assessing how closely two judges can agree on the total number of scorable elements in a large sample. For each of the following scoring classifications, we will report the total number of elements scored by each judge for a sample of either 50 or 100 dreams. Wherever possible, we shall also try to report a correlation coefficient based upon ten pairs of judges' scores for the number of elements contained within units of five or ten dreams. These two figures, the total number of scores per judge and the correlation coefficient between the number of their scores, should provide an indication of how similar the frequency counts listed in the norms would have been if a different judge had scored them.

In order to demonstrate how similarly the judges scored each individual dream, a percentage-of-perfect-agreement figure will be reported for each scoring classification. This figure will always be based upon just those elements which were scored as present and will not refer to any agreement about absence of elements. The numerator will contain the number of scoring agreements and the denominator will consist of the number of agreements and the number of scoring disagreements. This measure would be computed identically to the way it was. for Table 13-1 when a percentage figure of 5% was obtained for the number and types of aggressive incidents in each dream.

SETTINGS

The reliability of scoring settings was investigated by having both authors independently score 100 dreams. Throughout these tables, the two authors will be labeled as Judge A and Judge B. As shown in Table 13-2, Judge A scored a total of 139 settings in this 100 dream sample, while Judge B scored a total of 142 settings.

Table 13-2
Scorer Reliability for Settings

Class	O	I	A	NS	Total	F	D	G	U	Q
Judge A	59	63	17	0	139	56	7	9	22	45
Judge B	58	63	20	1	142	56	6	8	20	51
r	.90	.95	.85	-	.90	.80	-	-	.89	.83

The correlation coefficient of .90 reported for Total Settings was obtained by correlating the number of settings scored by each judge for groups of 10 dreams. Judge A and Judge B both scored 13 settings for the first group of 10 dreams, Judge A scored 15 settings for the second group of 10 dreams while Judge B scored 16 settings, and for the third group of 10 dreams Judge A scored 17 settings while Judge B scored 16 settings, etc. The correlation coefficient was then computed for the 10 pairs of scores obtained in this fashion. A similar procedure was followed to obtain the reliability coefficients for the various classes which comprise settings. It can be seen in Table 13-2 that these values ranged between .80 and .95 for the individual classes. Coefficients were not computed for those classes containing a low number of scores.

Unanswered by the figures in Table 13-2 is the question regarding how often the judges agreed exactly on their scoring of settings. It will be recalled that each of the three location classes (Indoor, Outdoor, Ambiguous) can be combined with each of the five familiarity classes (Familiar, Distorted, Geographic, Unfamiliar, Questionable) making a total of 15 combinations. With the additional score of No Setting, a total of 16 possible settings can be scored. Between the two judges a total of 146 different settings was scored, and both agreed exactly on which of the 16 possible scores were involved on 106 of these settings. This represents 73% perfect agreement on the scoring of settings.

Table 13-3
Scorer Reliability for Objects

Class	CL	HH	AR	TR	BH	Total[a]
Judge A	38	36	35	27	25	298
Judge B	40	31	36	27	25	300

[a]Includes figures for all 24 object classes

OBJECTS

A somewhat different procedure was followed to obtain an index of scoring reliability for objects. It was not feasible to analyze by groups of 10 dreams because most of the object classes were represented too infrequently with such a breakdown. Analysis was therefore made for a single group of 50 dreams. Judge A scored a total of 298 objects and Judge B scored a total of 300 objects. The number of objects each scored for the five most frequently appearing classes is shown in Table 13-3. The correlation coefficient computed between the pairs of judges' scores for each of the 24 possible object classes was .99. Of the 320 different objects scored by the two judges, they agreed exactly on which of the 24 object classes was involved in 265 instances. This provides a figure of 83% perfect agreement on scoring classes of objects.

CHARACTERS

The reliability figures for scoring characters were determined from 100 female dreams. Note in Table 13-4 that the total number of characters scored by each judge is exactly the same. If the number of characters scored by each judge for groups of five dreams is correlated, a coefficient of .99 is obtained. To give an idea of how closely judges would agree on classifying characters, the number of times each judge scored those characters with a frequency tally of 10 or more is shown in Table 13-4.

Quantification of the exact agreement of judges in assigning character scores is provided through the percentage figures listed in Table 13-5. A total of 286 characters was scored between the judges, and they agreed that a character was present on 266 occasions or 93% of the time. As indicated in Table 13-5, if the judges agreed that a character was present, they generally agreed as to the age and sex of the character as well as whether it was a single or group character, but they had more difficulty in agreeing on the identity of the character. Deciding among the hundreds of possible character combinations, the judges were able to agree exactly on the number, sex, identity, and age of 76% of the characters.

SOCIAL INTERACTIONS

The reliability figures for the social interactions, computed on the basis of 50 dreams, are shown in Table 13-6. The judges agreed almost perfectly on the total number of social interaction scores. The correlation coefficients for the number of scores were computed on 10 groups of dreams, each containing five

Table 13-4

Scorer Reliability for Characters

Type	1FKA	1MKA	1FMA	1MSA	1FSA	1MOA	1FUA	2JSA	1MUA	Total[a]
Judge A	35	24	18	14	11	11	11	10	9	276
Judge B	32	23	17	15	14	12	9	11	10	276

[a]Includes figures for all characters

Table 13-5
Percent Agreement for Scoring Characters

Presence of Character	Single vs. Group	Sex	Identity	Age	Perfect
93%	92%	89%	81%	92%	76%

dreams. The percentage of perfect agreement is in the neighborhood of 60%, but it must be remembered that scoring a social interaction involves a number of components. In order for perfect agreement to occur, the judges must agree that a social interaction was present, they must agree as to the scoring for the characters who initiated the interaction and those to whom the interaction was directed, as well as the appropriate subclass of the interaction and whether it was an initiated, reciprocated, mutual, or self-directed interaction. If a more lenient criterion were followed whereby the judges could disagree on some single component such as the subclass number, the level of agreement listed in Table 13-6 would reach slightly over 70%.

Table 13-6
Scorer Reliability for Social Interactions

	Number of scores for Judge A	Number of scores for Judge B	r for number of scores	One detail wrong	Perfect agreement all details
Aggressive	45	46	.97	72%	54%
Friendly	38	38	.91	70%	61%
Sexual	12	12	–	71%	64%

ACHIEVEMENT OUTCOME AND ENVIRONMENTAL PRESS

Since small frequencies are involved for both the achievement outcomes and environmental presses, the figures on scorer reliability for 50 dreams will be shown in the same table. As indicated in Table 13-7, the judges agree fairly closely on the number of scores for these classifications, although they differ slightly on the number of misfortunes scored. The percentages of perfect agreement vary considerably and are probably somewhat unstable because of the small frequencies involved.

Table 13-7
Scorer Reliability for Achievement Outcome
and Environmental Press

		SU	FL	MF	GF
Number of scores	Judge A	6	4	23	5
Number of scores	Judge B	8	4	18	6
Perfect agreement		56%	100%	71%	83%

ACTIVITIES

The number of activities scored by each judge for 50 dreams was quite large and virtually the same, 245 vs. 251. If the number of activities scored by each judge is compared by groups of five dreams, the correlation coefficient, as shown in Table 13-8, reaches a value of .92. A similar comparison for the three classes of activities having the highest frequencies also leads to coefficients of .92 or higher. The percentage of perfect agreement for

Table 13-8
Scorer Reliability for Activities

	P	V	M	L	S	A	C	E	Total
Judge A	86	49	50	18	22	9	6	5	245
Judge B	88	52	43	23	23	9	8	5	251
r	.92	.98	.92						.92

the type of activity class as well as the characters involved was 85% between the two judges.

EMOTIONS

Reliability for emotions was based upon 100 dreams. Table 13-9 shows that the total number of emotions scored by each judge was fairly similar but they did not agree very closely on several of the subclasses. The number of emotions scored by each judge for groups of 10 dreams correlated .76. The amount of perfect agreement on the classes of emotion was 63%.

Table 13-9
Scorer Reliability for Emotions

	AN	AP	SD	HA	CO	Total
Judge A	12	27	13	13	13	78
Judge B	11	20	8	13	18	70

MODIFIERS

A total of 50 dreams was used for the reliability estimates of modifiers. The number of modifiers scored in each subclass was almost identical for each judge. The percentage of perfect agreement shown in Table 13-10 is generally quite high for most of the classes.

TEMPORAL, NEGATIVE, AND ORAL SCALES

Table 13-11 contains the percentage figures for the remaining two descriptive element scales and the oral scales. The number of scores assigned by each judge was quite similar for

Table 13-10
Scorer Reliability for Modifiers

	C	S	D	T	V	A	L	E	I	Total
Judge A	9	30	5	0	5	7	1	7	33	97
Judge B	9	29	5	0	5	6	1	8	31	94
Perfect agreement	80%	91%	100%	–	100%	86%	0%	87%	71%	81%

the scales shown in Table 13-11. The reliability figures for the castration scales were published in an earlier article (Hall and Van de Castle, 1965).

Table 13-11
Scorer Reliability for the Temporal, Negative, and Oral Scales

	Temporal	Negative	Oral Incorp.	Oral Emphasis
Judge A	26	91	9	5
Judge B	25	87	11	5
Perfect agreement	75%	96%	82%	67%

The preceding tables indicate that judges can obtain high levels of scoring agreement for most of the scales described in our classification system. Correlation coefficients indicating agreement on the total number of elements present as well as the number of elements within separate classes were generally in the nineties. With coefficients of this magnitude, it would have been possible to substitute one judge for another, as they obtained approximately equivalent scores. It should be·recognized that this equivalency is obtained on samples containing at least 50 dreams and that the judges may not agree exactly on the scoring of every detail in a single dream. The figures on perfect agreement that are reported in the tables would be applicable to the latter case. These figures range from about 60% to 90%, depending upon the complexity of the scale being scored. The reliability figures described in this chapter for the various dream scales are generally higher than those reported for most projective techniques, and the authors feel that they are substantial enough to warrant their use in a broad spectrum of research studies.

REFERENCE

HALL, C. S. and VAN DE CASTLE, R. L. An empirical investigation of the castration complex in dreams. *J. Pers.*, 1965, *33*, 20-29.

14

Norms

The norms presented in this chapter were obtained from a content analysis of 1000 dreams collected from undergraduate students at Western Reserve University and Baldwin Wallace College during the years 1947-1950. The Western Reserve dreams were collected by Calvin Hall from students in his psychology classes, while the Baldwin Wallace dreams were collected by Roland Cook from his psychology classes. Both instructors had assigned the recording of dreams as a project to be completed during the semester. Alternative projects were also available for those who did not wish to report their dreams but few students availed themselves of these options. We make it a practice to assign code numbers to students so that the identity of the dreamer is known only to the instructor. It has been our experience that students do not object to reporting their dreams under such conditions and many of them enjoy this type of project.

Dreams composing the normative sample were selected in the following manner. Five dreams were picked from each of 100 male and 100 female dream series. These dream series contained between 12-18 dreams. The selection procedure was a random one with the exception that any dream less than 50 words or more than 300 words in length was rejected. The ages of the dreamers ranged from 18 to 25.

These norms should be appropriate for dream series collected in a similar fashion from college students. They may not be appropriate for single dreams because when a person is asked to report just one dream, he usually relates one that has some unusual or outstanding quality or one that possesses strong emotional intensity.

In our sample, female dreams were, on the average, eight

Table 14-1
Settings

	Male		Female	
	f	p	f	p
Total no. of settings	644		654	
Average no. per dream	1.29		1.31	
Total indoor	284	.440	362	.552
Total outdoor	302	.469	229	.351
Total ambiguous	46	.072	56	.086
No setting	12	.019	7	.011
Total familiar	197	.305	241	.369
Total distorted	14	.022	38	.058
Total geographical	51	.079	23	.035
Total questionable	247	.384	280	.429
Total unfamiliar	123	.190	65	.099
Indoor familiar	118	.183	167	.255
Indoor distorted	5	.008	23	.035
Indoor geographical	8	.012	3	.005
Indoor questionable	95	.148	129	.196
Indoor unfamiliar	58	.090	40	.061
Outdoor familiar	74	.115	64	.098
Outdoor distorted	7	.011	12	.018
Outdoor geographical	33	.053	15	.023
Outdoor questionable	128	.199	114	.174
Outdoor unfamiliar	60	.093	24	.037
Ambiguous familiar	5	.008	10	.015
Ambiguous distorted	2	.003	3	.005
Ambiguous geographical	10	.016	5	.008
Ambiguous questionable	24	.037	37	.057
Ambiguous unfamiliar	5	.008	1	.001

percent longer than male dreams. This is a fairly typical difference. Because of this difference in length of reports, it can be expected that the following tables will generally show more dream elements present for females.

SETTINGS

Table 14-1. This table contains the norms for all of the possible types of settings. The first column under Male gives the frequencies, the second column the proportions. The proportions

Table 14-2
Number of Objects Per Dream

Number of objects	Male	Female
	f	f
0	20	11
1	29	24
2	48	46
3	68	75
4	82	63
5	83	68
6	51	60
7	41	52
8	24	35
9	26	23
10	13	16
11	7	10
12	0	5
13	3	2
14	1	1
15	0	4
16	2	0
17	0	3
18	1	1
19	0	1
20	1	0

were obtained by dividing each frequency by the total number
of settings in male dreams. For example, the proportion of total
indoor settings in male dreams is .440. This figure was obtained
by dividing 284 by 644. The same procedure was followed for

Table 14-3
Objects

	Male		Female	
	f	p	f	p
Total number of objects	2422		2659	
Average no. per dream	4.8		5.3	
Architecture	655	.271	843	.317
AR Residential	272	.113	389	.146
AV Vocational	117	.048	138	.052
AE Entertainment	75	.031	69	.026
AI Institutional	28	.012	39	.015
AD Detail	152	.063	186	.070
AB Building materials	6	.002	3	.001
AM Miscellaneous	5	.002	19	.007
HH Household articles	197	.082	278	.104
FO Food or drink	44	.018	55	.021
Implements	160	.066	52	.020
IT Tools	35	.014	7	.003
IW Weapons	73	.031	20	.008
IR Recreational	52	.021	25	.009
TR Travel	271	.112	223	.084
ST Streets	163	.067	118	.044
RG Regions	135	.056	126	.047
NA Nature	221	.091	199	.075
Body Parts	246	.102	314	.118
BH Head	80	.033	161	.061
BE Extremities	90	.038	91	.034
BT Torso	34	.014	31	.012
BA Anatomy	20	.008	28	.011
BS Sex	22	.009	3	.001
CL Clothes	139	.057	271	.102
CM Communication	95	.039	112	.042
MO Money	36	.015	19	.007
MS Miscellaneous	60	.025	49	.018

female dreams. The figures in the second line were obtained by dividing the total number of settings by the number of dreams —500 for males and 500 for females.

It will be observed that few dreams are without a setting. Although the total number of settings in male and female dreams is about the same, there are sex differences in the various classes of settings. The most notable difference is the greater proportion of indoor settings in female dreams and of outdoor settings in male dreams.

OBJECTS

The norms for objects are presented in two tables, 14-2 and 14-3.

Table 14-2. This table shows the distribution of the number of objects per dream in male and female dreams. For example, there were 82 male dreams and 63 female dreams in which four objects were mentioned. There were 31 dreams in which no object was mentioned. The largest number of objects reported in any dream was 20 and this occurred in only one dream. There are no

Table 14-4
Number of Characters per Dream

Number of characters	Male	Female
	f	f
0	31	15
1	122	95
2	150	119
3	98	126
4	58	72
5	21	35
6	14	21
7	4	13
8	1	3
9	0	1
10	1	0

striking sex differences. Both distributions are positively skewed.

Table 14-3. This table contains norms for all classes and sub-classes of objects. The proportions were obtained by dividing the frequencies in each column by the total number of objects (line 1) in that column. There are approximately nine percent more objects mentioned by women than by men. Within class and sub-class proportions, a number of sex differences will be noted.

An alphabetical listing of every object mentioned in dreams and its frequency will be found in Appendix A.

CHARACTERS

Norms for characters are presented in three tables, 14-4, 14-5, and 14-6.

Table 14-4. The distribution of the number of characters per dream for male and female dreams appears in this table. Few dreams, less than 5 percent, are without any characters aside from the dreamer. The highest number of characters in the 1000 dreams is ten. On the average, there are more characters in female dreams.

Table 14-5. The norms for large groupings of characters, e.g., all male characters, all animals, all familiar characters, etc., are shown in this table. The proportions in Lines 3-7 were obtained by dividing frequencies by the total number of characters (Line 1). The proportions in Lines 8-27 were computed by dividing the various frequencies by the total number of human characters (Line 7). In this table and all other tables, familiar characters are those who are scored in one of the following four identity subclasses: Family, Relatives, Known, and Prominent. Unfamiliar characters are those who are scored in the following identity subclasses: Occupational, Ethnic, Stranger, and Uncertain. Imaginary and dead characters, as well as those involved in a metamorphosis, are classified as familiar or unfamiliar according to their identity class. Sex differences are pervasive.

Table 14-6. All characters represented in our sample are listed in this table along with their respective frequencies and proportions. The frequencies and proportions for each of the identity subclasses, e.g., family members, relatives, known characters, etc., also appear in Table 14-6. All proportions were figured by dividing each frequency by the total number of human characters—1108 in the case of male dreams and 1363 in the case of female dreams.

Table 14-5
Summary of Characters

	Male		Female	
	f	p	f	p
Total characters	1180		1423	
Average no. per dream	2.4		2.8	
Total animals	71	.060	60	.042
Total creatures	1	.001	–	
Single animals	43	.036	41	.029
Plural animals	28	.024	19	.013
Total human characters	1108	.939	1363	.958
Total single human characters	761	.687	980	.719
Total plural human characters	347	.313	383	.281
Total Male	587	.530	507	.372
Total Female	286	.258	547	.401
Total joint sex	145	.131	181	.133
Total indefinite	90	.081	127	.093
Total familiar	501	.452	796	.584
Total unfamiliar	607	.548	567	.416
Familiar males	280	.253	308	.226
Unfamiliar males	307	.277	199	.146
Familiar females	178	.161	392	.288
Unfamiliar females	108	.097	155	.114
Familiar indefinite	14	.013	33	.024
Unfamiliar indefinite	76	.069	94	.069
Familiar joint sex	29	.026	62	.045
Unfamiliar joint sex	116	.105	119	.087
Total adults	1078	.973	1271	.933
Total teenagers	7	.006	20	.014
Total children	20	.018	57	.042
Total babies	3	.003	15	.011

Table 14-6
Frequencies and Proportions for
All Character Subclasses

	Male		Female	
	f	p	f	p
I. Family	105	.095	201	.147
1MFA Father	28	.025	44	.032
1MBA Brother	12	.011	12	.009
1MBT Brother	2	.002	4	.003
1MBC Brother	1	.001	4	.003
1MHA Husband	–		13	.009
1MNC Son	1	.001	–	
1FMA Mother	27	.024	63	.046
1FTA Sister	9	.008	22	.016
1FTT Sister	–		9	.007
1FTC Sister	1	.001	3	.002
1FWA Wife	9	.008	–	
2JXA Parents	12	.011	18	.013
2JYA Family members	3	.003	9	.007
II. Relatives	25	.023	62	.045
1MRA	13	.012	18	.013
1MRC	–		1	.001
1MRB	–		1	.001
1FRA	8	.007	30	.022
1FRT	–		2	.001
1FRC	2	.002	3	.002
1IRB	–		2	.001
2FRA	–		1	.001
2JRA	1	.001	3	.002
2IRA	1	.001	–	
2IRC	–		1	.001
III. Known	347	.313	502	.368
1MKA	162	.146	179	.131
1MKT	2	.002	–	
1MKC	2	.002	5	.004
1FKA	113	.102	193	.141
1FKC	–		6	.004
1FKB	–		1	.001

	Male		Female	
	f	p	f	p
1IKA	6	.005	16	.012
1IKC	–		1	.001
1IKB	1	.001	1	.001
2MKA	38	.034	8	.006
2FKA	3	.003	49	.036
2FKC	1	.001	–	
2JKA	13	.012	30	.022
2JKC	–		2	.001
2IKA	6	.005	9	.007
2IKC	–		2	.001
IV. Prominent	_18_	_.016_	_14_	_.010_
1MPA	14	.013	9	.007
1FPA	3	.003	4	.003
1IPA	–		1	.001
2MPA	1	.001	–	
V. Occupational	_189_	_.171_	_116_	_.085_
1MOA	85	.077	39	.029
1FOA	17	.015	22	.016
1IOA	9	.008	10	.007
2MOA	58	.052	18	.013
2FOA	1	.001	8	.006
2JOA	11	.010	10	.007
2IOA	8	.007	9	.007
VI. Ethnic	_22_	_.020_	_29_	_.021_
1MEA	7	.006	6	.004
1FEA	–		6	.004
1FEC	–		1	.001
1IEA	1	.001	–	
2MEA	10	.009	4	.003
2MEC	–		1	.001
2FEA	–		3	.002
2JEA	4	.004	8	.006

	Male		Female	
	f	*p*	*f*	*p*
VII. Strangers	257	.232	233	.171
1MSA	60	.054	60	.044
1MST	1	.001	–	
1MSC	3	.003	5	.004
1MSB	–		1	.001
1FSA	49	.044	42	.031
1FST	–		1	.001
1FSC	2	.002	1	.001
1ISA	28	.025	16	.012
1ISB	1	.001	2	.001
2MSA	25	.023	11	.008
2MST	1	.001	–	
2MSC	1	.001	2	.001
2FSA	10	.009	15	.011
2FST	–		1	.001
2FSC	–		2	.001
2JSA	67	.060	56	.041
2JSC	2	.002	5	.004
2JSB	–		1	.001
2ISA	7	.006	11	.008
2ISC	–		1	.001
VIII. Uncertain	132	.119	181	.133
1MUA	29	.026	32	.023
1MUT	–		2	.001
1MUC	3	.003	1	.001
1FUA	21	.019	35	.026
1FUC	–		1	.001
1FUB	–		1	.001
1IUA	16	.014	23	.017
1IUB	–		3	.002
2MUA	18	.016	13	.009
2MUT	–		1	.001
2FUA	7	.006	13	.009
2JUA	31	.028	32	.023
2JUT	1	.001	–	
2JUC	–		7	.005
2IUA	5	.005	15	.011
2IUC	1	.001	2	.001

	Male		Female	
	f	p	f	p
IX. Dead, Imaginary, and Metamorphoses	_14_	_.013_	_26_	_.019_
Dead	3MKA		3MKA	
			3MSA	
			3FEA	
			3ISA	
			4FEA	
			4ISA	
Imaginary	5FTB		5MNB	
	5MPA		5FTB	
	5MPA		5MPA	
			5MPA	
			5FPA	
			5FPA	
			5FPA	
Metamorphoses	7ANI	8ANI	7MFA	8MPA
	7MKA	8MKA	7MKA	8MKA
	7MOA	8MOA	7MKA	8MKA
	7MOA	8MOA	7MSA	8ANI
	7MUA	8MUA	7D	8FEA
			7FMA	8MSA
			7FKA	8FRA

Table 14-7
Number of Aggressions per Dream

	Male	Female
Number of Aggressions	f	f
0	265	278
1	133	137
2	59	63
3	27	15
4	11	6
5	5	1

Characters that were classified as dead, imaginary, or showing metamorphoses were included as a separate section, but they have also been included in the appropriate age, sex, and identity summations in Table 14-5.

SOCIAL INTERACTIONS

The norms for the three types of social interactions, aggressive, friendly, and sexual, will be found in Tables 14-7 through 14-21.

AGGRESSIONS

The norms for aggressions are presented in six tables.

Table 14-7. This table shows the distribution of the number of aggressions per dream for males and females. Both distributions are J-shaped with five as the maximum number of aggressions in any dream.

Table 14-8. In this table appears the frequency for each subclass of aggression. The proportions were computed by dividing each frequency within a column by the total number of aggressions in that column. The main sex difference is found in the last two lines which contain the frequencies and proportions for physical and nonphysical aggression. The frequency of physical aggressions was obtained by summing the frequencies for subclasses 5 through 8 and that for nonphysical, subclasses 1 through 4. Males have an equal proportion of physical and nonphysical aggressions while females have approximately twice as much nonphysical aggression in relation to physical aggression.

Table 14-9. This table summarizes the frequencies and proportions, as well as the proportion of physical aggression, for broad types of aggression. The proportion of physical aggression is always determined in this table as well as in Tables 14-10, 14-11, and 14-12 by dividing the number of aggressions in subclasses 5 through 8 by the total number of aggressions.

The first line shows the number and proportion of dreams in which at least one aggression occurred. The frequency and proportion of total aggression in male and female dreams appear in the second line. Total aggressions consist of all types of aggressions—reciprocal, mutual, self, witnessed, and dreamer-involved. The proportions for reciprocal, mutual, and self-aggressions as well as aggressions in which the dreamer was involved (Lines 3-6) were computed by dividing the frequencies by the total aggressions (Line 2).

The second group of aggressions are those in which the dreamer was involved. In this table, as well as all other relevant tables, the category of dreamer includes the dreamer acting alone or in association with other characters. For example, if the dreamer and his brother were involved simultaneously in a fight with a group of strangers, this would be counted as a dreamer-involved aggression. It would be counted as just one aggressive interaction. That is, it would not also be counted as an aggression for the brother. There were very few interactions in which the dreamer acted in association with other characters.

The proportions for dreamer as aggressor, as victim, as a

Table 14-8
Number and Proportion of Aggressions
by Subclasses of Aggression

Subclass	Male		Female	
	f	p	f	p
8 Murder	24	.06	7	.02
7 Attack	89	.22	49	.15
6 Chasing-confining	62	.15	43	.13
5 Destruction	26	.06	15	.04
4 Serious threat	19	.05	15	.04
3 Rejection	71	.18	122	.36
2 Verbal	70	.18	50	.15
1 Covert	41	.10	36	.11
Total Aggressions	402	1.00	337	1.00
Total 5-8	201	.50	114	.34
Total 1-4	201	.50	223	.66

reciprocator, in a mutual aggression, or as self-aggressive were obtained by dividing the frequencies by the total number of dreamer-involved aggressions.

Witnessed aggressions, it will be recalled, are those in which the dreamer is not in any way involved. The proportion of witnessed aggressions was computed by dividing the frequency by the total number of aggressions. Witnessed aggressions were classified according to the sexes of the combatants. Any aggressive encounters in which males, either singly or in groups, aggressed against males, either singly or in groups, were classified under "Witnessed male to male." If males aggressed against females, it was classified as "Witnessed male to female," and if females aggressed against males, it was classified as "Witnessed female to male." Encounters between females were classified under "Witnessed female to female." The proportions for these

Table 14-9
Summary of Aggressive Encounters

	Male		Female		Male	Female
	f	p	f	p	p 5-8	p 5-8
Dreams in which A occurs	235	.47	222	.44	–	–
Total aggressions	402		337		.50	.34
Reciprocal aggressions	48	.12	33	.10	.56	.39
Mutual aggressions	19	.05	16	.05	.42	.37
Self-aggressions	13	.03	4	.01	.23	.00
Dreamer-involved aggression	321	.80	272	.80	.47	.30
Dreamer as aggressor	100	.31	76	.28	.45	.15
Dreamer as victim	153	.48	155	.57	.50	.34
Dreamer as reciprocal	43	.13	27	.10	.56	.44
Dreamer mutual	15	.05	10	.04	.40	.20
Dreamer self-aggression	12	.04	4	.01	.17	.00
Witnessed aggression	81	.20	65	.20	.61	.51
Witnessed male to male	32	.39	14	.21	.56	.71
Witnessed male to female	5	.06	7	.11	.00	.43
Witnessed female to male	3	.04	4	.06	.00	.00
Witnessed female to female	1	.01	4	.06	.00	.25

four classes were computed by dividing frequencies by total witnessed aggressions. Many witnessed aggressions did not fit into the foregoing four classes. Some involved joint sex groups, some indefinite characters, and some were mutual aggressions or reciprocated aggressions.

The last two columns of Table 14-9 contain the proportions of physical aggressions for male and female dreams. For example, in the line for "Dreamer-involved aggression," 47 percent of the aggressions in male dreams and 30 percent of the aggressions in female dreams were scored as being in subclass 5 through 8 (see Table 14-8 for a description of the subclasses).

Table 14-10. This table shows with whom the dreamer interacted aggressively either as aggressor, victim, mutually, or re-

Table 14-10
Aggressions in which Dreamer is Involved

	Male		Female		Male	Female
	f	p	f	p	p 5-8	p 5-8
Total	321	1.00	272	1.00	.47	.30
Reciprocal aggressions	43	.13	27	.10	.56	.44
Mutual aggressions	15	.05	10	.04	.40	.20
Self-aggressions	12	.04	4	.01	.17	.00
D with males	165	.51	112	.41	.50	.31
D with females	50	.15	78	.29	.12	.19
D with familiar characters	94	.29	140	.51	.23	.10
D with unfamiliar characters	165	.51	97	.36	.53	.49
D with familiar males	57	.18	60	.22	.28	.07
D with unfamiliar males	108	.34	52	.19	.63	.60
D with familiar females	29	.09	58	.21	.07	.15
D with unfamiliar females	21	.07	20	.07	.19	.30
D with joint sex familiar	6	.02	19	.07	.33	.05
D with joint sex unfamiliar	21	.07	12	.04	.38	.25
D with indefinite familiar	2	.01	3	.01	1.00	.00
D with indefinite unfamiliar	15	.05	13	.05	.47	.54
D with animals	27	.08	20	.07	.85	.55
D with creatures			None			
D with question mark	24	.07	11	.04	.79	.45

ciprocally. The proportions in the third and fifth columns were determined by dividing each frequency by the total number of aggressions (Line 1). The proportions in the last two columns are those for physical aggressions.

Table 14-11. The frequencies, proportions, and proportion of physical aggression in which the dreamer was the aggressor appear in this table.

Table 14-12. The normative data for the dreamer as victim are presented in this table.

FRIENDLINESS

The normative data for friendly interactions are presented in six tables, Tables 14-13 through 14-18. They are constructed in an identical manner with the tables for aggressive interactions, except that there is nothing comparable in friendliness with physical aggression.

Table 14-11

Aggressions in which Dreamer is Aggressor

	Male		Female		Male	Female
	f	p	f	p	p 5-8	p 5-8
Total D as aggressor	100	1.00	76	1.00	.45	.15
D to males	47	.47	29	.38	.45	.07
D to females	19	.19	30	.39	.16	.17
D to familiar characters	34	.34	47	.62	.26	.09
D to unfamiliar characters	43	.43	22	.29	.44	.14
D to familiar males	20	.20	18	.24	.30	.00
D to unfamiliar males	27	.27	11	.14	.55	.18
D to familiar females	11	.11	24	.32	.09	.17
D to unfamiliar females	8	.08	6	.08	.25	.17
D to joint sex familiar	1	.01	5	.07	.00	.00
D to joint sex unfamiliar	5	.05	2	.03	.40	.00
D to indefinite familiar	2	.02	0	.00	1.00	.00
D to indefinite unfamiliar	3	.03	3	.04	.00	.00
D to animals	13	.13	4	.05	.77	.75
D to creatures		None				
D to question mark	10	.10	3	.04	.70	.33

Table 14-13. This table shows the distribution of friendly scores. The distributions are J-shaped like those for aggression. Females, on the average, have more friendly encounters in their dreams than do males.

Table 14-14. The frequencies for each subclass of friendliness appear in this table. Helping and protecting interactions constituted the main friendly encounters.

Table 14-15. This is a summary table for friendly encounters. The proportions in Lines 3, 4, 5, 6, and Line 11 were obtained by dividing the frequencies by the total number of friendly encounters (Line 2). The proportions in Lines 7-10 were obtained by dividing the frequencies by the frequency in Line 6, and the proportions in Lines 12-15 were computed by dividing the frequencies by the frequency in Line 11.

Table 14-16. This table shows with whom the dreamer inter-

Table 14-12
Aggressions in which Dreamer is Victim

	Male		Female		Male	Female
	f	p	f	p	p 5-8	p 5-8
Total D as victim	153	1.00	155	1.00	.50	.34
D from males	82	.53	66	.43	.51	.42
D from females	21	.14	37	.24	.10	.11
D from familiar characters	42	.27	72	.46	.21	.07
D from unfamiliar characters	85	.56	62	.40	.53	.58
D from familiar males	29	.19	32	.21	.27	.13
D from unfamiliar males	53	.35	34	.22	.64	.71
D from familiar females	11	.07	27	.17	.00	.04
D from unfamiliar females	10	.07	10	.06	.20	.30
D from joint sex familiar	2	.01	10	.07	.50	.00
D from joint sex unfamiliar	13	.09	9	.06	.23	.22
D from indefinite familiar	0	.00	3	.02	.00	.00
D from indefinite unfamiliar	9	.06	9	.06	.67	.78
D from animals	12	.08	14	.09	.92	.57
D from creatures			None			
D from question mark	14	.09	7	.05	.86	.57

Table 14-13
Number of Friendly Acts per Dream

Number of Friendly Acts	Male f	Female f
0	309	289
1	149	139
2	29	54
3	10	9
4	3	8
5	0	1

acted in a friendly manner either as befriender or befriended, or in a mutual or reciprocal interaction. The proportions were figured by dividing each frequency by the total number of friendly interactions (Line 1).

Table 14-17. The normative data for the dreamer as befriender are presented in this table.

Table 14-18. The normative data for the dreamer as befriended are presented in this table.

Table 14-14
Number and Proportion of Friendly Interactions
by Subclasses of Friendliness

Subclass	Male f	p	Female f	p
7 Marriage	11	.04	23	.08
6 Physical	23	.09	25	.08
5 Inviting, dating	19	.08	47	.15
4 Helping, protecting	106	.42	99	.32
3 Gift, loan	27	.11	32	.10
2 Verbal	50	.20	59	.19
1 Covert	14	.06	23	.08
Total	250	1.00	308	1.00

AGGRESSION AND FRIENDLINESS

One problem in connection with comparing male and female dreamers or any other groups, for that matter, on social interactions is the different number of characters in male and female dreams. Since females tend to report more characters than males do, the probability of their having a social interaction is greater than it is for males.

Two ways of solving this problem are shown in Tables 14-19 and 14-20.

Table 14-19. The figures in this table were obtained by dividing the number of aggressions by the number of aggressions and friendly encounters combined. For example, there were 321 dreamer-involved aggressions (Table 14-9) and 222 dreamer-involved friendliness (Table 14-15) in male dreams. Dividing the

Table 14-15
Summary of Friendly Encounters

	Male		Female	
	f	p	f	p
Dreams in which F occurs	191	.38	211	.42
Total friendliness	250		308	
Reciprocal friendliness	6	.02	4	.01
Mutual friendliness	20	.08	21	.07
Self-friendliness		None		
Dreamer-involved friendliness	225	.90	258	.84
Dreamer as befriender	102	.45	106	.41
Dreamer as befriended	101	.45	119	.46
Dreamer reciprocal	6	.03	3	.01
Dreamer mutual	15	.07	10	.04
Witnessed friendliness	25	.10	50	.16
Witnessed male to male	5	.20	2	.04
Witnessed male to female	6	.24	8	.16
Witnessed female to male	2	.08	3	.06
Witnessed female to female	0	.00	3	.06

321 aggressions by a combination of aggressions and friendliness (321 + 222) yields a proportion of .59. A proportion greater than .50 indicates a preponderance of aggressions; a proportion less than .50 indicates a preponderance of friendliness. Sex differences are noticeable.

Table 14-20. Another method for controlling number of characters is to divide the number of aggressions or the number of friendly interactions involving a particular subclass of characters by the number of characters in that subclass. This has been done for some of the principal character classes, and the results are presented in Table 14-20. The figures from which these proportions were computed will be found in Tables 14-5, 14-10, and 14-16. For example, from Table 14-10 we learn that female dreamers were involved in 112 aggressions with male characters. There

Table 14-16
Friendliness in which Dreamer is Involved

	Male		Female	
	f	p	f	p
Total	225	1.00	258	1.00
Reciprocal friendliness	6	.03	3	.01
Mutual friendliness	15	.07	10	.04
D with males	97	.44	121	.47
D with females	84	.37	80	.31
D with familiar characters	115	.51	169	.65
D with unfamiliar characters	99	.44	82	.32
D with familiar males	55	.24	90	.36
D with unfamiliar males	42	.19	31	.12
D with familiar females	52	.23	53	.21
D with unfamiliar females	32	.14	27	.10
D with joint sex familiar	6	.03	22	.09
D with joint sex unfamiliar	14	.06	13	.05
D with familiar indefinite	2	.01	4	.01
D with indefinite unfamiliar	11	.05	11	.04
D with animals	6	.03	6	.02
D with creatures	1	.01	0	.00
D with question mark	3	.01	1	.01

were a total of 507 male characters in women's dreams (Table 14-5). Dividing 112 by 507 yields a proportion of .221. This proportion means that a female dreamer in our sample had an aggressive encounter with about one out of every five males in her dreams.

SEXUAL INTERACTIONS

We feel that our norms for sexual interactions do not accurately reflect the actual incidence of this type of social interaction. In our opinion, neither sex is completely candid in reporting sex dreams, and females are probably less frank than males. The norms may have some use, however, since dreams collected under similar conditions to those prevailing for our sample may be compared with our norms.

Table 14-21. This single table contains all of the norms that

Table 14-17
Friendliness in which Dreamer is Befriender

	Male		Female	
	f	p	f	p
Total D as befriender	102	1.00	106	1.00
D to males	35	.34	39	.37
D to females	46	.45	41	.39
D to familiar characters	61	.60	62	.59
D to unfamiliar characters	27	.27	38	.36
D to familiar males	24	.24	28	.26
D to unfamiliar males	11	.11	11	.10
D to familiar females	35	.34	23	.22
D to unfamiliar females	11	.11	18	.17
D to joint sex familiar	2	.02	11	.10
D to joint sex unfamiliar	5	.05	5	.05
D to indefinite familiar	None			
D to indefinite unfamiliar	6	.06	4	.04
D to animals	5	.05	6	.06
D to creatures	1	.01	0	.00
D to question mark	2	.02	0	.00

Table 14-18
Friendliness in which Dreamer is Befriended

	Male		Female	
	f	p	f	p
Total D as befriended	_101_	_1.00_	_119_	_1.00_
D by males	59	.59	54	.45
D by females	23	.23	36	.30
D by familiar characters	44	.44	81	.68
D by unfamiliar characters	55	.55	37	.31
D by familiar males	29	.29	40	.34
D by unfamiliar males	30	.30	14	.12
D by familiar females	9	.09	27	.23
D by unfamiliar females	14	.14	9	.08
D by joint sex familiar	4	.04	11	.09
D by joint sex unfamiliar	8	.08	8	.07
D by indefinite familiar	2	.02	3	.03
D by indefinite unfamiliar	3	.03	6	.05
D by animals	1	.01	0	.00
D by creatures		None		
D by question mark	1	.01	1	.01

Table 14-19
Proportion of Aggressions to Aggressions plus Friendliness

	Male	Female
	p	p
Total	.62	.52
Dreamer involved	.59	.51
Witnessed	.76	.57
D with males	.63	.48
D with females	.37	.49
D with familiar characters	.45	.45
D with unfamiliar characters	.62	.54
D with familiar males	.51	.40
D with unfamiliar males	.72	.63
D with familiar females	.36	.52
D with unfamiliar females	.39	.43
D with animals	.82	.77
D with question mark	.89	.92

are warranted. The proportions in Lines 3 and 4 and those under classes of sexual interaction were obtained by dividing the frequencies by total sexual interactions (Line 2). The proportions in Lines 5-8 were computed by dividing the frequencies by the number of sexual interactions in which the dreamer was involved (Line 3). It will be observed that female dreamers had more sexual interactions with familiar males, whereas male dreamers had more with unfamiliar females.

ACTIVITIES

Norms for activities are set forth in Tables 14-22 and ¡14-23.

Table 14-20
Aggressions and Friendliness Divided
by Number of Characters

	Aggressions No. of Characters		Friendliness No. of Characters	
	Males	Females	Males	Females
Total	.341	.237	.212	.216
D with males	.281	.221	.165	.239
D with females	.175	.142	.294	.146
D with familiar characters	.188	.176	.230	.212
D with unfamiliar characters	.272	.171	.163	.145
D with familiar males	.204	.195	.196	.292
D with unfamiliar males	.352	.261	.137	.156
D with familiar females	.163	.148	.292	.135
D with unfamiliar females	.088	.129	.134	.174
D with familiar indefinite characters	.143	.091	.143	.121
D with unfamiliar indefinite characters	.197	.138	.145	.117
D with joint sex familiar characters	.207	.306	.207	.355
D with joint sex unfamiliar characters	.162	.101	.108	.109
D with animals	.380	.333	.084	.100

Table 14-22. The distribution of number of activities per dream for male and female dreams is presented in this table. There are no striking sex differences. The distributions are positively skewed.

Table 14-23. This long table requires some explanation. All of the proportions were computed by dividing the frequencies in each column by the total number of activities in that column. Male frequencies were divided by 2362 and female frequencies by 2470.

Frequencies and proportions for all verbal activities, physical activities, etc., are given under I. Any activity which the dreamer does alone or does in association with other characters is included under II. Any activity in which only male characters engage and which do not involve the dreamer in any way is included under

Table 14-21
Summary of Sexual Interactions

	Male		Female	
	f	p	f	p
No. dreams in which any sex occurs	58	.116	18	.036
Total sexual interactions	73	–	19	–
Dreamer-involved sexual interaction	68	.93	13	.68
Witnessed Sex	5	.07	6	.33
D with opposite sex familiar	22	.32	10	.77
D with opposite sex unfamiliar	37	.54	3	.23
D reciprocates	5	.07	0	.00
D to self	4	.06	0	.00
Classes of sexual interactions				
5 Sexual intercourse	20	.27	5	.26
4 Petting	13	.18	5	.26
3 Kissing	8	.11	4	.21
2 Sexual overtures	22	.30	3	.16
1 Sexual fantasies	10	.14	2	.11

III. The same holds for female characters in IV. Group V contains activities for all other character classes and combinations of classes, as, for example, joint sex, indefinite, animals, etc.

Groups VI-XIII include only those activities which are scored for interactions. These are the verbal and physical classes. Group VI consists of the dreamer's verbal and physical interactions with male characters only, Group VII the dreamer's interactions with female characters only, and Group VIII his interactions with all other character classes and combinations of classes.

Groups IX through XII contain frequencies and proportions for interactions not involving the dreamer, that is, for witnessed interactions. Group IX consists solely of witnessed interactions

Table 14-22
Number of Activities per Dream

Number of Activities	Male f	Female f
0	4	10
1	43	26
2	72	73
3	75	69
4	70	66
5	67	63
6	55	68
7	35	44
8	27	31
9	25	15
10	4	11
11	6	10
12	6	4
13	2	3
14	3	1
15	1	2
16	3	1
17	1	2
18	0	0
19	0	1
20	0	0
21	1	0

Table 14-23
Activities

	Male		Female	
	f	*p*	*f*	*p*
I. Total of all activities	2362		2470	
V Verbal	511	.216	646	.262
P Physical	627	.265	482	.195
M Movement	586	.248	621	.251
L Location change	194	.082	182	.074
S Visual	280	.118	307	.124
A Auditory	38	.016	36	.014
E Expressive	51	.022	83	.034
C Cognitive	75	.032	113	.046
II. Dreamer and dreamer + other characters	1249	.528	1212	.490
V Verbal	37	.016	46	.019
P Physical	308	.130	240	.097
M Movement	387	.164	367	.148
L Location change	140	.059	131	.053
S Visual	251	.106	257	.104
A Auditory	34	.014	32	.013
E Expressive	18	.008	30	.012
C Cognitive	74	.031	109	.044
III. Male characters	288	.122	256	.103
V Verbal	34	.014	27	.011
P Physical	77	.033	70	.028
M Movement	107	.045	101	.041
L Location change	39	.016	21	.008
S Visual	12	.005	16	.006
A Auditory	1	.000	1	.000
E Expressive	18	.008	17	.007
C Cognitive	0		3	.001
IV. Female characters	100	.041	216	.088
V Verbal	12	.005	20	.008
P Physical	30	.013	48	.019
M Movement	38	.016	84	.034

	Male		Female	
	f	p	f	p
L Location change	4	.002	18	.007
S Visual	8	.003	21	.008
A Auditory	1	.000	3	.001
E Expressive	6	.002	21	.008
C Cognitive	1	.000	1	.000
V. All other characters	*121*	*.052*	*148*	*.060*
V Verbal	15	.006	23	.009
P Physical	21	.009	16	.006
M Movement	54	.023	69	.028
L Location change	11	.005	12	.005
S Visual	9	.004	13	.005
A Auditory	2	.001	0	
E Expressive	9	.004	15	.006
C Cognitive	0		0	
VI. D or D + others with males				
V Verbal	165	.070	162	.066
P Physical	70	.030	43	.017
VII. D or D + others with females				
V Verbal	93	.039	162	.066
P Physical	57	.024	18	.007
VIII. D or D + others with all others				
V Verbal	40	.017	71	.029
P Physical	26	.011	18	.007
IX. Males with males				
V Verbal	14	.006	3	.001
P Physical	12	.005	4	.002
X. Males with females				
V Verbal	7	.003	10	.004
P Physical	7	.003	7	.003
XI. Females with females				
V Verbal	3	.001	5	.002
P Physical	2	.001	3	.001

	Male		Female	
	f	p	f	p
XII. All others				
V Verbal	8	.003	10	.004
P Physical	6	.002	12	.005
XIII. Reciprocals				
V Verbal	83	.035	107	.043
P Physical	11	.005	3	.001

of male characters with male characters, Group X of male characters with female characters, Group XI of females with females, and Group XII of all other character classes and combinations of classes.

All reciprocal interactions, both those involving the dreamer and those involving all other characters, are included under XIII.

ACHIEVEMENT OUTCOMES

Because the great preponderance of success and failure occurred to the dreamer, the analysis of the data was simplified. Two short tables, one for failure and one for success, suffice.

FAILURE

Table 14-24. Failure occurred in 13 out of every 100 dreams —a few more in male dreams, a few less in female dreams. Line 3 contains not only failure experienced by the dreamer alone but also failure by the dreamer in association with other characters. There are very few of the latter. Consequences of failure are rare. Proportions from Line 3 on were computed by dividing the frequencies in a column by the total number of failures in that column (Line 2). The proportions in Line 1 were obtained by dividing the frequencies by the number of dreams.

SUCCESS

Table 14-25. This table for success has the same format as the one for failure.

ENVIRONMENTAL PRESS

The norms for environmental press appear in three tables, two for misfortune and one for good fortune. Misfortunes were six times more numerous than good fortunes.

MISFORTUNE

Table 14-26. The frequencies and proportions for the six sub-classes of misfortunes are set forth in this table. There are no striking sex differences.

Table 14-27. Misfortunes to the dreamer (or to the dreamer plus other characters) and misfortunes to other classes of characters appear in this table. All proportions for the latter were figured by dividing the frequencies in each column by the total

Table 14-24
Summary of Failures

	Male		Female	
	f	p	f	p
No. of dreams with failure	77	.15	49	.10
No. of failures	80	–	54	–
Failure for dreamer	69	.86	45	.83
Failure for other humans	9	.11	9	.17
Failure for male characters	8	.10	3	.06
Failure for female characters	0	.00	2	.04
Failure for animals	2	.03	0	.00
Consequences				
Good Fortune	1	.01	1	.02
Success	5	.06	1	.02
Friendliness	1	.01	3	.06

Table 14-25
Summary of Succesess

	Male		Female	
	f	p	f	p
No. of dreams with success	75	.15	38	.08
No. of successes	81	–	38	–
Success for dreamer	72	.89	33	.87
Success for other humans	9	.11	5	.13
Success for male characters	7	.09	4	.11
Success for female characters	1	.01	1	.03
Success for animals		None		
Consequences				
Misfortune	1	.01	0	.00
Failure		None		
Aggression		None		

number of misfortunes to others (Line 4) in that column. This table also shows the consequences of misfortune. These are rare.

GOOD FORTUNE

Table 14-28. Good fortunes are rare and those that do occur usually happen to the dreamer.

Table 14-26
Number and Proportion of Misfortunes by
Subclasses of Misfortunes

Subclass	Male		Female	
	f	p	f	p
6 Death	17	.08	21	.10
5 Injured or ill	43	.21	51	.25
4 Accident, destruction, or loss of possession	51	.25	39	.19
3 Threat from environment	27	.13	26	.13
2 Falling	10	.05	7	.03
1 Obstacle	57	.28	62	.30

Table 14-27
Summary of Misfortunes

	Male		Female	
	f	p	f	p
Dreams with misfortune	181	.36	167	.33
No. of misfortunes	205	–	206	–
M to dreamer	146	.71	139	.68
M to other characters	59	.29	67	.32
M to male characters	23	.39	26	.39
M to female characters	23	.39	24	.36
M to familiar	24	.41	32	.48
M to unfamiliar	28	.48	23	.34
M to familiar male	13	.22	14	.21
M to unfamiliar male	10	.17	12	.18
M to familiar female	11	.18	16	.24
M to unfamiliar female	12	.20	8	.12
M to joint sex familiar	0	.00	2	.03
M to joint sex unfamiliar	3	.05	2	.03
M to indefinite familiar		None		
M to indefinite unfamiliar	3	.05	1	.01
M to animals	6	.10	12	.18
M to creatures		None		
M to question mark	1	.02	0	.00
Consequences				
Good fortune	14	.07	6	.03
Success	7	.03	5	.02
Friendliness	2	.01	3	.01

Table 14-28
Summary of Good Fortunes

	Male		Female	
	f	p	f	p
No. of dreams with good fortune	30	.06	28	.06
No. of good fortune	30	–	29	–
GF to D	27	.90	23	.79
GF to other humans	3	.10	5	.17
GF to animals	0	.00	1	.04

Table 14-29
Summary of Emotions

	Male		Female	
	f	p	f	p
I. Total no. of emotions	<u>282</u>		<u>420</u>	
Total Happy	55	.195	82	.195
Total Sad	26	.094	54	.129
Total Anger	44	.156	53	.126
Total Confusion	61	.215	75	.178
Total Apprehension	96	.340	156	.372
II. Dreamer				
Happy	51	.180	63	.151
Sad	21	.075	46	.110
Anger	29	.103	33	.078
Confusion	55	.195	69	.164
Apprehension	85	.302	140	.333
III. Characters other than dreamer				
Happy	4	.014	16	.038
Sad	5	.018	8	.019
Anger	9	.032	23	.055
Confusion	12	.043	6	.014
Apprehension	11	.039	16	.038
IV. Male characters				
Happy	0	.000	5	.012
Sad	2	.007	1	.002
Anger	3	.011	11	.026
Confusion	9	.032	4	.009
Apprehension	2	.007	5	.012
V. Female characters				
Happy	1	.004	5	.012
Sad	3	.011	6	.014
Anger	2	.007	9	.021
Confusion	0	.000	1	.002
Apprehension	6	.021	6	.014

	Male		Female	
	f	p	f	p
VI. All other characters				
Happy	3	.011	6	.014
Sad	0	.000	1	.002
Anger	4	.014	3	.007
Confusion	3	.011	1	.002
Apprehension	3	.011	5	.012

Table 14-30
Number of Modifiers per Dream

	Male	Female
Number of modifiers	f	f
0	107	60
1	108	113
2	105	90
3	84	77
4	41	49
5	21	42
6	9	32
7	10	13
8	6	10
9	2	4
10	3	3
11	2	1
12	2	2
13	0	2
14	0	1
15	0	1

EMOTIONS

The norms for emotions are presented in one table.

Table 14-29. All of the proportions in this table were obtained by dividing the frequencies in each column by the total number of emotions (Line 1) in that column.

Table 14-31
Modifiers

	Male		Female	
	f	p	f	p
Total no. of modifiers	1110		1458	
Average no. per dream	2.22		2.92	
C+ Chromatic	75	.067	166	.114
C− Achromatic	43	.039	67	.046
S+ Large	199	.180	194	.133
S− Small	106	.095	114	.078
I+ Intense	326	.295	439	.300
I− Weak	56	.051	55	.038
D+ Filled	18	.016	22	.015
D− Empty	9	.008	3	.002
L+ Straight	4	.004	7	.004
L− Crooked	13	.012	19	.013
T+ Hot	5	.005	12	.008
T− Cold	8	.007	11	.008
V+ Fast	40	.036	30	.021
V− Slow	8	.007	10	.007
A+ Old	46	.040	61	.042
A− Young	57	.051	61	.042
E+ Pretty, good	58	.052	103	.071
E− Ugly, bad	39	.035	84	.058

Table 14-32
Number of Negatives per Dream

	Male		Female	
	f	p	f	p
0	141	.282	93	.186
1	145	.290	134	.268
2	111	.222	117	.234
3	62	.124	68	.136
4	20	.040	43	.086
5	12	.024	22	.044
6+	9	.018	23	.046

Group II consists of emotions experienced by the dreamer alone or conjointly with other characters. Group III includes all emotions experienced by characters other than the dreamer. These are broken down into character classes in Groups IV, V, and VI. Group VI consists of joint sex, indefinite, animals, etc.

Table 14-33
Number of Temporal References per Dream

	Male		Female	
	f	p	f	p
0	328	.656	299	.598
1	119	.238	128	.256
2	38	.076	52	.104
3+	15	.030	21	.042

Table 14-34
Distribution of Oral Incorporation
and Oral Emphasis Scores

	Male		Female	
	f	p	f	p
Oral Incorporation				
0	420	.840	415	.830
1	50	.100	54	.108
2	21	.042	22	.044
3+	9	.018	9	.018
Oral Emphasis				
0	439	.878	438	.876
1	45	.090	53	.106
2	16	.032	5	.010
3+	0	.000	4	.008

Negative emotions, i.e., sad, angry, confused, and apprehensive, predominate over happiness.

DESCRIPTIVE ELEMENTS

The data for descriptive elements are presented in four tables.

MODIFIERS

Table 14-30. The distribution for the number of modifiers per dream is J-shaped for both males and females. There are more modifiers in female dreams than in male dreams.

Table 14-31. This table comprises frequencies and proportions for all modifiers. Several sex differences will be noticed.

NEGATION AND TEMPORAL

Table 14-32. The number and proportion of negative scores per dream appear in this table. Females have, on the average, higher negative scores.

Table 14-33. The distribution of temporal scores is a fairly truncated one. Females tend, on the average, to have more temporal references in their dreams.

ORALITY

Table 14-34. This table contains the distribution of scores for oral incorporation and oral emphasis.

CASTRATION COMPLEX

Table 14-35. The distribution of scores for castration anxiety, castration wish, and penis envy are presented in this table.

Table 14-35
Distributions of Castration Anxiety, Castration
Wish, and Penis Envy Scores

	Male		Female	
	f	p	f	p
Castration Anxiety				
0	399	.798	454	.908
1	94	.188	44	.088
2	6	.012	1	.002
3+	1	.002	1	.002
Castration Wish				
0	455	.910	461	.922
1	43	.086	38	.076
2	1	.002	1	.002
3+	1	.002	0	.000
Penis Envy				
0	475	.950	487	.974
1	24	.048	13	.026
2	1	.002	0	.000
3+			None	

15

Scales of Content Analysis Devised by Others

Although the system of classifying and scoring the contents of reported dreams presented in the preceding chapters is the most comprehensive one devised, it is by no means the first application of quantitative methodology to dream analysis. As far as we are able to determine, that honor belongs to two psychoanalysts, Franz Alexander and George Wilson, who thirty years ago published a trail-blazing article entitled "Quantitative Dream Studies: A Methodological Attempt at a Quantitative Evaluation of Psychoanalytic Material" (1935). They set up a classification of dreams based upon Alexander's vector theory of pregenital impulses. It consisted of the following ten types of dreams:

1. satisfied receptive
2. satisfied taking
3. satisfied giving
4. satisfied attacking
5. satisfied retaining

6. inhibited receptive
7. inhibited taking
8. inhibited giving
9. inhibited attacking
10. inhibited retaining

The inhibited version, in each case, represents a superego reaction which interferes with the satisfaction of the impulse. An example of an inhibited receptive dream is the following one.

"Dreamer is afraid there will not be enough chicken and she will not receive anything to eat."

An example of a satisfied giving dream is one in which the dreamer teaches his brother to play golf and tries to make him a better player than the dreamer is.

The dreams of 18 patients with gastrointestinal disturbances were scored. Not all of the dreams could be placed into one of the foregoing 10 classes, but no dream was placed in more than one class. When more than one theme appeared in a dream, the classifiers tried to locate a major tendency and to classify it according to this major tendency. Failing to find a major tendency, the dream was not classified.

With regard to scoring reliability, the investigators say, "After considerable practical experience we have found it possible to classify the majority of our patients' dreams in these groups without feeling that we have been arbitrary in our judgment" (p. 375). They note, however, some scoring difficulties. It was not always easy to differentiate between inhibited giving and retentive tendencies, and there was even greater difficulty in classifying some dreams which expressed attacking. Free associations were used to assist in clarifying some ambiguities in the dream contents.

In general, the results of this quantitative study of dreams bears out the conclusions arrived at by clinical studies of gastrointestinal cases. Patients suffering from constipation have more retentive dreams, those with peptic ulcers express a lot of passive receiving and aggressive taking in their dreams, and persons afflicted with chronic diarrhea, although resembling peptic ulcer patients, have more dreams of passive receiving than aggressive taking.

The authors are quite ambivalent about the application of quantitative methods to dream analysis. On the one hand, the quantitative approach is not proposed "as a substitute for the usual clinical approach. It can be employed only in conjunction with the usual techniques of psychoanalysis, without which it shows all the defects in statistical studies" (p. 393). Of "all the defects" the authors mention only one, namely, that statistics reveal correlation but not causality. They say that "the quantitative data obtained by this method can be evaluated and interpreted only in cases which have been competently psychoanalyzed" (p. 393). But on the other hand, there is some value to quantitative analysis "inasmuch as it contributes quantitative data, obtained by a reliable method, for estimating the intensity of dynamic tendencies which otherwise can only be roughly estimated" (p. 393).

It will be observed that the unit of classification employed in this pioneer study is the entire dream and that the scales are theoretical in character.

The example set by Alexander and Wilson has not been widely emulated by other psychoanalysts in spite of the fact that many of them must have files bulging with dreams which would lend themselves to quantitative analysis. See, however, the brief statistical treatment of dreams by Miller (1942) which was reprinted in *Studies in Psychosomatic Medicine* edited by Alexander and French (1948). Miller found that patients with skin disorders had more dreams of looking and/or exhibiting. That it has not been widely emulated may be due in part to the ambivalence and qualifications of these pioneer investigators regarding their methodology. Moreover, psychoanalysis probably has more than its fair share of disciples who suffer from number phobia. Notable exceptions, however, are Saul, Sheppard and their associates, and Beck and his associates, both groups connected with the University of Pennsylvania Medical School. In contrast to the cautious attitude of Alexander and Wilson regarding the use of reported (manifest) dreams, these investigators make no apologies for doing quantitative studies of reported dreams. Sheppard and Saul (1958) state flatly, "The manifest dream itself is an important subject for research" (p. 244). Beck's work demonstrates clearly and conclusively the value of quantitative studies of dreams reported by patients in psychoanalysis.

The first two scales constructed by the Saul-Sheppard group were designed to measure hostility (Saul, Sheppard, Selby, Lhamon, Sachs, and Master, 1954) and ego strength (Sheppard and Saul, 1958). The hostility scale consists of six subclasses of hostility arranged in order of intensity. They are:

6   Death of a person
5   Destruction of an object
4   Actual or threatened injury to a person
3   Actual or threatened damage to an object
2   Discomfort of a person
1   Minor impairment of an object

The unit of analysis is a conceptual element roughly equivalent to the independent clause of a sentence. Each such unit in a dream is scored for hostility, and the number of scores per dream is summed to give a hostility rating for that dream.

After training in the use of the hostility scale, three judges scored a set of dreams. Rank difference correlations among the scores of the three judges were .83, .84, and .85, all significant at better than the .001 level. The scale differentiated between the dreams of chronic hypertensive patients and normotensive college students.

The original ego rating scale (Sheppard and Saul, 1958), comprises ten categories. These ten categories deal with impulsive expression, logicality and reality, the health of the dream characters, and the dreamer's interrelationships with other characters in the dream. Each category is broken down into four subcategories which represent degrees of "distancing" of the dream representation from the dreamer's ego. For example, the source of the impulse may be (1) the dreamer himself, (2) another human being, (3) an animal, or (4) an inanimate object. If the dreamer is able to represent himself as the source of the impulse, presumably his ego is in better shape than if he has to displace the impulse onto someone or something else.

Preliminary validation of the scale consisted of comparing the dreams of psychotic patients, incarcerated criminals, and employees of an industrial firm. The ego rating scale differentiated among these groups.

Since these original studies, Sheppard (1964) has added three new scales. A summary of the five dream scales as given by Sheppard appears in Tables 15-1 through 15-5.

The scoring of a dream will be illustrated using the orality scale as an example. The orality scale consists of seven categories

Table 15-1
Hostility Scale

A. Intensity of Hostility
    4. Maximum: death
    2. Medium: injury
    1. Minimum: discomfort
B. Incidence of Hostility
    4. Repetitive hostile themes
    2. Dominant hostile themes
    1. Incidental hostile themes
C. Source (Aggressor)
    8. Inanimate, unspecified
    4. Animate
    2. Human
    1. Dreamer
D. Object (Victim)
    8. Inanimate, unspecified
    4. Animate
    2. Human
    1. Dreamer
E. Completion
    8. Denied, confused
    4. Contemplated, nonactual
    2. Incompleted, actual
    1. Completed, actual
F. Expression
    8. Character-setting
    4. Action
    2. Conversation
    1. Thought-feeling
G. Roots of Hostility
    8. Id
    4. Superego
    2. Ego
    1. Sublimated

(From Sheppard, 1964)

Table 15-2
Orality Scale

A. Intensity of Orality
   4. Maximum: bizarre, overwhelming
   2. Medium: realistic, benign
   1. Minimum: sublimated, symbolic
B. Incidence
   4. Repetitive oral themes
   2. Dominant oral themes
   1. Incidental oral themes
C. Source (Eater-Hungry one)
   8. Inanimate, unspecified
   4. Animate
   2. Human
   1. Dreamer
D. Object (Feeder)
   8. Inanimate, unspecified
   4. Animate
   2. Human
   1. Dreamer
E. Completion
   8. Denied, confused
   4. Contemplated, nonactual
   2. Incompleted, actual
   1. Completed, actual
F. Expression
   8. Character-setting
   4. Action
   2. Conversation
   1. Thought-feeling
G. Food
   8. Harmful: poison, drunkenness
   4. Nonnurturant: gum, smoking, cocktails
   2. Realistic: nurturant, essential
   1. Sublimated, symbolic

(From Sheppard, 1964)

Table 15-3
Anality Scale

A. Intensity of Anality
    4. Maximum: bizarre, overwhelming
    2. Medium: realistic, benign
    1. Minimum: sublimated, symbolic
B. Incidence of Anal Themes
    4. Repetitive
    2. Dominant
    1. Incidental
C. Source (Soiler)
    8. Inanimate, unspecified
    4. Animate
    2. Human
    1. Dreamer
D. Object (Cleaner)
    8. Inanimate, unspecified
    4. Animate
    2. Human
    1. Dreamer
E. Completion of Anal Impulse
    8. Denied, confused
    4. Threatened, nonactual
    2. Incompleted, actual
    1. Completed, actual
F. Expression of Anality
    8. Character-setting
    4. Action
    2. Conversation
    1. Thought-feeling
G. Dirt
    8. Harmful, bizarre
    4. Unrealistic, feces
    2. Realistic: waste materials
    1. Symbolic, sublimated

(From Sheppard, 1964)

Table 15-4
Genitality Scale

A. Intensity of Genitality
    4. Maximum: bizarre, overwhelming
    2. Medium: realistic, benign
    1. Minimum: sublimated
B. Incidence of Genital Themes
    4. Repetitive
    2. Dominant
    1. Incidental
C. Source (Seducer)
    8. Inanimate, unspecified
    4. Animate
    2. Human
    1. Dreamer
D. Object (Seduced)
    8. Inanimate, unspecified
    4. Animate
    2. Human
    1. Dreamer
E. Completion of Genital Impulse
    8. Denied, confused
    4. Threatened, nonactual
    2. Incompleted, actual
    1. Completed actual
F. Expression of Genitality
    8. Character-setting
    4. Action
    2. Conversation
    1. Thought-feeling
G. Type of Sexuality
    8. Bizarre, castration, animal
    4. Homosexual
    2. Autosexual
    1. Heterosexual

(From Sheppard, 1964)

Table 15-5
Ego Rating System

A. Reality ot Setting
 8. Bizarre
 4. Possible, improbable, terrifying
 2. Familiar setting altered, mild disturbance
 1. Realistic, benign
B. Body Image
 8. Bizarre, suicide, homicide, psychosis
 4. Mutilation, critical injury
 2. Ill, something wrong, anxiety
 1. Healthy
C. Interpersonal Relationships
 8. Solitary, nonproductive
 4. Dependent
 2. Rivalry, enmity, competition
 1. Friendly, work
D. Sequence of Themes: Logical Structure
 8. Illogical, confused
 4. Retreat, restitution, flight, shift of scene
 2. Repetition, similar theme
 1. Action reaction, cause and effect, logical
E. Problem in Dream
 8. Wish fulfillment
 4. Insoluble problem, confused, strange
 2. Anxiety, frustration, inability
 1. Interest, work, game

(From Sheppard, 1964)

divided into 26 subcategories. The dream report is read for evidence of orality which is defined by Sheppard in the following words:

"Orality is herein defined as a motivating factor derived from the somatic impulse of taking nourishment into the body by way of the mouth. In the dream the orality may be expressed directly in somatic terms, or in forms closely related to the somatic drive. The derivative forms may be recognized as items dealing with food, or the obtaining of food, as items dealing with the mouth, lips, teeth, and/or tongue. Indirectly related forms include items such as general shopping, emphasis on speech or conversation, and characters demonstrating obesity or greed. Concern with the mouth of either a pleasurable or unpleasurable nature is scored in the orality scale; e.g., kissing, tooth trouble, going to the dentist" (1964, p. 10).

If no evidence of orality is found, the dream is given a score of 0. If any orality whatsoever is found, then it must be scored under all seven categories. If there is more than one representation of orality in the dream, each such representation may be scored as long as the score falls in a different subcategory. That is, only one score per dream is permitted for each subcategory. In theory, a dream may be scored for all 26 subcategories which would yield a score of 89, the maximum score obtainable. The lowest possible score when any orality appears in the dream is 7.

The other scales are used in the same manner as the orality scale. No interscorer reliability studies have been published but we are informed by Dr. Sheppard that such studies have been made and will be published in the near future.

Two studies making use of these or similar scales have recently appeared (Sheppard, 1963; Sheppard and Karon, 1964). The first study comparing clinical judgment with objective measurement of ego strength is an extension of the investigation reported by Sheppard and Saul (1958). Two graduate students in industrial psychology were given eight hours of training in using the ego rating system. They then rated dreams collected from 28 psychotic patients and 30 persons without known disease. The ratings of the psychotic dreams were higher than those for normal dreams at a statistically significant level. The 58 dreams were then submitted to two psychiatrists and two psychologists and they were asked to separate the two samples. Three of the judges did not succeed at a statistically significant level. The fourth judge who did succeed was a psychiatrist who had been a member of the research seminar which formulated the ego rating system. Sheppard concludes that "clinically naive personnel using the ego rating system can distinguish between the dreams of psychotics and normals better than clinically experienced personnel who have not had training with the scale" (1963, p. 268).

Interscorer reliability in this study was quite high considering the complex judgments required. The two judges made a total of 2784 ratings for the 58 dreams. Of these, 2245 were exactly the same for the two judges which yields an overall agreement of 81 percent.

In the study by Sheppard and Karon (1964), the five scales were used to determine the relationship between manifest dreams and the associations given to the dreams. Dreams and associations to them were scored independently. Significant relationships between dreams and associations were found for certain aspects of the hostility scale and for genitality. No interscorer reliabilities are reported. A similar study by Reis is discussed later in this chapter.

Beck and Hurvich (1959) tested and confirmed the hypothesis that the first 20 dreams from six neurotic-depressed female patients in psychoanalytic therapy would show a greater incidence of masochistic content than the first 20 dreams from a matched group of six nondepressed female patients.

A scoring manual for masochism was developed, the authors state, by a combined theoretical and empirical approach. It consisted of formulating a number of categories reflecting a need to suffer. These scoring categories were expanded and refined by studying and comparing several hundred dreams of depressed and nondepressed patients for content that reflected a need to suffer and which was differentially represented in the two samples.

An abridgement of the scoring manual appears in Table 15-6.

TABLE 15-6
A MASOCHISM SCALE

The dream will score positive (+) "masochistic" if it falls into one of the following three categories.

A. The dreamer explicitly reports one of the following unpleasant affects accompanying the dream: bad, guilty, sad, hurt, disappointed, sorrow, unhappy, lonely, deserted, unwanted, worthless, rejected, humiliated, inferior, or inadequate.

B. The dreamer is crying or sobbing.

C. The dream action or the appearance of the dreamer is indicative of an unpleasant experience for the dreamer. In order to score positive in this category the unpleasant experience must fall into one of the following subcategories.

1. *Deprived, disappointed, or mistreated.* Examples: "I was in a restaurant but the waiters would not serve me." "I put a nickel in the coke machine but all I got was fizz, no syrup." "I got a hamburger but it was made of rubber." "The professor sprang an exam on us. He had told the other students about it but not me."

2. *Thwarted.* Examples: "I ran to make my appointment with you. I was one minute late and the door was locked." "I put some bottles of wine in the refrigerator. The corks fell out and the wine spilled over and spoiled everything." "I tried as hard as I could on the exam but I flunked it."

3. *Excluded, superseded, or displaced.* Examples: "Everybody was invited to the party but me." "My fiancee married somebody else." "My husband was making love to another woman."

4. *Rejected or deserted.* Examples: "You said 'Get out. I don't want to see you any more.'" "I was waiting for my friends all night but they never showed up."

5. *Blamed, criticized, or ridiculed.* Example: "He said I was a cry baby."

6. *Legal punishment.*

7. *Physical discomfort or injury.* Example: "Leeches were crawling all over me."

8. *Distortion of body image.* Examples: "My hair fell out." "I was large and fat."

9. *Being lost or losing something.*

No score is given for dreams with "threat," "anxiety," or "shame" content unless there is a specific "masochistic element" or theme as described above. No score is given for affects classified as "frightened," "anxious," "worried," or "apprehensive," or where there is a danger or threat but the dreamer is not actually harmed.

Examples of dreams that do *not* score:

"There was some dangerous force in the building."

"I fell off a cliff but I don't remember hitting bottom."

"There was a monster chasing me. I woke up before he caught me."

(From Beck and Hurvich, 1959)

The unabridged scoring manual is available on request from Aaron T. Beck, M.D., Department of Psychiatry, University of Pennsylvania, School of Medicine, Philadelphia, Pa.

Scoring reliability was determined in the following manner. The two investigators practiced scoring dreams using the manual until they had attained a high degree of agreement. For the final determination of reliability, the two authors scored the 240 dreams making up the experimental and control samples. A dream was scored as masochistic if it had at least one masochistic element in it. They agreed on the presence or absence of a masochistic element in 229 of the dreams which is 95% agreement.

The study was replicated (Beck and Ward, 1961) with 218 patients who were measured for depth of depression by a depression inventory (Beck, Ward, Mendelson, Mock, and Erbaugh, 1961) and by clinical ratings. Each patient reported the most recent dream he could recall. Patients with high clinical ratings for depression and/or high scores on the depression inventory reported more dreams with a masochistic element in them than did patients with low ratings and/or scores. Scoring reliability for presence or absence of a masochistic element between the two authors for the 216 dreams was 96%.

Other measures of masochism in addition to dreams are described in another article by Beck (1961). These measures consisted of masochistic elements in early memories and in stories told to pictures, and a masochism inventory. In this article, Beck comments upon the question as to whether the presence of masochistic elements in dreams might not simply reflect the subjective state of the depressed person. "While our studies have not progressed far enough as yet to answer this question definitely, we have some preliminary data that is worth noting. It has been found that a number of patients report masochistic dreams with the same degree of frequency during relatively long symptom-free periods between episodes of depression. Also it has been found that a number of individuals who have never been depressed but who show typical masochistic behaviors in their interpersonal relations report the masochistic dreams with a high degree of frequency. These observations suggest that masochistic dreams could be best regarded as a relatively persistent characteristic of individuals who are prone to develop depression and may be more directly related to certain personality features of depression-prone individuals than to the state of depression *per se*" (p. 169).

In our opinion, Beck's masochism scale is the most rigorous and careful application of quantitative methodology to a particular phase of dream analysis that has been made to date. His construction of a theoretical scale provides a model that other investigators would do well to emulate.

A method of measuring ego strength in reported dreams was devised by Polster (1950) eight years prior to the publication of the Sheppard and Saul scale. The system is set forth in Table 15-7.

TABLE 15-7
CRITERIA OF EGO STRENGTH IN DREAMS

A. Appropriateness of aggression

Classify each of the aggressive encounters involving the dreamer in one of the following categories.

1. Aggressive response to aggression (Appropriate)
2. Aggressive response to nonaggression (Inappropriate)
3. Nonaggressive response to aggression (Inappropriate)

B. Probability of Occurrence

Each dream is to be read with an eye toward judging the plausibility of the dream events. The dream is to be looked upon as telling a story about events in waking life, and it is to be decided whether it does so reasonably or plausibly and the degree to which it does. There should be no concern necessarily with the probability that the events actually do occur in waking life. For example, if the dream tells a story about a poor boy who works hard and becomes President of the United States it is no concern of the scorer that the probability of this occurring is low, but it is his concern whether the events are handled in a plausible way. The actual characteristics of the dreamer (e.g., intelligence, personality, etc.) will have to be ignored in this scoring arrangement, except in cases where they openly represent incongruous features of the situation, such as a six-year-old girl dreaming she is the mother of a ten-year-old child.

Rating	Categories
5	Very high degree of likelihood that the events of the dream could occur in waking life.
4	Probable except for some relatively unimportant feature, or moderate degree of likelihood that the dream events could occur in waking life.
3	Low degree of likelihood that dream events could occur in waking life, and lack of or unsuccessful effort to give the dream events reasonableness.
2	Very low degree of likelihood. Events border on impossible. Fantasy which has some reasonable features.
1	Impossible. Clearly unrealistic.

Give each dream a rating.

C. Ways of handling problems

Choose the event or events in a dream that are painful or present a problem which you feel is presented in a way that requires solution. The event may be an accident, illness, injury, emotional crisis, frustration, threat to safety, etc.

Rate the way of handling the problem on the following two scales.

I. Reasonableness of solution
1. Situation not handled in manifest content or handled by ending the dream.
2. Situation handled in an unrealistic, magical, unconvincing way.
3. Situation handled by a reasonable relationship of events.

II. Directness of action
1. No action, including ending the dream.
2. Indirect or inappropriate action.
3. Incompleted direct action; direct attempt at solution which is not completed in the dream.
4. Completed direct action.

(From Polster, 1951)

The dreams of four groups of subjects were scored for ego strength. The four groups were children between the ages of 5 and 10, adolescents between the ages of 12 and 16, adults over 30 years of age, and patients being treated at a mental hygiene clinic. It was predicted that ego strength would increase with age, and that the ego strength of the patient group would resemble that of children or adolescents. These predictions were confirmed. Interscorer reliability was satisfactorily high.

A study of attitudes toward the male and female sex organs as expressed in the dreams of college students was undertaken by Claire Rabe (1949). She scored male and female dream series (college students) for the categories shown in Tables 15-8 and 15-9. Her findings support Freud's formulation of the castration complex. The average percentage agreement between two scorers was 88%.

TABLE 15-8
ATTITUDES TOWARD THE PENIS

1. *Impaired:* Under this heading, all symbols where the context was one of mutilation to the phallic organ were included. For example, the dreamer's nose is cut or his car gets wrecked.

2. *Aggressive:* The symbol was pictured as a weapon which the dreamer was using in an aggressive fashion. For example, the dreamer shoots someone with a pistol.

3. *Insufficient:* The symbol was in a context of inadequacy in the sense of being a disappointment to the dreamer. For example, one dreamer sadly reflected on the size of a plane; it was a piper cub plane, much too small.

4. *Fear of:* The dreamer was the object of an attack by a symbolized phallus, such as guns threatening the dreamer.

5. *Wish:* The dreamer presented phallic symbols in a context of wanting them. Phallic gifts were included here. For example, the dreamer has received a powerful plane on his birthday. Stealing or borrowing a phallus as often occurred with the females was included under this column.

6. *Revulsion:* The symbol was given in a context of a strongly negative affect such as a very ugly tail.

7. *Neutral:* The writer could not discover any immediate emotional context in relation to the symbol. There was no action or affect directly involved. For example, the dreamer is carrying a pole or wearing a sword as part of a costume.

(From Rabe, 1949)

TABLE 15-9
ATTITUDES TOWARD THE VAGINA

1. *Impaired:* The vaginal symbol represents a more or less injured vagina. For example, a diamond ring has a stone missing.

2. *Rejection:* The dreamer either directly casts away the organ or unequivocally indicates that it ought to be cast away or rejected. For example, the dreamer throws shoes away or dreams that her house is being criticized.

3. *Dislike:* This differed from rejection since the dreamer did not indicate action or the need for action of any sort; instead these symbols symbolized an attitude as such. For example, a road is a messy place or a building is dilapidated in appearance.

4. *Fear of:* The symbol indicated that the vagina was considered as a punishing instrument.

5. *Valued:* The symbol was either a pleasant object, such as a flower, or the context showed that the vagina was considered valuable. For example, the dreamer is proud of her diamond ring.

6. *Neutral:* Here, as for the phallic symbols, were put the symbols without an emotional context. No discernible affect was attached to any aspect of the symbol in question. For example, a tunnel serves as a passage, or a suitcase is being carried.

(From Rabe, 1949)

Rychlak (1960) investigated the relationship between three dream themes, namely, affiliation, reward, and tension, and scores on the Cattell Junior Personality Quiz and a sociometric measure of popularity. The subjects were 30 fifth-grade and 29 eighth-grade children who wrote their dreams each week during classtime for a three-month period. The definition of each of the themes is set forth in Table 15-10.

Each dream was given a single scoring for one of the foregoing themes. Less than 5% of the dreams could not be scored as either affiliation, reward, or tension. Scoring reliability was obtained by having two trained scorers independently classify 32 dreams. They agreed in 94% of the cases.

Dream themes were shown to be related to personality test

TABLE 15-10
BRIEF DESCRIPTIONS OF DREAMS OF AFFILIATION, REWARD, AND TENSION

Affiliative: Dreams having relaxed or pleasurable interpersonal relations with other human beings as their major themes, regardless of the latter's relationship to S; e.g., relatives, peers, same or opposite sex, etc. There must be some form of interaction with the person, and not simply a recollection of seeing him in the dream.

Examples:

"I dreamed that my brother and I went swimming."

"I dreamed that a boy in our room took every girl out to a show."

"I dreamed that me and Stevie played catch."

Reward: Dreams with major themes involving a positive, pleasurable connotation *other than* that derived from strictly interpersonal contact. Reward themes include individual achievement and recognition, the receiving of gifts, and any fantasy-like tale of miraculous happenings.

Examples:

"I dreamed I got a new watch."

"I dreamed I scored 25 points against Panama City."

"I was on Arthur Godfrey's Talent Scouts."

Tension: Dreams reflecting anxiety, frustration, or hostility in their major themes.

Examples:

"I dreamed that Frankenstein was after me."

"I was riding my bike and the wheel came off."

"I dreamed some friends of mine were killed in an auto accident."

(From Rychlak, 1960)

scores and to sociometric measures. For example, dreamers who had relatively more reward themes seemed to be either outgoing and affable or fairly dominant and achievement oriented, whereas dreamers with more affiliative themes tended to be passive, conforming, and inhibited, and expressed a preference for close interpersonal relations.

In a second study involving college students using the same

dream themes of affiliation, reward, and tension, plus a miscellaneous category, Rychlak and Brams (1963) correlated themes with scores on the Taylor Manifest Anxiety Scale, the Edwards Personal Preference Schedule, and the MMPI. The only changes in the scoring manual used for adults as compared with the one for children (Table 15-10) were that sex dreams were classed under Affiliative, and the following qualifying sentence was added to the description of the tension theme: "There is often an element of these emotions in the Affiliative and Reward dream, but the general coloring of the major theme must have this feature before a Tension scoring is given to it" (p. 227). The miscellaneous class, or as the authors label it, Garden Variety, consists of dreams which do not have one of the three themes. They tend to be trite or vaguely recalled dreams.

With regard to scoring reliability, they say that "repeated reliability checks with two raters scoring dream themes independently have demonstrated that 90% agreement is not difficult to obtain" (p. 227).

It is of interest to compare the distribution of these themes for children and adults which appear in Table 15-11. The current dreams reported by adults are distributed in roughly the same manner as those reported by children. Children tend to have

Table 15-11

Distribution of Major Dream Themes for Children and Adults

	n	Affiliative	Reward	Tension	Miscellaneous
		% of _n_ reporting one or more themes in their dream series of			
Children	59	42	51	70	–
Adults (current)	41	54	41	66	27
Adults (recurring)	41	12	07	54	02

(Based on data given in Rychlak, 1960, and Rychlak and Brams, 1963)

somewhat more reward dreams, and adults somewhat more affiliative dreams, but the differences are not striking. The recurring
dream reported by adults is nearly always a tension dream.

Rychlak and Brams also developed a scale for measuring
what they call reactive content in dreams. Reactive content as
defined by them is anything in the dream that is unusual, peculiar,
or distorted. The determination of the amount of reactive content
in dreams is outlined in Table 15-12. It has similarities to the
method for measuring distortion in dreams developed by Perry
(1964) and discussed on p. 226 of this chapter.

TABLE 15-12
THE SCORING OF REACTIVE CONTENT IN DREAMS

In order to score a dream for Reactive Content, the dream is first
broken down into the following five categories.

Location: Where the dream is taking place; e.g., city, state, an
ambulance, on the desert, or the moon.

Actors: Human and/or other animate actors in the dream. This
scoring was much like identifying TAT heroes, although no distinction
was made between central or peripheral figures in the story line.

Action: This referred to the story line of the dream; e.g., dancing,
a war battle, an athletic contest.

Mood Terms: The emotions expressed in the dream report, either
as occurring in the actors or as representative of a given location, etc.;
e.g., angered (cop), scary (country road), silly (little house).

Implements: Inanimate materials used in the action of the dream;
e.g., hammer, gun, automobile (may also be the location), food and
drink.

When the dream is thus dissected, the entries under each category
are termed Representative Contents. The scorer then goes through
these Representative Contents and selects those which have Reactive
characteristics.

Reactive Contents are those which demonstrate an unusual quality, such as a shift, an alteration, an about-face, or a weird connotation
according to customary standards or expectations. Some examples of
Reactive Content would be when a location suddenly shifts from a
dance floor to a skating rink or when the actors may be unlike them-

selves in appearance or pop up in the dream at an unusual time or place. The action in a dream might shift abruptly or be entirely inappropriate as in feeding ice cream to a dead person. Inappropriate moods or violent shifts in emotion would also constitute Reactive Content; e.g., being pleased about the loss of one's arm. If S dreams that he is wearing a dog collar, this would suggest a Reactive Implement Content. A score on any of the five categories consisted of the percentage (decimal removed) of Representative Content which was also judged to be Reactive in nature.

(From Rychlak and Brams, 1963)

The writers have this to say about reliability. "Over 150 comparisons were made in pretesting of dream contents as a scoring reliability check, with the two authors scoring the same series of dreams independently. The percentages of agreement on these comparisons (agreement divided by total comparisons) were as follows: Representative Content, 79%; Reactive Content, 81%. . . . Broken down by the five categories, the percentages of agreement approximate these overall figures, and in no case did they fall below 70%" (1963, p. 228).

In their study of the effects of drugs on the dreams of college students, Whitman, Pierce, Maas, and Baldridge (1961) devised seven scales for rating the contents of reported dreams. The seven scales are reproduced in Tables 15-13 through 15-19. The hostility scale was an adaptation of the Saul and Sheppard one (1956) and the anxiety scale was modified from the one developed by Hamburg, Sabshin, Board, Grinker, Korchin, Basowitz, Heath, and Persky (1956). A dream is scored by breaking it down into clauses and rating each clause with the appropriate scale.

TABLE 15-13
SCALE FOR MEASURING HOSTILITY

Rating
6   Human: Death or death threat by stabbing, shooting, pushing, striking, hit by car, drowning, illness, warfare, animal attack, mutilation, driven to insanity, violence.

5   Nonhuman: Equivalent destruction of animate or inanimate objects other than human.

4   Human: Injury or injury threat by fight, accident, illness, abandonment, helplessness, robbery.

3   Nonhuman: Equivalent injury of animate or inanimate objects other than human.

2   Human: Discomfort or discomfort threat by minor difficulty, hurt, annoyance, failure, inappropriate behavior.

1   Nonhuman: Equivalent discomfort of animate or inanimate objects other than human.

(From Whitman *et al.*, 1961)

TABLE 15-14
SCALE FOR MEASURING DEPENDENCY

Rating

6   Total reliance on an object or institution (including specific references to eating or food).

5   Total reliance on a group.

4   Total reliance on an individual.

3   Partial reliance on an object or institution.

2   Partial reliance on a group.

1   Partial reliance on an individual.

(From Whitman *et al.*, 1961)

TABLE 15-15
SCALE FOR MEASURING ANXIETY

Rating

6   Most extreme ever reported (Panic).

5   Extremely intense (Dread).

4   Unusually intense (Danger).

3   Intense (Foreboding).

2   Impressive (Apprehension).

1   Distinct but not impressive (Unpleasant anticipation).

(From Whitman *et al.*, 1961)

TABLE 15-16
SCALE FOR MEASURING MOTILITY

Rating

6 Accelerated animate motor activity (sprinting, racing, sexual intercourse, etc.).

5 Vigorous animate activity (walking rapidly, running, jumping, etc.).

4 Moderate animate activity (walking, driving a car, going some place by own motor power, etc.).

3 Minimal animate activity (talking, watching, eating, etc.).

2 Vigorous inanimate activity (rapidly-growing things, cars moving, boats racing, etc.).

1 Minimal inanimate activity (light winds, etc.).

(From Whitman *et al.*, 1961)

TABLE 15-17
SCALE FOR MEASURING HOMOSEXUALITY
(SUBSTITUTE WOMAN FOR MAN WITH FEMALE SUBJECTS)

Rating

6 Direct sexual expression with a man.

5 A man being alone with another man in situation with overt sexual possibilities or overtones (sleeping, lying down, brushing together, etc.).

4 Involved interchange between men including manipulation, joking, teasing, or intimate conversation.

3 The appearance of men (two or more) with active interchange.

2 The appearance of two men but without active interchange.

1 The appearance of more than two men but without active interchange.

 (Minus 2 from each score if the male or female in the dream is a child.)

(From Whitman *et al.*, 1961)

TABLE 15-18
TABLE FOR MEASURING HETEROSEXUALITY
(SUBSTITUTE MAN FOR WOMAN WITH FEMALE SUBJECTS)

Rating

6   Direct sexual expression with a woman (coitus). (Including symbolic references.)

5   Sex of foreplay type with a woman (including symbolic references).

4   Dating or being alone with a woman and/or in a sitution with sexual possibilities.

3   Involved interchange with a woman including posing and conversation.

2   The appearance of one or more women in which he is the only male.

1   The appearance of one or more women in the dream but one or more other males are present.

(Minus 2 from each score if the male or female in the dream is a child.)

(From Whitman *et al.*, 1961)

TABLE 15-19
SCALE FOR MEASURING INTIMACY

Rating

6   A person is with people in an intimate relation with them (including touching and sexuality).

5   A person is with people with close interaction with them (talking, working together, common task, etc.).

4   A person is with animals in close interaction.

3   A person is with people at a distance but with interaction with them or close with animals without interaction.

2   A person is with people at a distance without interaction with them (visual, etc.).

1   A person is alone in a dream without other people, or with living things but without interaction with them.

(From Whitman *et al.*, 1961)

The investigators report interjudge reliability of .75 but do not give any details as to how this figure was obtained. The investigators wish to emphasize "that although these scales all rate the manifest content of the dreams, they are constructed from clinical knowledge of the implicit latent content" (p. 220). Moreover, they found "in contrast to Saul, that a good deal of psychodynamic training was necessary to score doubtful phrases and to be alert to symbolic or other allusions to important affective material" (p. 220). They do not say what amount of training is necessary or the nature of the training.

Goldhirsh (1961) tested and confirmed the hypothesis that eight imprisoned sex offenders undergoing therapy would report more dreams in which a sexual element appeared than would eight criminals of other types, e.g., burglars, who were also undergoing therapy. A brief version of the scoring system used to identify sexual themes in dreams is presented in Table 15-20. The unabridged scoring manual has been deposited with the American Documentation Institute, No. 6862.

TABLE 15-20
A SYSTEM FOR SCORING SEXUAL THEMES IN DREAMS

The dream text will score positive (+) "sexual" if it contains words, slang expressions, activity, or references to the following items:

1. "Wet dreams" or any form of sex play.
2. Sexual organs or their activity (erection, masturbation).
3. Nakedness, or body description of any erotic nature:
      Sexy, lovely, beautiful, or well-built breasts, hips, thighs, legs, nipples, body, etc.
4. Kissing, hugging, petting, necking, or erotic feelings from body contact.
5. Sex crime: Any form of sex play with a child or teenager until 16 years of age. Any activity involving incest, rape; homosexuality, or sodomy (oral or anal genital contacts). An uncamouflaged "sex crime" dream also receives a double score (++).

(From Goldhirsh, 1961)

Scoring reliability was determined by having two scorers classify the dreams for presence or absence of a sexual element as defined by the manual. One scorer was the investigator who constructed the scale; the other scorer who was unfamiliar with the research, the cases, and their dreams, was given "a few minutes of clarification" before scoring the 80 experimental and 80 control subjects' dreams. These dreams consisted of the first 10 dreams reported during therapy. The scorers agreed as to the presence or absence of a sexual element on 158 of 160 dreams and the presence or absence of a sex crime on 156 out of 160 dreams.

Framo, Osterweil, and Boszormenyi-Nagy (1962) tested and confirmed the hypothesis: "If threat in the manifest content of the psychotic's dreams is directed toward the self, the overt behavior of the patient will be largely characterized by overactivity, and if threat is directed toward others in the dream, the overt behavior will be largely characterized by pathological passivity" (p. 42). At least one dream was related verbally by each of 92 patients in a research and training psychiatric institute. These patients were also rated by nurses and aides for manifestations of active and passive behavior. The threat scale for classifying dreams is given in Table 15-21.

TABLE 15-21
A SCALE FOR MEASURING THREAT IN DREAMS

I. The first judgment to be made about each dream is whether the dream is a "threat" (T) dream or a "nonthreat" (NT) dream. A "threat" dream, in general, is defined as one in which at any point in the dream any one of the following appears: A dangerous action or image, or an affect indicating fear or anxiety, or a dangerous situation threatening or potentially detrimental to the survival, health, or way of life of anyone in the dream. A dream should be judged a threat dream under the following conditions:

(a) Where the survival of some person or persons is at stake or where some actual or imminent or completed state of death, injury, or illness occurs to someone in the dream. (Examples: "I dreamt my mother died," or "I saw that my uncle was blind," or "I was being chased by a monster," or "I had to go to the hospital," or "My baby was sick.")

(b) Psychological or "way of life" threats—continued marriage being threatened, financial security, career or job, social ostracism, rejection from or loss of significant relationships, etc. (Examples: "They were brainwashing me," or "I was becoming insane," or "My boss fired me," or "My husband divorced me," or "I told my small son to leave home.")

(c) Fear or anxiety mentioned in dreams with or without appropriate cause. (Examples: "I was frightened," or "I was walking through the park; the sun was shining, and the children were afraid.")

(d) Natural disasters, fires, explosions, wild animals, or fearful abstractions are considered threatening provided human beings as either the source or the target are being affected in the dream. (Examples: "The city full of people was on fire," or "A tiger was chasing my brother," or "Damnation was on my soul.")

(e) Although there may be no explicitly dangerous content in the dream, threat may be implied by a *potentially* dangerous situation or by some major aspect of one's life situation being potentially altered detrimentally. (Examples: "I was sitting in the car my four-year-old was driving," or "I was standing on top of a cliff," or "I dreamt my husband was going to Tibet," or "I felt that I may have to look for another job.")

Threat may be determined by the actual or potential anxiety-generating nature of a dream element, relative gravity of several dream elements, or by the dream's emotional context. Resentment, arguing, irritation, annoyance, and other expressions of hostility, as well as words expressing worry, concern, insult, rebuke, frustration, feelings of rejection, and sarcasm, *may or may not* be considered threat depending on the significance of the relationships in the dream or the dangerousness of the situation.

II. The second judgment, direction of threat, is to be made only on the "threat" dreams. The whole dream should be summarily evaluated for this purpose.

(a) Threat is directed toward the dreamer *from any source* (Label S for Self).

(b) Threat is directed toward some other person or persons *from any source* (Label O for Other).

(c) The Complex category is used when dreams with more than one dream element have threats going in different directions. If this is judged to be the case it is rated as *C* for complex with the direction of the most serious or grave threat sublabeled as the dominant one. (For example, *Cs* would be rated for the following dream: "I was trying to hurt this tiger, jabbing at it with a stick, when he turned around and he ran after me and I woke up scared." Example of threat rated as *Co*. "I felt very sick and weak and I couldn't prevent my baby from dying.")

(d) Threat is involved but direction is unspecified, unable to be determined, or gravity is equally serious to Others and to Self (Label *U*). (Examples: "There was great destruction all around," or "The building was on fire," or "We were killing each other.")

(From Framo *et al.*, 1962)

The authors independently classified all of the 189 dreams for the presence or absence of threat. The three scorers agreed among themselves on 169 dreams or 89% of the cases. Using just the dreams that contained a threat, scorers agreed on the direction of threat 92% of the time.

Lott (1963), in an honors thesis written at Brandeis University under the direction of R. M. Jones, set out to study the identity crisis in adolescence which is one of the stages in Erikson's developmental scheme. He identified six configurations (Table 15-22) in manifest dreams which were related in some manner to the identity crisis.

Table 15-22

Six Configurations in Dreams Related to the Identity Crisis in Adolescents

I. *Painful isolation*
    1. Dreamer is isolated from other dream characters throughout the dream
        A. Dreamer is ignored by population
            1. He tries to communicate
            2. He remains silent and expressionless

     B. Dreamer is isolated by being "different"
        1. As a result of an activity performed by him through-
        out the dream
        2. As a result of being involved in an event which de-
        scends upon him from the immediate environment

This configuration of painful isolation is a reflection of the fear of identity diffusion and a working through of the problems of choice and commitment in the identity crisis.

II. *Self-made isolation*
    1. The dreamer isolates himself from other dream characters as a result of a specific action
       A. The action is aggressive
          1. Dreamer is isolated by being ignored
          2. Dreamer is isolated by receiving reprimands
       B. The action constitutes a refusal on the part of the dreamer
          to do what the rest of the dream characters are doing
       C. The action is a voicing of criticism

This configuration represents the repudiation process which is part of identity formation.

III. *Identification with group*
    1. An isolated dreamer joins other dream characters
       A. Simply as a part of the dream sequence with no reason
          given
       B. As a result of a stated action on the part of the dreamer
IV. *Isolation of another dream character*
    1. A person other than the dreamer is isolated and the dreamer observes this isolated character
       A. The character isolates himself by performing an action
       B. The character is isolated through an inherent quality in
          his personal appearance or through a misfortune which
          befalls him in the dream
V. *Race against time*
    1. The dreamer is trying to finish an action before time runs out and makes completion impossible
       A. Time does, in fact, run out, making the intended action
          impossible and making the dreamer affectively experi-
          ence the resulting frustration
       B. The resolution of the race does not occur in the dream

This configuration reflects the sense of urgency underlying the everyday psychopathology of the identity crisis.

VI. *Absence of affect*
   1. The dreamer does not report emotions for himself or for others in dream situations that ordinarily would evoke emotion

This configuration reflects the adolescent's attempt to deal with the identity crisis by impersonalization, withdrawal, and suppression.

(Adapted from Lott, 1963)

Three studies that we know of have attempted to construct scales for identifying unrealistic elements in dreams, in addition to the one devised by Polster (Table 15-7), the reactive content scale of Rychlak and Brams (Table 15-12), and references to bizarreness in some of the scales devised by Sheppard (Tables 15-2 through 15-5).

Domhoff (1962) identified three broad classes of bizarre elements in dreams: metamorphoses, unusual acts, and magical occurrences. Subclasses of each of these and examples are presented in Table 15-23. This scale, along with other scales, was

TABLE 15-23
BIZARRE ELEMENTS IN DREAMS

I. Metamorphoses
   1. Person to another person ("a man yelled 'Larry' and the lady changed into my best male friend")
   2. Animal to person and vice versa ("the foot-high dwarf changed into a crocodile-shaped animal")
   3. Inanimate to animate and vice versa ("the statue came to life," "the refrigerator turned into my friend and then into foam rubber")
   4. Object to another object ("baseball bats into swords")
II. Unusual Acts
   1. Using object in way seldom or never used ("the bed was in the kitchen," "there was a trailer tied to the tail of the airplane")

    2. Doing something seldom or never done ("packed a huge trunk with all her belongings for a picnic," "walking around nude")

III. Magical Occurrences

    1. Flying

    2. Animals doing things they can't ("a horse talking," "a swan lecturing a hunter," "a mouse bouncing up and down")

    3. Babies talking

    4. Distortions, disappearances

(From Domhoff, 1962)

used by Domhoff in a comparative study of dreams collected throughout the night using objective EEG indicators and dreams spontaneously remembered in the morning. For male subjects, although not for female subjects, there were more bizarre elements in dreams collected throughout the night than in dreams remembered in the morning.

In a dissertation written by Goldenberg (1963) at Wayne State University, a seven-point scale for assessing primary process thinking in reported dreams was developed. The criteria for primary process thinking consisted principally of bizarre features. Descriptions of the scale points are given in Table 15-24. Two judges independently rated 30 dreams and the reliability of their ratings was .87.

TABLE 15-24
A Scale for Measuring Primary Process Thinking in Dreams

    1. The dream as a whole is logical and there is nothing unusual occurring within it.

    2. The dream is still logical and orderly but some of the events are unusual yet possible.

    3. Some event in the dream is impossible or contradictory; or there is the presence of obvious symbolization; or the transitions in

time, space, and sequence are not explained; or something about the dream is mildly uncanny such as a feeling of not being able to move.

4. One of the following characteristics is present in the dream: rapid shifts in time, locale, or sequence without any linkage provided by secondary revision; highly illogical or impossible series of events; the attribution of human qualities to animals or nonliving things; the report that a person is dead but comes back to watch the living with nothing otherwise bizarre in the dream; the dream as a whole is moderately bizarre or uncanny.

5. There are one or more instances of metamorphosis or condensation; the dream as a whole is bizarre and primarily a production of fantasy.

6. The dream as a whole is very bizarre, extremely uncanny, and autistic, but there are still some logical linkages in the dream.

7. The dream as a whole is extremely bizarre, uncanny, and autistic, and there are no logical linkages of any kind.

(From Goldenberg, 1963)

In Perry's study (1964) of distortion in dreams, he began by breaking down a dream into standard units and then scoring each unit for the presence or absence of a distortion. He could then compute the relative amount of distortion in dreams.

A scoring unit is defined as something *happening* to a specific *agent* in a particular *location*. If a particular dream contains ten A (agent), H (happening), L (location) units, and three of these units contain a distortion, then the proportion of distortion is .3. Should there be twenty such units and six distortions the proportion would still be .3. One may also compute the proportion of distortions for each constituent element within a unit, that is, for agents or happenings or locations separately.

Although it is not feasible to present Perry's complete system of content analysis here, we will describe some of its main features. It resembles our system in some respects. This is not surprising because any empirically derived system for analyzing the contents of dreams is going to find pretty much the same classes of events in dreams. There *are* settings, and objects, and characters, and actions and interactions, and modifiers in reported dreams no matter what theoretical preference an investigator may have.

Agents consist of characters, either human or animal, objects, and syntheses which are any of the following when they are spoken of as though they were "things": emotions, evaluations, qualities and attributes, perceptual terms, actions and processes, communication terms, physical terms, and impersonal pronouns. A happening is something that takes place, i.e., an event in a dream. Happenings are verbs. A location is the place in which a happening occurs to an agent.

Another class of events in dreams not covered by the foregoing classes is that of speech and thought. These are designated by the code letter V, scored separately, and are not analyzed into AHL units, although it is possible to do so.

When all of the AHL units and V's have been scored in a dream, each unit and V is scored for the presence or absence of a distortion. Distortion is defined as something appearing in a dream which is not something that can and typically does occur in the real world. The main types of distortion occurring in dreams are presented in Table 15-25. Examples of each of these

TABLE 15-25
TYPES OF DISTORTIONS IN DREAMS

1. An alteration in the typical appearance or dimensions of an agent.
2. Incongruous or impossible behavior of an agent.
3. Implausible behavior of a specific agent. (It may not be implausible for other agents.)
4. An agent is located in an atypical place for that agent.
5. An incongruous element appears in a situation.
6. Appearance or disappearance of an element in defiance of physical laws.
7. An agent changes in sex or identity; disembodiment.
8. An agent is dressed in inappropriate clothing.
9. Verbal peculiarities.
10. False or unrealistic ideas are expressed in the dream.

(From Perry, 1964)

types of distortion are given in the manual. In actual practice, a third kind of scoring is made for distortion. This is called "equivocal distortion" and is employed when the scorer is in doubt as to whether there is or is not a distortion. No information regarding scorer reliability for either scoring units or the analysis of distortion is given in the manual.

It may be pointed out that Perry's criteria for distortion in dreams are not tied to his system of classifying dream contents. The criteria for distortion may be used with any classificatory system.

In the preceding scales, the unit of analysis has been either the dream as a whole or some element of the dream, and usually there has been some attempt to be analytical rather than global in devising a system of classifying and scoring dream contents. Moreover, the categories formulated have been, for the most part, both empirical and theoretical in character.

We will now discuss several studies which represent methodological extremes in the content analysis of dreams. One of these studies was carried out by K. Colby (1958), in which the unit of analysis was the word, or infrequently a phrase.

Colby's list consists of 752 words. These 752 words are grouped under the six main headings of settings, objects, action, affects, thought, and properties. Settings are further subdivided into time, space, and motion, and objects are subdivided into human beings including human body parts, nonhuman animate objects, and inanimate objects. The classification system with examples is given in Table 15-26. The number in parentheses is

TABLE 15-26
CLASSIFICATION OF WORDS IN REPORTED DREAMS WITH EXAMPLES

1. Settings (97)
   - (a) Time (35): afternoon, early, gradually, old, suddenly, winter
   - (b) Space (30): above, back, edge, inside, left, narrow, right, top, under
   - (c) Motion (32): ascent, enter, leave, pull, push, towards, up
2. Objects (384)

    (a) Human and human body parts (123): actress, arm, baby, man, Negro, pus

    (b) Nonhuman animate (47): dog, flowers, fruit, tree, woods

    (c) Inanimate (214): auto, fork, mirror, pencil, room, stairs, tool, window

3. Actions (160): arrest, cry, eat, give, stand, throw, vomit, wish, write
4. Affects (73): amazement, enjoy, laughter, paralysis, shame
5. Thought (9): associate, decide, forget, think
6. Properties (29): beautiful, heavy, red, thin

(From Colby, 1958)

the number of different words (elements) in each category and subcategory.

    Colby used this system to make a study of sex differences in dreams. He compared the dreams of 200 male and 200 female patients undergoing psychoanalysis, and 200 male and 200 female college students. For the patient groups, five of the 752 categories (words) differentiated between males and females at the 5% level of significance, and for the college groups, seven of them were significant. Five of the seven significant differences for college males and females were the same as the five significant differences for male and female patients. These five elements were wife, husband, vehicle travel, auto, and hit. Men have higher frequencies for all of these elements with the exception of husband. The two other significant differences for the college groups are home and cry, both of which appear more frequently in the dream reports of college women.

    Another word analysis used on folktales and being used on dreams, so we are informed, is B. Colby's adaptation (1963) of the General Inquirer System (Stone, Bales, Namenwirth, and Ogilvie, 1962). This system feeds verbal material into the IBM 7090, a high speed digital computer. The main interest in Colby's study was to determine the incidence of words, classified under 180 headings in the folktales of five cultures. Each heading constitutes a theme and includes a family of related words. An example is as follows:

Theme: *Dominate*

Bribe, coerce, command, compel, conquer, control, convince, demand, deny, direct, dissuade, dominate, forbid, influence, insist, lead, manage, manipulate, obligate, overcome, persuade, prohibit, tempt, triumph, triumphant.

The use of computers is a welcome addition to content analysis because it promises to reduce some of the drudgery of present hand methods. (See also a recent article by Harway and Iker, 1964, which describes a computer method for analyzing the contents of therapy protocols.)

The other methodological extreme is represented in an investigation comparing series of dreams with and without free associations by Reis (1951, 1959). Reis set out to devise a rating scale that would have the following features.

"The rating scale should reflect the psychoanalytic personality theory since this is a theoretical framework within which this writer thinks. The rating scale should also be adapted as much as possible to the way a practical clinical psychologist operates in his daily work. Specifically, the clinician does not think in terms of isolated traits, but in terms of the total personality. For this reason the categories should be as global as the thinking of the psychoanalytically oriented clinician who describes personality in terms of orality, oedipus complexes, etc. Lastly, since this writer feels that reliable global judgments are possible, provided raters are taught the technique in personal training sessions rather than by a scoring manual, the units of the rating scale should reflect a fairly high level of abstraction" (1959, p. 214).

The rating scale that Reis devised is presented in Table 15-27.

TABLE 15-27
SCALES FOR RATING DREAMS FOR PSYCHOSEXUAL DEVELOPMENT, FAMILY RELATIONS AND PRESENT ADJUSTMENT

A. Psychosexual Development

1. Oedipus resolution
   (a) positive (b) unresolved or otherwise (c) negative
2. (a) Males: castration fear
   (a) strong (b) moderate (c) weak or absent

2. (b) Females: penis envy
   (a) strong (b) moderate (c) weak or absent
3. Primary dominant stage of psychosexual development
   (a) oral (b) anal (c) phallic or genital
4. Secondary stage of psychosexual development
   (a) oral (b) anal (c) phallic or genital
5. Degree of narcissism
   (a) strong (b) moderate (c) weak or absent
6. Type of sexual orientation
   (a) homosexual (b) bisexual (c) heterosexual
7. Quality of sexual adjustment
   (a) good (b) moderate (c) poor

B. Family Relations

8. Intensity of relation to mother
   (a) strong (b) moderate (c) weak
9. Quality of relation to mother
   (a) harmonious (b) medium (c) unharmonious
10. Intensity of relation to father
    (a) strong (b) moderate (c) weak
11. Quality of relation to father
    (a) harmonious (b) medium (c) unharmonious
12. Quality of relation to siblings
    (a) harmonious (b) medium (c) unharmonious

C. Present Adjustment

13. Intensity of relation to same sex
    (a) strong (b) moderate (c) weak
14. Quality of relation to same sex
    (a) harmonious (b) medium (c) unharmonious
15. Intensity of relation to opposite sex
    (a) strong (b) moderate (c) weak
16. Quality of relation to opposite sex
    (a) harmonious (b) medium (c) unharmonious
17. Ego strength
    (a) strong (b) moderate (c) weak
18. Id strength
    (a) strong (b) moderate (c) weak
19. Superego strength
    (a) strong (b) moderate (c) weak

20. Emotional control
    (a) rigid (b) moderate (c) weak
21. Aggression toward others
    (a) strong (b) moderate (c) weak
22. Aggression toward self
    (a) strong (b) moderate (c) weak
23. Anxiety
    (a) strong (b) moderate (c) weak or absent
24. Emotional maturity
    (a) mature (b) moderately mature (c) immature
25. Degree of psychopathology
    (a) strong (b) moderate (c) weak or absent

(From Reis, 1959)

It is estimated that it took eight to ten hours to rate a series of ten dreams and their accompanying associations. Interjudge agreement on the scale was made the subject of a thesis written by Ellen Lane (1951). Agreements between raters was satisfactorily high on most of the items. This is the most theoretically global and least empirical scale we have found in the literature of content analysis.

Another unique approach to the content analysis of dreams is that of D. Eggan (1952) who has fashioned a system of classification for one long dream series. Mrs. Eggan has been collecting dreams from the Hopi Indians for a number of years and correlating them with characteristic features of Hopi society. Although she has not published any quantitative studies of Hopi dreams, she does refer to her continuing study of the dreams obtained from a single Hopi person in several articles (e.g., 1952). With reference to this study she describes a chart on which she enters content items from successive dreams in the series.

On it (the chart) each dream is numbered in the order in which it was recorded, and the elements in the dream are distributed in horizontal columns across the page. These columns record among some fifty-five items, various Freudian symbols, and symbols mentioned by the Hopi in their discussion of dream meanings, as well as personalities, situations, and concepts of particular significance to the Hopi.

Primarily, however, the categories were empirically derived from a preliminary analysis of the data (i.e., the dreams) themselves (our italics) (1952, p. 481).

Mrs. Eggan points out that by "reading across this chart, one finds therefore, a fairly comprehensive summary of the manifest elements which make up the dream, its affectual import, and its factual contents. Reading down the chart, all of these items are seen in relation to those in other dreams, so that the massing of elements is self-evident" (1952, p. 482). A partial list of categories and the frequency of occurrence are shown in Table 15-28.

Some investigators who set out to study the relationship between dreams and other types of protocols such as the TAT or Rorschach impose upon dreams a system of scoring that has been devised for the TAT or Rorschach. This is what both Gordon (1953) and Catanzaro (1962) did in their comparisons of dreams and TAT stories, and what Bolgar (1954) did in her comparison of dreams and Rorschach responses. Gordon used an adaptation of the need-press system of scoring TAT stories devised by Aron (1949), for scoring both stories and dreams. Catanzaro employed a need-press system adapted from the Murray system (1938) and from Karen Horney's theory of interpersonal relationships (1945). In Catanzaro's study, each dream and each story was scored for just one need, one press, one direction of interpersonal interaction, one role of the central character, and one outcome. The percentage of agreement between two scorers on a sample of 25 dreams and 25 TAT stories ranged from 64 to 88, with an overall average of 78 percent. In Bolgar's study of the consistency of affect and symbolic expression, dreams and Rorschach responses were scored by a method developed by De Vos (1952).

Some investigators who have compared dreams with other methods of personality assessment have used methods of analysis devised primarily for use with dreams. Grotz (1950) analyzed dream series and TAT protocols for desires, frustrations, conflicts, and outcomes. Osterberg (1951) made use of the earlier manuals prepared by Hall to compare the occurrence of aggression and misfortune in dreams and TAT stories. A structured set of 84 Q-sort items based upon Hall's theory of conceptual systems was

Table 15-28
Summary of Frequencies of Elements in 254 Dreams of an Adult Male Hopi
Reported between 1939 and 1945

Elements of security support		260
Personal strength, wisdom, and bravery	53	
"Guardian Angel"	51	
Support of Whites	49	
Miscellaneous (including clowning, dancing,		
dead mother, spirits, praise, sex, etc.)	107	
Elements of Persecution and Conflict		169
Personal, with Hopi	55	
With Hopi because of whites	30	
General Hopi-white	26	
General, among Hopi	26	
Police and soldiers	21	
With Navajo or other Indians	10	
Personal, with whites	1	
Physical hazard		136
Accidents or danger	95	
Violence or murder	41	
Heterosexual Elements		67
Frustrated	38	
Successful	14	
Casual	15	
Flying		10
Falling		6
Gifts and material possessions		57
Crops and Stock		96
Water		64
Streams and lakes	32	
Rain	32	
Religion and Ceremonies		101
Supernatural (Other than "Guardian Angel")		185
Dead	83	
Gods	39	
Vague spirits	39	
Witches	15	
Dead Animals	9	
Repeated Theme of Previous Dream		107
Dreamer's Reaction to Dream		254
"Bad" Dream	136	
"Good" Dream	84	
Indifferent or "mixed"	34	

Dreamer's Emotion on Awakening	254
Described as "scared," "crying," "upset," "ears ringing," etc.	170
Described as "happy," "good," "excited," etc.	46
Not Described	38

(From Eggan, 1952)

employed by Shulman (1955) for comparing dreams with TAT stories and with self-conceptions.

Dreams may be classified by the occurrence of a particular happening as well as by the analysis of content. This has been done for the so-called typical dreams which everyone is supposed to have experienced at one time or another, often repeatedly. Griffith, Miyago, and Tago (1958), and Ward, Beck, and Rascoe (1961) have made studies of the prevalence of such dreams. Griffith, Miyago, and Tago's list consisted of 34 dream happenings, and 250 American college students were asked if they had ever dreamed of these 34 happenings. The percentage who had is given in Table 15-29. For only 13 of the 34 did the percentage exceed 50. Ward, Beck, and Rascoe presented 748 psychiatric patients with a list of 17 happenings and asked them to check those which they could remember having had. The percentage responding to each item in the list is given in Table 15-30. Only two types of dreams were reported as having occurred by more than 50 percent of those questioned.

Other investigators who have made use of earlier editions of the manuals prepared by Hall may be mentioned. Paolino (1964) made an extensive investigation of aggression in the dream series of 42 male and 42 female undergraduates. Cook (1956) did the same for characters. Meer (1952, 1955) scored the dream series of students making high scores on the F (Fascism) scale and those making low scores for a number of content variables. Pope (1952) compared the person's conceptions of his own aggression and friendliness with the expression of aggression and friendliness in his dreams. Domhoff (1962) used some of Hall's scales in

Table 15-29
Percentage of 250 American College Students Reporting Dreams

Have you ever dreamed of . . . ?	%
1. being attacked or pursued	77.2
2. falling	82.8
3. trying again and again to do something	71.2
4. school, teachers, studying	71.2
5. being frozen with fright	58.0
6. sexual experiences	66.4
7. eating delicious food	61.6
8. falling with fear	67.6
9. arriving too late, e.g., missing train	63.6
10. fire	40.8
11. swimming	52.0
12. dead people as though alive	46.0
13. being locked up	56.4
14. loved person to be dead	57.2
15. snakes	48.8
16. being on verge of falling	46.8
17. finding money	56.0
18. failing an examination	38.8
19. flying or soaring through air	33.6
20. being smothered, unable to breathe	44.4
21. falling without fear	33.2
22. wild, violent beasts	30.0
23. being inappropriately dressed	46.0
24. seeing self as dead	33.2
25. being nude	42.8
26. killing someone	25.6
27. being tied, unable to move	30.4
28. having superior knowledge or mental ability	25.6
29. lunatics or insane people	25.6
30. your teeth falling out	20.8
31. creatures, part animal, part human	14.8
32. being buried alive	14.8
33. seeing self in mirror	12.4
34. being hanged by neck	2.8

(From Griffith, Miyago, and Tago, 1958)

Table 15-30
Percentage of 748 Psychiatric Patients Reporting Dreams

Which of the following types of dream can you remember?	%
1. A person being hurt, in danger, dead, or dying	57
2. Yourself falling or falling through space	52
3. Yourself being chased by people or animals	45
4. Yourself swimming or being in water	33
5. Yourself eating or about food	27
6. Yourself finding money	27
7. Being lost	25
8. Fire	24
9. Yourself being naked or scantily clothed in public or before other people	21
10. Something happening to any of your teeth	19
11. Yourself flying through the air, being able to fly; not in airplane but with own body	19
12. Yourself taking a test or examination	17
13. Losing objects	17
14. Yourself missing a train or plane, bus, trolley, or other ride that you had planned on	12
15. Yourself being rescued	11
16. Yourself passed through a narrow space	9
17. caves	6

(From Ward, Beck, and Rascoe, 1961)

order to compare dreams collected throughout the night with dreams recalled in the morning.

Finally, we should like to call attention to a method of dream analysis which has been developed by Richard M. Jones. Based upon Erik Erikson's stages of development, Jones (1962) has devised what he calls an epigenetic method of dream analysis. Of it he writes:

"Our complete hypothesis states that a manifest dream is the product of a confluence of psychodynamic forces: (1) a motivating repressed wish of infantile origin; (2) the defense ego which so discharges the energy of the repressed wish as to maintain a healthy state of sleep; and (3) the synthesis ego which so governs the setting, style, and rhythm of the dream's formation as to support a subsequently adaptive state of wakefulness. We describe this third process as the preconscious re-differentiation and re-integration of pre-adaptive epigenetic successes and failures in the context and under the problematic pressure of phase-specific re-adaptive crises" (p. 43).

In his book, Jones presents an epigenetic analysis of a specimen dream series in qualitative terms. In a monograph that he is now readying for publication, a quantitative scoring system will be described. Jones characterizes his method as one for analyzing dream *structure* as contrasted with our method for analyzing dream *content*.

This completes our survey of the literature which, if not exhaustive in scope, is representative of the many approaches made to objective and quantitative analyses of dreams. The temerity with which investigators have approached dreams in the past seems to be diminishing, and today there is a frank acceptance of the reported dream as a significant form of behavior in its own right, independent of its "latent content." We fully anticipate in the years to come that objective dream analysis will verify many current hypotheses regarding personality as well as reveal new dimensions of man. We are committed to the belief that dream analysis is one of the most powerful tools for comprehending the dynamics of human behavior.

REFERENCES

ALEXANDER, F. and FRENCH, T. M. (Eds.). *Studies in psychosomatic medicine.* New York: Ronald Press, 1948.

ALEXANDER, F. and WILSON, G. W. Quantitative dream studies: A methodological attempt at a quantitative evaluation of psychoanalytic material. *Psychoanal. Quart.,* 1935, *4,* 371-407.

ARON, BETTY. *A manual for analysis of the Thematic Apperception Test.* Berkeley, Calif.: Berg, 1949.

BECK, A. T. A systematic investigation of depression. *Comprehen. Psychiat.,* 1961, *2,* 163-170.

BECK, A. T. and HURVICH, M. S. Psychological correlates of depression. I. Frequency of "masochistic" dream content in a private practice sample. *Psychosom. Med.,* 1959, *21,* 50-55.

BECK, A. T. and WARD, C. H. Dreams of depressed patients: characteristic themes in manifest content. *Arch. gen. Psychiat.*, 1961, *5*, 462-467.

BECK, A. T., WARD, C. H., MENDELSON, M., MOCK, J., and ERBAUGH, J. An inventory for measuring depression. *Arch. gen. Psychiat.*, 1961, *4*, 561-571.

BOLGAR, HEDDA. Consistency of affect and symbolic expression: A comparison between dreams and Rorschach responses. *Amer. J. Orthopsychiat.*, 1954, *24*, 538-545.

CATANZARO, GERALDINE A. A comparative study of the content expressed in dreams and Thematic Apperception Test stories. M.A. thesis, Cornell University, 1962.

COLBY, B. N., COLLIER, G. A., and POSTAL, SUSAN K. Comparison of themes in folktales by the General Inquirer System. *J. Amer. Folklore*, 1963, *76*, 318-323.

COLBY, K. M. Sex differences in dreams: a contribution to the masculinity-femininity problem. In *A skeptical psychoanalyst*, New York: Ronald Press, 1958, 107-145.

COOK, W. R. Nomothetic personality patterns in dreams. Ph.D. dissertation, Western Reserve University, 1956.

DEVOS, G. A quantitative approach to affective symbolism in Rorschach responses. *J. Proj. Tech.*, 1952, *16*, 133-150.

DOMHOFF, G. W. A quantitative study of dream content using an objective indicator of dreaming. Ph.D. dissertation, University of Miami, 1962.

EGGAN, DOROTHY. The manifest content of dreams: a challenge to social science. *Amer. Anthropologist*, 1952, *54*, 469-485.

FRAMO, J. L., OSTERWEIL, J., and BOSZORMENYI-NAGY, I. A relationship between threat in the manifest content of dreams and active-passive behavior in psychotics. *J. abnorm. soc. Psychol.*, 1962, *65*, 41-47.

GOLDENBERG, G. M. An investigation of primary-process thinking in the manifest dream report. Ph.D. dissertation. Wayne State University, 1963.

GOLDHIRSH, M. L. Manifest content of dreams of convicted sex offenders. *J. abnorm. soc. Psychol.*, 1961, *63*, 643-645.

GORDON, H. L. A comparative study of dreams and responses to the Thematic Apperception Test: A need-press analysis. *J. Pers.*, 1953, *22*, 234-253.

GRIFFITH, R. M., MIYAGO, O. and TAGO, A. The universality of typical dreams: Japanese vs. Americans. *Amer. Anthropologist*, 1958, *60*, 1173-1179.

GROTZ, R. C. A comparison of Thematic Apperception Test stories and manifest dream narratives. M.A. thesis. Western Reserve University, 1950.

HAMBURG, D. A., SABSHIN, M., BOARD, F. A., GRINKER, R. R., KORCHIN, S. J., BASOWITZ, H., HEATH, H., and PERSKY, H. Classification and rating of emotional experiences. *A.M.A. Arch. Neurol. and Psychiat.*, 1956, 79, 415.

HARWAY, N. I. and IKER, H. P. Computer analysis of content in psychotherapy. *Psychol. Rep.*, 1964, 14, 720-722.

HORNEY, KAREN. *Our inner conflicts.* New York: W. W. Norton, 1945.

JONES, R. M. *Ego synthesis in dreams.* Cambridge, Mass.: Schenkman, 1962.

LANE, ELLEN. The reliability of personality ratings based on dream series. M. A. thesis. Western Reserve University, 1951.

LOTT, I. T. Identity formation in the manifest dreams of late adolescents: an exploratory study. Honors thesis, Brandeis University, 1963.

MEER, S. J. A study of the dynamic relationship between ideology and dreams. Ph.D. dissertation. Western Reserve University, 1952.

MEER, S. J. Authoritarian attitudes and dreams. *J. abnorm. soc. Psychol.*, 1955, 51, 74-78.

MILLER, M. L. A psychological study of a case of eczema and a case of neurodermatitis. *Psychosom. Med.*, 1942, 4, 82-93.

MURRAY, H. A. *Explorations in personality.* New York: Oxford Univer. Press, 1938.

OSTERBERG, MARY N. A comparison of aggression in dreams and TAT stories. M.A. thesis. Western Reserve University, 1951.

PAOLINO, A. F. Dreams: sex differences in aggressive content. *J. proj. Tech.*, 1964, 28, 219-226.

PERRY, C. A manual of procedures for analyzing manifest dream content into narrative elements and for classifying such elements with respect to distortion from reality. Mimeographed. Department of Psychology, The University of Sydney, 1964.

POLSTER, E. An investigation of ego functioning in dreams. Ph.D. dissertation. Western Reserve University, 1951.

POPE, H. L. Prohibitions, self-conceptions, and dreams. Ph.D. dissertation. Western Reserve University, 1952.

RABE, CLAIRE F. A study of sexual attitudes as revealed by symbols in dreams. M.A. thesis. Western Reserve University, 1949. Reprinted as Research Report No. 2 of the Institute of Dream Research, 1963.

REIS, W. A comparison of the interpretation of dream series with and without free association. Ph.D. dissertation, Western Reserve University, 1951. Abridged version in *Dreams and personality dynamics*. M. F. DeMartino, (Ed.) Springfield, Ill.: Thomas, 1959, 211-225.

RYCHLAK, J. Recalled dream themes and personality. *J. abnorm. soc. Psychol.*, 1960, *60*, 140-143.

RYCHLAK, J. and BRAMS, J. M. Personality dimensions in recalled dream content. *J. proj. Tech.*, 1963, *27*, 226-234.

SAUL, L. J. and SHEPPARD, EDITH. An attempt to quantify emotional forces using manifest dreams: a preliminary study. *J. Amer. Psychoanal. Ass.*, 1956, *4*, 486-502.

SAUL, L. J., SHEPPARD, EDITH, SELBY, DOROTHY, LHAMON, W., SACHS, D, and MASTER, REGINA. The quantification of hostility in dreams with reference to essential hypertension. *Science*, 1954, *119*, 382-383.

SHEPPARD, EDITH. Systematic dream studies: clinical judgment and objective measurements of ego strength. *Comprehen. Psychiat.*, 1963, *4*, 263-270.

SHEPPARD, EDITH. *Dream rating scales*. Mimeographed. July, 1964, 1-55.

SHEPPARD, EDITH and KARON, B. Systematic studies of dreams: relationship between the manifest dream and associations to the dream elements. *Comprehen. Psychiat.*, 1964, *5*, 335-344.

SHEPPARD, EDITH and SAUL, L. J. An approach to a systematic study of ego function. *Psychoanal. Quart.*, 1958, *27*, 237-245.

SHULMAN, H. S. Congruences of personality expression in self-conceptions, Thematic Apperception Test, and dreams. Ph.D. dissertation. Western Reserve University, 1955.

STONE, P. J., BALES, R. F., NAMENWIRTH, J. Z., and OGILVIE, D. M. The General Inquirer: a computer system for content analysis and retrieval based on the sentence as a unit of information. *Behav. Sci.*, 1962, *7*, 1-15.

WARD, C. H., BECK, A. T., and RASCOE, E. Typical dreams: incidence among psychiatric patients. *Arch. gen. Psychiat.*, 1961, *5*, 606-615.

WHITMAN, R. M., PIERCE, C. M., MAAS, J. W., and BALDRIDGE, B. Drugs and dreams II: Imipramine and procholorperazine. *Comprehen. Psychiat.*, 1961, *2*, 219-226.

Objects and their
Frequencies in Dreams

An alphabetical list of 1170 objects mentioned in 1000 dreams and their frequencies for male and female dreamers is presented in this appendix.

In Chapter 13, the frequencies for broad classes of objects were given. In this appendix, the frequencies listed are for specific objects mentioned in dreams.

The definition of an object used for compiling this appendix is the same as the one given in Chapter 4 with the exception that animals are also included here. When the same type of object was referred to by different names, the frequencies were combined under one name. For example, car, automobile, and Ford were included under "automobile." Few such combinations were made, however, because we wanted to preserve the specificity of objects in these norms. We did not include taxi or bus under automobile but gave each of them a separate heading. Cross references are made to objects that were combined. No object was entered under more than one heading.

There are three capitalized objects in the list. These are Country, State, and University, and in each instance they include all references to a specific country, e.g., England, a specific state, e.g., Michigan, or a specific university, e.g., Western Reserve University.

	Male	Female	Both
abdomen		2	2
abutment	1		1
accelerator, car	3	1	4
accordion	1		1
adrenalin	1		1
advertisement	1	1	2
aerial	1		1
afterbirth		1	1
aircraft carrier	2		2
airfield	1		1
airplane	16	8	24
aisle	4	6	10
alcohol		1	1
alley	1	2	3
alfalfa		1	1
albums, record		1	1
altar	2	3	5
ambulance	2	1	3
ammunition	2		2
anastomosis	1		1
anatomy		1	1
animal	10	8	18
ankle		2	2
anklets		1	1
antiques		1	1
apartment	6	10	16
ape	1		1
aperture	1		1
apparatus		1	1
appendix	1		1
apple		2	2
arches	1		1
archway		1	1
area	6		6
arena	1		1
arm	24	20	44
armholes	1		1
armor	1		1
arrows	1		1

	Male	Female	Both
arsenic	1		1
artillery, weapons	1		1
attic	1	2	3
attire	2		2
ashtray	1		1
auditorium	4	5	9
automobile	86	63	149
avenue (see street)			
bag	3	2	5
bag, mail	1		1
bag, golf	1		1
baggage		3	3
back, body	4	4	8
back, chair	1		1
back, couch	1		1
backstage (see stage)			
backyard (see yard)			
bacon		1	1
bait	2		2
balcony	1	2	3
ball, any type	11	2	13
ballfield		1	1
balloon	1	1	2
bakery		1	1
bandages	1	2	3
bank, building		2	2
bank, river	4	1	5
bankbook		1	1
bar, ballet		2	2
bar, tavern	6	4	10
barn	5	2	7
barracks, army	4		4
barrel, container	1		1
base, baseball	2		2
basement	7	3	10
basket	1	2	3
bassinet		1	1
bat, baseball		1	1
bathtub		5	5
battlefield	3		3
battleship	1		1

	Male	Female	Both
bay	3		3
bayonet		1	1
beach	6	5	11
beads		1	1
beak	1		1
bear, animal	3	1	4
beard	1		1
beams	1		1
bed	21	20	41
bedspread	1	1	2
beer	4	3	7
bell	4	8	12
bellows	1		1
belly		1	1
belongings	1	1	2
belts		1	1
bench		3	3
bible		1	1
bicycle	9	8	17
billboard		1	1
billfold		2	2
bills, money	5	1	6
bills, store		1	1
binoculars		1	1
birds	4	1	5
blackboard	2	1	3
blackheads		1	1
blankets	3	1	4
bleachers		2	2
blimp	1		1
blinds, venetian	1	1	2
blisters, body		1	1
block, city	2	5	7
blood	6	5	11
blouse	1	1	2
boar	1		1
board	3	1	4
boat	10	12	22
body, human or animal	18	6	24
bolt, hardware	2		2
bomb, explosive	4	6	10
bond, security		1	1

	Male	Female	Both
bone, collar		1	1
bone, hip		1	1
bone, jaw		1	1
bonfire		1	1
book	10	7	17
bookcase		1	1
booth, restaurant	3	1	4
boots	3	2	5
bouquet, flower		1	1
bottle	2	3	5
boulder	2		2
bouy		1	1
bowl	1	1	2
bowling alley		2	2
box	5	8	13
box, music	1		1
bra		1	1
bracelet		3	3
brains	1		1
brakes, car	3	2	5
branch, tree	1		1
bread		1	1
breakwater		1	1
breasts	4	1	5
breath	2	1	3
brick	1	2	3
bridge	12	7	19
bristle, brush	1		1
brooches		1	1
brook	1	1	2
broom	1		1
brush	2		2
bugs		2	2
building	27	36	63
bullets	4	2	6
bulletin	1		1
bump		2	2
bumper	1		1
bunks	2		2
bus	6	14	20
butter		1	1
button	3		3
button, firing	1		1

	Male	Female	Both
cabana		1	1
cabbage		1	1
cabin	5	2	7
cabinet	1	1	2
cable	1		1
cafeteria	5	4	9
cage	2		2
cake	3	2	5
calf, animal		1	1
camelia		1	1
camera	1		1
camp	1	3	4
campus	7	4	11
canal	1	3	4
can	1		1
cancer		3	3
candles	1		1
candy	3	2	5
canoe	4	1	5
canyon		1	1
cap, head gear	1	1	2
capsules		1	1
car (see automobile)			
carbuerator	2		2
card, AGO	1		1
card, calling	1		1
card, christmas	2		2
card, class		1	1
cards, playing	4	5	9
cardboard	1		1
carnations		1	1
carnival	1		1
carpet	1	3	4
carriage	1		1
cart		4	4
cartoon		1	1
cases, container		3	3
cash register	1		1
castle	2		2
cat	2	7	9
cattails		1	1
cave	5	1	6

	Male	Female	Both
cavity, tooth	1		1
ceiling	3	2	5
cellar	2	2	4
cement	1	1	2
cemetery	2	1	3
chair	10	17	27
champagne	1		1
chandeliers		1	1
chapel		1	1
chart	1		1
cheek		3	3
cheese	1		1
chest, body	2	2	4
chickens	1		1
church	6	11	17
chute	1		1
cigarette	1	1	2
city	64	64	128
clearing	1		1
cliff	7	5	12
clock	1	1	2
closet	2	9	11
cloth	1	1	2
clothes	15	21	36
clot	1		1
clouds	5	1	6
club, country	4		4
coal	2	1	3
coat	9	15	24
cockpit	1		1
cockroaches		1	1
cocktail	1		1
coffee	3	1	4
coke		2	2
coin, (see money)			
collar	1	1	2
college	5	11	16
cologne		3	3
compartment, house	1	1	2
condom	1		1
containers	1		1
contraption	1	2	3

	Male	Female	Both
contrivance	1		1
controls, airplane	1	1	2
convertible (see automobile)			
cookies	1	1	2
cooler, boston	1		1
co-op, store	2		2
copper		1	1
corral	1		1
cord	1	1	2
corner, street	14	13	27
corridor	2	6	8
corset		1	1
costume	3	8	11
cot	1	1	2
cottage		1	1
cotton	1	1	2
couch	2	4	6
counter	7	5	12
Countries	25	5	30
country	11	9	20
coupe (see automobile)			
court, basketball	1		1
court, tennis		1	1
cover, slide rule	1		1
cows	1		1
crack	1	1	2
crackers	2		2
cradle		1	1
cream	1		1
creek	1		1
crevasse	1		1
crocodiles	1		1
cross, red	1		1
cross, religious		1	1
crossing, railroad	1	1	2
crow		1	1
crown	2		2
cruiser, police (see automobile)			
cup	1	1	2
cupboards		3	3
cupcake	1		1
curb	1	3	4

	Male	Female	Both
curls		1	1
currency (see money)			
curtain	2	2	4
cut	3	1	4
cutlass	1		1
dam	1		1
dance hall	1	1	2
darts	1	1	2
davenport	1		1
deck, boat	3		3
decorations		3	3
deer	3		3
den, room	1	1	2
depressor, tongue		1	1
desert	1		1
desk	8	13	21
destroyer	1		1
diagram	1		1
diamonds	1	3	4
diapers		2	2
diner		1	1
dining hall		1	1
dinosaur		1	1
diploma		1	1
dirt	2	1	3
dish	1	3	4
display	2	2	4
district	1	2	3
ditch		1	1
divan		1	1
diving board		2	2
dock		1	1
dog	9	10	19
doll	1	2	3
dollars (see money)			
donkey		1	1
door	46	57	103
doorbell (see bell)			
doorknob		1	1
doorway	2	2	4
dope		1	1

	Male	Female	Both
dormitory	4	42	46
doughnut	3		3
downspout	1		1
downstairs	13	10	23
downtown	7	9	16
drain, water	1	1	2
drapes	2		2
drawer	2	7	9
drawstring	1		1
dress	8	31	39
dresser		5	5
drink	6	5	11
driveway	6	4	10
drug	1		1
duck	2	1	3
dummy	1	1	2
dungarees		1	1
dynamos	1		1
earrings		2	2
ears	2	1	3
earth	1	1	2
eaves	1		1
egg		2	2
elbow	1	1	2
elephants	2		2
elevator	5	8	13
embankment		1	1
emeralds		1	1
engine	3	1	4
engine, fire	1	1	2
entrails		1	1
entrance	3	4	7
envelope	1	1	2
equipment	3	2	5
equipment, fire	1		1
eraser		1	1
escalator		2	2
escape, fire	1	2	3
excavations	1		1
extinguisher, fire	1		1
eyes	8	16	24

	Male	Female	Both
eyebrows		1	1
eyelashes	1	1	2
eyelid	1		1
facade	1		1
face	14	32	46
factory		1	1
fair	2		2
fare		1	1
farm	3	1	4
feathers	1		1
features, facial	1		1
feelers		1	1
feet	5	6	11
fence	4	3	7
fender	3		3
field	15	4	19
file, box		1	1
film	1		1
figurine	1	1	2
finger	3	4	7
fingerprints	1		1
fingertip	1		1
fire	7		7
firecrackers	1		1
fireplace	1		1
fish	5	3	8
flames	2	2	4
flamethrower	1		1
flashlight	1		1
flask		1	1
fleas	1		1
float, homecoming		1	1
flood	1	1	2
floor	29	30	59
flooring	1		1
flower	2	8	10
flowerpot	1		1
fluid	1		1
foliage	1	1	2
food	7	5	12
foot	2	3	5

	Male	Female	Both
forearm	1		1
forehead	2	1	3
forest	8	8	16
fork		1	1
formation	1	1	2
forts		1	1
foundation		1	1
fountain	1	1	2
fox	1	1	2
foxhole		1	1
frame, glasses		1	1
frame, wooden	1		1
frog		2	2
fruit	1		1
fur	1	3	4
furnace	2		2
furnishings	1	2	3
furniture	1	3	4
furrows		1	1
fuselage	1		1
gangplank		1	1
garage	5	2	7
garden		2	2
garden, beer	1		1
garnets		1	1
gas, anesthetic	2		2
gas, tear	1		1
gasoline	6	1	7
gate	1		1
gear, belongings	1		1
gear, landing	2		2
genital	3		3
gift		4	4
giraffes	1		1
girders	1		1
glass, container	2	1	3
glass, window	3		3
glasses, eye	2	7	9
gloves	2	1	3
gold	2	3	5
golf club	3		3

	Male	Female	Both
gondola	1		1
goods, material	1		1
gown	1	7	8
grass	2	5	7
grave		1	1
graveyard		1	1
grease	1		1
grill		1	1
groin	1		1
ground	19	13	32
guinea pig		1	1
gully	1		1
gum		1	1
gums		1	1
gun	18	4	22
gym	7	1	8
hail	1		1
hair	8	24	32
hall	10	20	30
halter		1	1
hammer	1		1
ham	1		1
hand	26	33	49
handbag	2	1	3
handbook	1		1
handcar	1		1
handle	2		2
hanger, clothes	1		1
harbor	1	1	2
hat	6	4	10
hawk	2		2
head	17	19	36
headlights	4		4
headquarters	1		1
heart	4	3	7
heels	2		2
helicopter	2		2
helmet	1		1
herd	1		1
highway	12	1	13
hill	17	18	35

	Male	Female	Both
hinges	1		1
hips	1	1	2
hole	5	8	13
home	47	71	118
hometown	3		3
hood, car	4		4
hood, parka		1	1
horn	2		2
hornet		1	1
horse	4	5	9
horse, water	1	1	2
hospital	4	13	17
house	83	77	160
house, club	1		1
house, court		1	1
house, export		1	1
house, farm	1	1	2
house, fraternity	10	1	11
house, movie	3	1	4
housecoat		1	1
hotel	6	13	19
hubcap	1		1
hull	1		1
hurricane	1		1
hymn		2	2
ice	4		4
iceberg		1	1
icebox	2		2
ice cream	3		3
ice cubes		1	1
icing, cake	1		1
ink		2	2
insect		2	2
instruments	1		1
intersection	1		1
invitation, wedding		1	1
iron		1	1
island	5		5
jack, car	1		1
jacket	5	4	9

	Male	Female	Both
jail	2		2
jars		1	1
jeans, blue		3	3
jello		1	1
jelly		1	1
jewelry		3	3
jewels	1	1	2
juice	1	1	2
jungle	2		2
junk		2	2
kayak		1	1
kettle	1		1
keys, door	4	2	6
keys, piano	1		1
kidney		1	1
kit, tool	1		1
kitchen	13	12	25
kitten		3	3
kleenex	1	1	2
knees	2	4	6
knitting		1	1
knife	8	3	11
laboratory		8	8
lace		1	1
lace, football	1		1
ladder	4		4
lake	9	18	27
lambs		1	1
lamps	1	2	3
lance	1		1
land	1	3	4
landmarks		1	1
landscape	1	1	2
lane		1	1
lap	4	1	5
lapels		1	1
launch		1	1
laundrateria		1	1
lawn	2	4	6
lean—to	1		1

	Male	Female	Both
leather	1	1	2
leaves		2	2
ledge	4	1	5
legs	14	17	31
legs, pant		1	1
lens		2	2
leotards		1	1
letter	5	7	12
lettuce		1	1
library	2	2	4
license	2	1	3
lid		1	1
light	12	14	26
light, street	1		1
light, traffic	1	1	2
lighter, cigarette	1		1
lighthouse		1	1
lightning	3		3
limbs, legs or arms		2	2
limbs, tree	1		1
linens		1	1
lingerie		1	1
linoleum		1	1
lions	1		1
lips	1		1
lipstick	1	2	3
liquor	1	1	2
liver		1	1
lobby	2	3	5
locker	3	2	5
locomotives	1	2	3
loft	1		1
log	1	2	3
lot	2	2	4
lot, parking	4	7	11
loud speaker		1	1
lounge	2		2
lumber	1		1
lumps	1		1
machine	6	1	7
machinery	2	1	3

	Male	Female	Both
magazine	2	4	6
mail	3	3	6
mailbox	2		2
mainland	1		1
mansion	4		4
marble	2	1	3
marshland	2		2
mascara		1	1
mask		2	2
mats	1	2	3
mattress	1	1	2
maze	1	1	2
meadow	1		1
meat	1		1
medal	1		1
medicine		2	2
membrane		1	1
merchandise	1	1	2
mercury		1	1
mezzanine		1	1
microphone	2		2
milk	2		2
mill	1		1
mine		1	1
mint, money		1	1
mints, candy		1	1
mirror	2	4	6
mist	2	1	3
moccasins		1	1
model, replica		1	1
molding	1		1
money	27	16	43
monument		1	1
moon		2	2
mop	1		1
moss	1		1
motel		1	1
motor	3	1	4
motorboat	1		1
motorcycle	1	2	3
mounds	1		1
mountain	6		6

	Male	Female	Both
mouth	7	5	12
mouthpiece		1	1
movies	6	9	15
muck		1	1
mud	3	1	4
mugs	1		1
murals		1	1
muscles	1		1
mustache		1	1
nails	3		3
napkin		2	2
neck	4	6	10
necklace		2	2
neckpiece	1		1
needle	1	1	2
negatives	1		1
negligee	1	2	3
neighborhood	4	1	5
nerve	1		1
nest	1		1
newspaper	2	2	4
nightgown	1	1	2
nightclub	1	1	2
nipples	1		1
nose	3	2	5
notes	2	1	3
nozzle		1	1
ocean	4	5	9
octopus		1	1
office	8	9	17
oil	1		1
ointment	1		1
opening	1	2	3
orchard	1		1
orchid		2	2
organs, body	4	2	6
organs, sense		1	1
orifice	1		1
outfit, clothes	2	4	6
overalls		1	1

	Male	Female	Both
overcoats	1	1	2
owl		1	1
package	3	5	8
paddle		1	1
page	4	3	7
paint	6	2	8
painting		1	1
pajamas	1	3	4
pan		4	4
panel	1	1	2
pants	14	16	30
paper	10	11	21
park	5	5	10
passageway	2	3	5
passport		1	1
patches	1		1
path	5	3	8
peaches		1	1
peanut butter	1		1
pearls	1	1	2
peas	1	2	3
pebbles	1	1	2
peepholes		1	1
pen		1	1
pencil		2	2
penis	2		2
perfume	1	1	2
pew	1	1	2
pheasant	1		1
piano	3	4	7
pickles	1		1
piccolo		1	1
picture	8	7	15
pie	1		1
pier	3		3
pig		1	1
pile	3	3	6
pill	1		1
pillar	1	1	2
pillow	1	2	3
pimple		2	2

	Male	Female	Both
pin	2	2	4
pin, bowling		1	1
pipe	3		3
pistol	2	1	3
pit		2	2
plain	2		2
planet	1		1
planks		1	1
plants	1		1
plant, power	1		1
plaster	1		1
plate, license	2	1	3
plate, baseball	1		1
plate, charge		1	1
platform	9	2	11
playground		1	1
plumbing	1		1
plums		1	1
plywood	1		1
pocket	10	2	12
poker	1		1
pole	3		3
pole, fishing	1		1
pole, telephone		1	1
pond	1	4	5
pool	3	12	15
pool hall	1		1
popcorn		1	1
porch	2	6	8
port	2		2
possum		1	1
post		1	1
post office	1	2	3
potatoes	1	2	3
pot		3	3
powder	1	2	3
precipice	1		1
pretzel		1	1
print, foot	1		1
prison	1	1	2
projection	1		1
puddle		2	2

	Male	Female	Both
pulpit		1	1
pump	2		2
puppy	1	1	2
purse		7	7
python	1		1
quail		1	1
quarters, rooms	2	1	3
rabbit	1		1
rack	2	1	3
radio	5	2	7
rafters	1		1
rags		1	1
railing	3	4	7
railroad	1		1
rain	6	2	8
raincoat	1		1
raisins		1	1
ramp	2		2
ranch	1		1
rapids	1		1
rat		1	1
rattlesnake		1	1
ravine	1	2	3
ray	1		1
receptacle	1		1
record, phonograph	2	1	3
residence	1		1
resort	1	3	4
restaurant	4	5	9
revolver	3		3
ribbon		5	5
rifle	5	1	6
ring	4	15	19
ring, boxing	1		1
ring, napkin		1	1
river	7	8	15
road	27	17	44
roadblock		1	1
roast	1		1
robe	3	1	4

	Male	Female	Both
rock	3	3	6
rocket	1		1
rod	1	2	3
rod, fishing	1	1	2
roof	4	6	10
room	57	68	125
room, back		4	4
room, ball	1	4	5
room, basement		1	1
room, bath	8	14	22
room, bed	12	16	28
room, boiler	1	1	2
room, class	10	8	18
room, dining	4	10	14
room, dressing		3	3
room, front	2	1	3
room, home	1		1
room, hotel	2	2	4
room, ironing		1	1
room, living	10	18	28
room, locker	2	1	3
room, operating	2	1	3
room, pool	1		1
room, reception	1		1
room, recreation	1		1
room, recitation	1		1
room, school	1		1
room, shower		1	1
room, sitting	1		1
room, smoking		1	1
room, stock	1		1
room, sun		1	1
room, waiting		2	2
room, wash	1		1
roots		1	1
rootbeer	1		1
rope	2		2
roses		2	2
rubber	1	1	2
rubberbands		1	1
rubies		1	1

	Male	Female	Both
sack	1		1
salad	1	2	3
saloon	1		1
salt		1	1
sand	1	3	4
sand dune	1		1
sandwiches	1	1	2
sapphires	1		1
sauerkraut	1		1
saw	1		1
sawdust	1		1
scale	1		1
scarf		2	2
school	13	34	47
school, jr. high		3	3
school, high	3	12	15
school, grade		1	1
school, medical	1		1
school, sunday		1	1
schoolyard	1		1
scissors	1	2	3
score, musical		1	1
scrapbook	1		1
screen	2		2
sea	3	1	4
seal, official		1	1
seal, animal		1	1
seashore	1		1
seats	13	18	31
seat cover	1		1
seaweed		1	1
sedative		1	1
seed		1	1
semen	1		1
serum	1		1
setting, jewel		1	1
seven up		1	1
sewing		1	1
shacks	3		3
shade	2	2	4
shadows		2	2
shaft	1		1

	Male	Female	Both
shavings		1	1
sheaf	1		1
shed	2		2
sheep	1		1
sheet	4	3	7
shell, sea		1	1
shell, gun	2		2
shelf	1	2	3
shelter		3	3
ship	5	5	10
shirt	5	10	15
shoe	4	5	9
shooting gallery	1		1
shop	9	3	12
shore	2	4	6
shorts	1	1	2
shoulder	7	5	12
shovel	1		1
showcase	1		1
shrimp	1		1
shrubbery		2	2
sidewalk	8	5	13
sign		3	3
signal	2		2
sill		1	1
sink	1	2	3
siren	1	1	2
skates		1	1
ski run	1		1
skin	2	1	3
skin, bear	1		1
skirt	2	4	6
ski jump		1	1
skis	2		2
skull		1	1
slab	1		1
sled		2	2
sleeves	2	1	3
slide rule	1		1
slip, clothes		3	3
slugs	1		1
smoke	5	4	9

	Male	Female	Both
snake	7	4	11
snow	7	6	13
snowballs	1	1	2
soap	1	1	2
socket	1		1
soda fountain		1	1
sofa	4		4
solution, cleaning		1	1
sores	2		2
space, parking		1	1
speedometer	1		1
spinal cord		1	1
spine		1	1
splinter		1	1
stable		1	1
stack		1	1
stadium	4	2	6
stage	5	17	22
stairs	29	45	74
stake	1		1
stalk	1		1
stalls	1		1
star	1	1	2
State	12	12	24
station	1	1	2
station, bus		1	1
station, gas	5		5
station, police	1		1
station, radio	1		1
station, railroad	6	2	8
stationary		1	1
statue	1		1
steak		2	2
steamer		1	1
steel	1		1
stepladder		1	1
sticks	1	2	3
stock		1	1
stockings	2	6	8
stomach	9	2	11
stone	4	5	9
stool	1	1	2

	Male	Female	Both
store	16	25	41
store, antique		1	1
store, book	2	1	3
store, clothing	2		2
store, department	2	2	4
store, drug	6	4	10
store, fruit	1		1
store, furniture		1	1
store, grocery		1	1
store, jewelry	2		2
store, shoe		1	1
stories, building	3	2	5
strap		1	1
stove	1	1	2
straw	1		1
stream	1		1
street	78	71	149
streetcar	3	8	11
string	5		5
structure	3	1	4
student union, building		1	1
studio		2	2
study, room	1	1	2
stump		1	1
submarine		1	1
substation	1		1
suburb	2	1	3
subway		1	1
suit	4	6	10
suit, bathing	2	3	5
suitcase	1	9	10
suite	3	7	10
sun	5	7	12
sundae	1		1
surf	1		1
squirrel	1	1	2
swamp	1	2	3
seat	1		1
sweater	3	2	5
swing		1	1
switch, light	3	1	4
sword		1	1
syringe	1		1

	Male	Female	Both
table	24	30	54
tackle, fishing	1		1
tadpoles		1	1
tag, price		1	1
tail	1	1	2
tank	2		2
tape	2		2
target	1		1
tavern	3	1	4
taxi cab		1	1
tear, rip		1	1
tears		3	3
teaspoon		1	1
teeth	7	13	20
telephone	2	6	8
telephone booth	1		1
telephone book	1		1
telephone wires	1		1
television	2		2
temple, building		1	1
temple, head		1	1
tent	1		1
terrace		2	2
terrain	1		1
territory	2		2
theater	2	7	9
theme	1	1	2
thermometer		1	1
threshold		1	1
throat	1	1	2
throne	1	1	2
throttle		1	1
thumb	1		1
ticket	4	6	10
tie	1	4	5
tiger	1	1	2
tile		1	1
timberland	1		1
tires	4		4
toast		1	1
tobacco	1		1
toes		2	2

	Male	Female	Both
tomatoes	1	1	2
tomb	1		1
tongue	1		1
tonic	1		1
tonsils		1	1
tools	1		1
toothbrush		1	1
toothpaste	1		1
tornado	1	1	2
towel	1	2	3
toy	1		1
track, deer	1		1
track, race	2		2
track, railroad	4	1	5
track, streetcar	2	1	3
trail	2	1	3
trailer	1		1
train	8	7	15
tray	1		1
tree	17	10	27
tricycle		1	1
trigger	2		2
trimming		1	1
trousers	1	4	5
truck	7	4	11
trunk	2		2
tub		1	1
tube	5		5
tunnel	3	1	4
turbine	1		1
turtle	1		1
tusks	1		1
tuxedos	1	1	2
typewriter		2	2
umbrella	1	2	3
underbrush	1		1
underclothes	4	2	6
uniform	12	3	15
University	11	7	18
upstairs	4	13	17
uptown	1		1
urethra	1		1

	Male	Female	Both
vagina	4		4
valise	1		1
valley	2	2	4
vases	1	2	3
vault		1	1
vegetables		1	1
vegetation		2	2
vehicles		1	1
veranda		1	1
vest	1		1
vestibule		1	1
village	1	1	2
violin	1	1	2
vulture		1	1
wagon		1	1
waist	2	4	6
walk, side	3	1	4
wall	9	19	28
wallet	1	1	2
wallpaper		2	2
ward		1	1
wash, laundry	1		1
washbowl	2		2
washing machine		1	1
wastebasket	1	2	3
watch, timepiece		5	5
water	27	35	62
watertower	1		1
waves	2	4	6
weapon	2	1	3
well	1		1
wheel	3	1	4
whip		1	1
whirlpool		1	1
whiskers		3	3
whiskey	1		1
whistle	1	1	2
window	25	37	62
windshield	1		1
wine		2	2
wings	1	1	2

	Male	Female	Both
wires, communication	1		1
wires, streetcar	1		1
wolf	2		2
wood	2	6	8
wool		1	1
worm		1	1
wreath		1	1
wreckage	1		1
wrist	3	2	5
writing		1	1
yacht		1	1
yard	2	8	10
yard, back	4		4
yard, railroad		1	1
yard, school	1		1
yearbook	1		1
zipper	1		1
zone	1		1

An Example
of Scoring a Dream Series

In order to illustrate how our classification system is used in actual practice, we have appended this series of ten dreams and an explanation of the scoring rationale for each dream. These ten dreams were obtained from a 21-year-old unmarried male college student who was working as a Fuller Brush salesman part-time. This particular dream series was selected because it contained an unusually large number of scoring problems, and it was hoped that by discussing the rationale followed in resolving some of these problems, the potential user would gain a clearer understanding of our classification system.

DREAM 1

I was in a classroom teaching girls several things about cosmetics, hair care, etc. I remember getting into a big discussion on the virtues of natural hair brushes vs. nylon ones and the correct way to brush hair. The class was about 30 girls about age 18 in a classroom much like we had in high school (fixed desks, and old building). The girls all paid attention and discussed things well.

Before proceeding to a discussion of the scoring rationale, it is necessary to comment first about the format of the scoring card. This card has been designed so that all of the symbols needed for scoring a usual dream can be handled on one 5 x 8 card. The arrangement of the columns follows the same sequence as the scales in this book, with the exception that objects pre-

Scoring Card for Dream 1

O	S	Char	Aggressive		Friendly		Sexual			Activities		Success
AV	IQ	2FSA			D 4>2FSA					D V=2FSA		
HH												
HH												
HH												
BH												
HH												
AV												

O	Failure	M-Fort	G-Fort	Emot	M	T	N	OI	OE	CA	CW	PE	Activities	LI	WD
					I+										
					A+										

cede settings. One half of a column length is generally sufficient for scoring most of the scales, but it will be noted that in the case of objects and activities, a full column length is provided. Since the scoring for each scale appears under the column heading identifying it, it is not necessary to repeat the scoring symbol for all of the classes. For example, in the Achievement Outcome chapter it was stated that the method of scoring success was to place a capital SU before the characters who had achieved success. This, however, was done only for the purpose of clarity in the text and these symbols are not necessary on the actual scoring card. In the lower right hand part of the card only a single space is necessary to record the scores for the temporal, negation, and each of the oral and castration scales. The total score for these scales is placed directly under the letters identifying each scale and this number therefore appears above the heavy dark line. In the spaces below the dark line the scorer may place tally marks while he is tabulating for the total frequency score. A brief explanation of how the format of this card facilitates machine tabulation of scores will be found in Appendix C.

In the Objects column, the two AV scores for Dream 1 were given for the classroom and old (high school) building. The four HH scores are for cosmetics, natural bristle hair brushes, nylon brushes, and desks. The BH score is for mentioning hair. The dreamer's high school was not scored because it is contained within the scoring for building.

It is clear that the setting was an indoor one in a classroom; a Q score was given for familiarity because there is some doubt as to whether the dreamer has ever been in this setting before. On the other hand, there is the possibility that he may use this classroom more or less regularly, and it may even be that the dreamer perceived it as the same classroom that he attended in high school. Since a Q score is intended specifically to reflect these situations where it cannot be ascertained from the report how familiar a setting is, it was the score given here.

The scoring of characters raises somewhat of a problem in this dream. It is clear that it is a group character and that the group consists of all females. Since no indication was given of any sort that he might be familiar with any of these girls, the group was scored as consisting of strangers. There is some question about age, but since the statement about age 18 was made, this information was used to score the group as an adult one. It will be recalled that age 13 through 17 is the age range covered in the teenage subclass. Since 18-year-olds are considered adults, this was the scoring assigned here. It is possible that some of the girls in this group may have been younger than 18, but our convention has been to score a group in accordance with the characteristics possessed by the majority of the members.

The only social interaction which occurred was a friendly one. This was scored as an F4 because it was considered that the dreamer was performing a helpful act by instructing the girls about personal grooming. Even though such instruction is part of his employment role as a Fuller Brush man, Rule 1 under scoring Friendliness states that "It is considered to be a friendly act even though the befriender may be acting in a societal or professional role."

In contrast to most dreams, this dream contains a paucity of activity. The only activity involved is a mutual verbal discussion that takes place between the dreamer and the girls on the virtues of various types of hair brushes.

The next scorable classification is that of modifiers. The I+ score was assigned for the "big" discussion. Big in this sentence does not refer to size but to a quality of intensity. The A+ score was given for describing the building as old. Although the comment that the girls discussed things well might seem to be an evaluative statement, it was not scored as such because it could not be considered as belonging in either the aesthetic or moral realm of evaluation. The same rationale explains why teaching the girls the correct way to brush hair was not scored.

There are no scorable elements for any of the remaining scales. The column headed LI is used for the number of lines, and the column headed WD for the number of words in a dream. These scores might be used in case an investigator wished to use either of these measures of dream length for matching or other experimental design purposes.

DREAM 2

I remember driving up a hill on a paved road. It was a steep hill, probably in Maine. The road made a right hand turn, but I kept right on going in the same direction I was going. I was going up a trail that was very steep. I kept right on going till I reached the top of this hill. There was no road up there, just a trail and a lot of rocks. I felt rather foolish driving all the way up, and I came back down. Then the setting changes. It was flat-seeming, like Florida is. Then I stopped to see one of my customers, but this is no customer that I recognized. As I saw she was just a customer, I never even got out of the car. She just came to the car window and I rolled it down to talk to her. She was a woman about 45 and had brown hair. I don't remember the conversation. It was pleasant though. It only lasted a few minutes. I drove on and that's about all I can remember.

In the Objects class for Dream 2, the two NA scores are for hill and rocks. The two ST scores were given for road and trail. Two TR scores were assigned; one for the car and one for the car window. The BH score was entered for the woman's hair. An interesting scoring problem is raised by the dreamer's reference

Scoring Card for Dream 2

O	S	Char	Aggressive	Friendly	Sexual	Activities	Success
NA	OQ	1FOA				P	
ST	OQ					L	
RG						S	
ST						M, 1FOA	
NA						P	
RG						D V=1FOA	
TR						P	
TR						L	

O	Failure	M-Fort	G-Fort	Emot	M	T	N	OI	OE	CA	CW	PE	Activities	LI	WD
BH		M1,D			I+	1	4								
					C+	x	x								
							x								
							x								
							x								
							x								

to Maine and Florida because in both cases he is careful to insert
a comment indicating that these are not necessarily those regions.
If he had stated that he was in Maine and in Florida, two separate
RG scores would definitely be indicated. However, they do seem
to qualify as mentioned objects even though they do not exist
with any substantive reality in the dream, and therefore they
were scored. Rule 2 under scoring Objects states that "Any object that is mentioned in the dream is scored. An object does not
need to be physically present to be scored." Hill is only scored
once even though it is mentioned in three instances, because it is
clear that the dreamer is referring to the same hill. If he described
a different hill, one off in the distance, for example, another NA
score for the additional hill would have been awarded. Even
though the top of the hill might be considered to be a subunit of
the larger unit, i.e., hill, it was felt that it was not a sufficiently
demarcated part of the larger unit to warrant being scored in this
case.

Two settings were scored in this dream: one for the steep
hill which the dreamer was attempting to drive up, and the other
for the flat area where the dreamer was in his car talking to a

customer. The first hill setting is obviously an outdoor one, and the second one appears to be some sort of outdoor street setting since the dreamer mentions driving away after the conversation. Both settings were scored as Q, because in each, the dreamer indicates some vague familiarity with the settings by being able to classify them approximately geographically, but on the other hand he never provides sufficient information to indicate his exact locale. The Q scoring seems best to handle this questionable level of familiarity.

The only character appearing in this dream is the 45-year-old woman. She was scored as O because she was known in a customer role to the dreamer. The subclass of Occupational Identification is not intended to include only long term occupational pursuits such as doctor, teacher, or policeman; it also serves to cover temporary vocational or avocational roles such as athlete, student, cheerleader, or customer. The psychological rationale underlying the use of the O subclass is that characters so identified have some degree of familiarity in that the dreamer can expect them to behave in a manner consistent with their role characteristics.

No social interactions were scored although it might be considered that a borderline case of friendliness existed when the woman came to the dreamer's car and he rolled down the car window to converse with her. Had this involved some effort on her part, such as coming downstairs from an upstairs apartment and going out of her way to approach the dreamer, her actions would have been scored as F5 for a friendly visit. Since the dreamer is not very specific about this, it is possible that she was already standing there and made no unusual efforts to initiate a friendly interaction. We do know that the dreamer rolled down his car window to talk to her which would seem to indicate some minimal friendliness on his part. However, in the preceding sentence, he says that he never even got out of the car when he saw that she was "just a customer," so that it seems quite doubtful that he was expressing any scorable degree of friendliness toward her.

The activities will be discussed in the same sequence that they were scored within the dream. Both a P and L were given for the dreamer driving up a hill. The L score is clear because the dreamer is changing his physical location; the P is included for the physical activity of driving the car under these circumstances. The dreamer's descent down the mountain was considered a part of this same driving activity and therefore was not scored. The S score was given for seeing the customer, and the customer was given an M for coming to the car window since she would have done this through some sort of walking activity. The P was given for the dreamer rolling down the window, and then a mutual V was scored for the dreamer and the customer having a conversation. The final P and L scores were given for the dreamer driving on after the conversation.

In turning our attention to Environmental Presses, a problem presents itself as to whether an M1 score should be given for the lack of a road on top of the hill. After considering the sentence about the dreamer feeling rather foolish when he had to drive down after his long trip up, it was felt that he perceived he had encountered an obstacle or barrier which prevented him from continuing his drive. Since minor environmental barriers are scored M1, this score was utilized although this situation would be considered a borderline one.

No emotions were scored although it might be debated that the dreamer experienced some degree of pleasure or contentment because the conversation was described as pleasant. Since we warned against making inferences about emotional states, we followed our own advice here and refrained from inferring an emotion when the dreamer did not specifically state that this was his reaction. He did say he felt foolish as his reaction to driving up the hill, but this reaction is not classifiable as one of our five scored emotions.

Several scoring problems are also raised with regard to modifiers. Some might consider a paved road to be a straight road with regard to its surface quality, but because a paved road can also be a winding road, a score for linearity would be inappropriate. Similarly, mention of a steep hill might be considered as a size referent, since we score tall or high objects as S+. However, since it seems more appropriate to consider steep as referring to angularity rather than exclusively to height, it was not scored. An I+

was included because the trail was referred to as being very steep. The reference to a "lot of" rocks was not scored as D+ because this subclass requires that a type of bounded area or container must be involved with the implication of fullness or some pressure being exerted against the sides. A lot of rocks in a box would therefore qualify for scoring, but a lot of rocks lying on the top of a hill would not. The dreamer's comments about feeling "rather" foolish were not scored as I+ because it's not clear from the word "rather" that he felt strongly or intensely foolish. Foolish was not scored as an evaluative reference because it did not seem to refer to either an aesthetic or a moral judgment. No V− score was awarded for the dreamer when he "stopped," because a V− score is given only for a reference to moving slowly, not to stopping. The C+ score was assigned for the brown hair. The final scoring problem occurs in connection with the mention of "pleasant" conversation. Although the aesthetic criteria involved in scoring E+ are broad enough to allow any sensation which is pleasant to the senses, the enjoyment here seems to be more a matter of intellectual enjoyment rather than visual, auditory, or other sensual enjoyment.

One temporal score was awarded for mention of the conversation "lasting a few minutes." The four items scored on the negative scale were: "no" road up there, "no" customer that I recognized, I "never" even got out of the car, and I "don't" remember the conversation.

DREAM 3

In the beginning of this dream I was in the back of a large open truck with a bunch of other boys. It seems that we were going back to school. I cannot remember what we were talking about. We stopped at the edge of a small town and everyone was getting out to go swimming. I threw down the helmet to my skin-diving wet suit and said "five dollars." Immediately a boy took it and gave me the $5 (which was for renting it). The place we swam at was much like a place we used to go to in Colorado when I was in summer camp. It was a gorge full of deep pools and a lot of fast moving water. The boy I rented the helmet to was in the place I wanted to go, but it was so small only I could fit. Finally he moved out and I got in. I had my mask on so I was doing some diving. I remember thinking I could really earn a lot if I rented out my whole suit. The dream becomes hazy now, but I do remember something about a red and white '57 Ford going up the road. It had a N.Y. plate on it.

Scoring Card for Dream 3

O	S	Char	Aggressive	Friendly	Sexual	Activities	Success
TR	OU	2MUA				L, D +	
RG	OQ	1MUA				2MUA	
CL						V, D +	
MO						2MUA	
RG						M, D +	
RG						2MUA	
NA						P	
NA						V	

O	Failure	M-Fort	G-Fort	Emot	M	T	N	OI	OE	CA	CW	PE	Activities	LI	WD
IR					S+		1						P, 1MUA		
CL					S−	x							1MUA P>D		
TR					S+								M, 1MUA		
ST					V+								M		
TR					S−								M		
					I+								C		
					C+										
					C−										

Since so many objects are mentioned in Dream 3, they will be discussed in the same sequential order that they appeared in the dream. The TR score was given for truck, but no separate score was given for mention of the back of the truck since this was not considered to represent a clearly demarcated part of the vehicle. No score was given for the school reference since the word school here was used in a generic sense and not to denote a specific building. The RG was given for town, but the edge of town is not a scorable region item since it does not represent a distinguishable part of a larger unit. The wet suit helmet was scored CL, although a strong argument might be offered in favor of considering this as a recreational item which would then be scored as IR. IR is used more for sporting goods items such as

an aqualung, football, or tennis racquet. The MO score was given
for the reference to five dollars. Both Colorado and summer camp
were scored as RG and are examples of mentioned objects rather
than objects that tangibly appear within the dream. Two NA
scores were given for the gorge and the pools, but no NA score
was given for the mention of water. We do score water as an
NA object if it is mentioned in isolation, but do not score it if a
body of water is also mentioned, e.g., a reference to the water in
the ocean. This convention is followed because the ocean consists
of water and does not exist independent of it, and to score both
mention of the ocean and the water as well leads to double scoring of the same item. We do, however, score separate and relatively independent parts of a larger unit, as for example, in this
dream when the helmet and the whole wet suit are separately
scored. The word "place" was not scored because it is too vague
and does not seem to refer to any clearly bounded area that would
qualify for an RG score. The diving mask was scored as IR because it seemed to be closer to the sporting goods category than
it did to the clothing one. A clothing score was given for the mention of the whole wet suit, however. The two TR scores were
given for the '57 Ford and for the N. Y. plate, and the ST score
was for the road.

The scoring problems posed by settings revolve first about
the issue of how many settings are present. It is clear that there
is one outdoor setting present where the various swimming activities take place, but it is less clear whether a separate setting score
should be given for the initial part of the dream involving the
open truck. Since the truck did seem to represent a different
locale and the dreamer was apparently there long enough to become engaged in some unremembered conversation with the other
boys, it was decided that two outdoor settings should be scored.
The truck setting was scored as U because the dreamer does not
give any indication that the area they were passing through was
in any way familiar. The swimming setting was scored as Q because apparently it was very similar and yet also dissimilar to a
familiar place, so that its degree of familiarity to the dreamer remains questionable.

The two characters involved in the dream are a bunch of
boys and the boy who rented his helmet. Since there is a good

possibility that the boys may have been familiar to the dreamer although they were not so identified, a U scoring is relevant. Both characters were scored as adults because this is our convention when no other information is given. Describing them as boys is not a sufficient basis to classify them as teenagers or as children.

No social interactions were scored. A question might be raised as to whether there was a friendly act on the part of the dreamer in renting out his helmet, but this was not scored. The dreamer says that he threw the helmet down and then announced the price. His actions were impersonal in nature and intended more to benefit himself rather than some individual that he had selected to be the recipient of his friendliness.

The activities will be described in the same sequence in which they appeared within the dream. The L score for the dreamer and the bunch of boys was given for riding in the back of the truck. Although the dreamer does not say specifically that the truck was moving, it becomes evident that it was when he does refer to it stopping. The V score was included for the talking in which the dreamer and the boys engaged, since the wording of the report strongly suggests that some talking was going on while they were in the truck. Getting out of the truck was scored as an M for the dreamer and the boys. The dreamer then engages in a P when he throws down his helmet and a V when he mentions the five dollars. The boy who took the helmet was given a P score for this action. He receives another P score when he gives the dreamer the five dollars. This is scored as a physical interaction because both characters become a part of the physical activity. The boy next receives an M score for moving out of the place where the dreamer wanted to be and the dreamer receives an M score for getting into this place. An M score is also credited to the dreamer for his diving activities. The dreamer receives a C for thinking about how he could earn a lot of money. The latter is a rather marginal case as C scores are generally reserved for more sustained cognitive activity than that described in this report. However, it seems that the dreamer was calculating how much he could get for the whole suit at the rate of five dollars for just the helmet and this would require some degree of concentration.

There were no achievement outcomes or environmental

presses scored for this dream. Although the dreamer does acquire five dollars in the dream, this is accomplished through his own efforts and therefore cannot be scored as a Good Fortune. On the other hand, these efforts cannot be treated as a Success because the dreamer does not have to expend any effort pursuing some stated goal.

In scoring for modifiers, an S+ score was given for the large truck and an S— for the small town. There may be a question regarding whether density should be scored for mention of the bunch of boys in the truck. As indicated earlier, a D+ score is generally reserved for situations where there is an implication of pressure or fullness. If the dreamer had said that the boys were bunched up in the truck, a D+ score would have been appropriate. This same rationale for not scoring density also applies for the description of the gorge as full of pools. An S+ score was indicated for the pools being deep, since a description of any one of the three dimensions is sufficient for a size score. The fast moving water was scored V+, and the place that was so small was given an S— for being small and I+ for the intensifying term "so." The colors on the '57 Ford were handled by assigning a C+ score for the red and a C— score for the white color. The modifier "really" was not scored as I+ because it seems to carry the meaning of realistically rather than any intensity connotation.

One negative score was credited for "I *cannot* remember what we were talking about." No PE score was given for the dreamer acquiring five dollars in this dream because in order to do so he had to give up a possession which apparently had an equivalent value. If the dreamer had found this sum of money or if someone had given it to him as a friendly act in the dream, it would have been scored PE.

DREAM 4

The time is winter and a group of students and myself are on a field trip. The instructor is telling us about the formation of sand dunes and snow drifts as we walk through the snow. We all have a drawing board and are making a drawing of the areas he tells us about.

The lecture then seems to get more artistic than scientific as the beauty of the drifts, trees, and few buildings is pointed out. I remember I was making my drawing with a Bic pen just like the one I am using on this report. I tried to show the way the snow looked as it formed little clouds at the lips of the snowbanks as it blew. The ones we were seeing were in beautiful pastels of red, green, and blue. The instructor also pointed out the beauty of the noise of the wind. I made a slight whistle which sounded much like it and someone else did the same. Just before I awakened, the instructor told us about a canoe that was awarded to the student at Yale who could make the best academic recovery and hold it for a month.

Scoring Card for Dream 4

O	S	Char	Aggressive	Friendly	Sexual	Activities	Success	
NA	OU	2JOA		1MOA 4>D +		1MOA V>D +		
NA		1MOA		2JOA		2JOA		
CM		1IOA				M, D +		
CM						1IOA +		
RG						2JOA		
NA						P, D +		
AM						˙2JOA		
CM						S, D +		
CM						2JOA		
TR						P		
						P, 1IOA		

O	Failure	M-Fort	G-Fort	Emot	M	T	N	OI	OE	CA	CW	PE	Activities	LI	WD
					E+	2			2				1MOA V>D +		
					S−	x			x				2JOA		
					E+	x			x						
					C+										
					C+										
					C+										
					E+										
					I−										

Objects will be taken up in the same order that they appeared in Dream 4. Two NA scores were given for the sand dunes and snow drifts. The next reference to snow was not scored separately as it was felt that snow and snow drifts were not different

objects just as the water and pools of the previous dream did not
receive two separate NA scores. The two CM scores were given
for the drawing board and the drawing. An RG score was given
for the areas the instructor tells them about. This represents
borderline acceptability as a more specific designation of some
region should generally be provided to receive such a score. The
next NA score was given for the trees but the drifts were not
scored because they were scored earlier. The buildings are given
an AM score because no information is provided as to what types
of buildings they might be. The two CM scores are for the Bic
pen and for report. No score was allowed for snow or snowbanks
since snowdrifts had previously been scored. Clouds were not
scored because they were clouds of snow rather than celestial
clouds which would have received an NA score. Similarly lips
were not scored because they obviously do not refer to a body
part. Neither noise nor whistle are scorable items because it was
pointed out in the chapter on scoring objects that sounds and
things with temporal boundaries were not included in the object
class. The final item which was scored was the canoe as a TR
object. Yale is not scorable as an object because it does not have
a specific enough referent such as a campus or building.

Only a single setting is involved in this dream and this is
clearly an outdoor one. This setting was scored as being unfamiliar to the dreamer because although he devoted a great deal
of description to it, he never at any point indicated that any part
of it was familiar to him. The more lengthy the description of a
setting becomes without any indication of familiarity being provided, the greater is the likelihood that a setting is unfamiliar to
the dreamer.

The first character is the group of students scored as J because there is no reason to believe that the group would not be
composed of both male and female students. Being identified as
students is sufficient to warrant a scoring of O, as pointed out in
Dream 2. The instructor is scored as a male because in the third
sentence, the dreamer uses the masculine pronoun to identify
this instructor. Being an instructor clearly qualifies for an O identification score. Had the dreamer indicated he knew the instruc-

tor, the scoring would have been K, since K takes precedence over O. The remaining character is the someone who whistled after the dreamer whistled. Since no indication of this person's sex was given, an I score is necessary. Although no information is provided as to this character's identity, it seems reasonable to assume that it must have been a student since they are the only persons, except for the instructor, mentioned in the report. It also seems unlikely that anyone else would have been close enough to hear the dreamer's slight whistle unless this person were also a student. If this had been a field trip to a city, it is much more probable that other people would have been nearby, and in that situation, a U score would have been given. The student at Yale was not scored as a character because this is an example of a generic reference as no actual student was referred to.

A friendly interaction was scored for the instructor telling the students about the formation of sand dunes. His explanation is considered as a helpful act and therefore scored F4, even though the instructor is only carrying out his teaching role. This point was explained in the discussion of Dream 1.

The first activity is a verbal one when the instructor tells the dreamer and the students about the sand dunes. An M score is given for the dreamer, students, and instructor, who are all walking through the snow. The dreamer and the students engage in a physical activity when they make drawings of the areas that are pointed out. No score is given for pointing out because it is not clear whether this is done through physical or verbal means. No additional P score was used for the dreamer explaining in the report how he proceeded to make his drawing, since this was the same drawing activity for which the earlier P score was assigned. An S score was given to the dreamer and the students for seeing the little clouds of snow. The whistling engaged in first by the dreamer and later by someone else was scored as two separate physical activities since it was not done jointly but separately by each character. Another V score was given for the instructor telling the dreamer and the students about the canoe. This was scored as a different verbal activity even though it seems as if there were a continuing dialogue between the instructor and the students, because in this instance it refers to an entirely different topic unrelated to the preceding nature talk and because there were some intervening activities.

Although a success theme was mentioned in the latter part of the dream, no SU scoring was introduced because no specific character experienced it. The Yale student was treated as a generic nonscorable character and therefore cannot be associated with any other elements in the dream. Success, in our classification system, can only be dealt with when it is achieved by some scorable character.

The first modifier is an E+ for the reference to the beauty of the surroundings. S— was given for the little clouds and another E+ for the mention of the beautiful pastels. Red, blue, and green are each given separate C+ scores since they refer to different colors. Another E+ score was entered for the reference to the beauty of the noise of the wind. I— was used for the mention of the slight whistle that the dreamer made.

Two temporal scores were given, one for indicating the time is winter, and the second for the mention of one month in the last sentence. No negative scores were present which is unusual in a dream report of this length. Two scores for oral emphasis were tallied because of the whistling engaged in by the dreamer and later by the other person.

DREAM 5

The first part of this dream I can remember was about grade school children voting on some issue. They were using red ballots so that collection would be easier. It seems that the ballots were left by the doors of their houses. While this was going on, I was talking with a street sweeper. He was quite well informed and had run for several offices. The last one he ran for had something to do with assisting the town manager. He said he had really done a job at cleaning out the corruptions in the offices then. (This man was a gas station attendant and school bus driver in my home town.)

Just three objects were scored in Dream 5: the ballots (CM), the doors (AD), and the houses (AR). The mention of offices

Scoring Card for Dream 5

O	S	Char	Aggressive		Friendly		Sexual		Activities		Success
CM	AQ	2JUC							D	V = 1MKA	1MKA
AD		1MKA									
AR		1MOA									

O	Failure	M-Fort	G-Fort	Emot	M	T	N	OI	OE	CA	CW	PE	Activities	LI	WD	
					C+											

was not scored because it does not refer to rooms in a building, but to political positions.

The setting for this dream is very ambiguous, and although it seems as if the dreamer were probably out of doors on some street, this would be making too much of an inference. The fuzziness of the locale description for this setting is best handled by scoring it as AQ.

The grade school children were scored as J because there is no reason to believe that they do not consist of both male and female children. These children were scored as possessing uncertain identity, because although they were identified as grade school children, they were not identified as pupils. Had they been identified as pupils, the scoring would have been O. Since all children of grade school age are scored as C, this presents no scoring problem. The next two characters are both single male adult characters, and it is evident from the dreamer's remarks in parentheses that one of them was personally known to him. However, it is not clear whether it was the street sweeper or the town manager. It seems somewhat more probable that he is referring

to the street sweeper, since the dreamer does describe some interaction with him but not with the town manager. The street
sweeper was therefore given a K scoring and the town manager
an O scoring.

The only scorable activity in this report is the mutual verbal
interaction between the dreamer and the street sweeper. Although
voting and ballots being used were mentioned, it is not clear if
the children were actually voting during the dream or just planning to do so. The reference to "this going on" was ambiguous
as to whether it refers to the voting or the ballots being left. With
regard to the ballots which were being left, no information is provided as to what characters were engaged in this activity, so it is
therefore unscorable. The reference to cleaning out the corruptions is also too vague about what activities were involved to be
scored.

A score for success was given for "really having done a job
of cleaning out the corruptions." Exactly who cleaned them out,
the street sweeper or the town manager, is uncertain but it seems
as if it were the street sweeper. The only scorable modifier was
a C+ for the red ballots. No intensity scores were given for quite
and really because these words represent an indeterminate
amount of intensity.

DREAM 6

I was in a coed boarding school or college by the edge of the
sea. Many of the classes were outside. I remember one in which about
50 of us were all on one big rock next to the water. I cannot remember
the subject of the class, however. We had some classes inside also. In
one, I remember I had an assignment to deliver a short talk on the
value of the education I was getting at the school and how it differed
from other schools. I did a very poor job preparing, but I was sure I
would not be called. As it turned out the professor (female) stopped
just one person before me. For this class we were in a large room
somewhat like a cafeteria. In the corner I was sitting in there were
some strange foods which had just been brought in for dinner. I remember one was mastodon meat. After that class we had one outside
on the rocks. I left early and did not clean up the things I was work-

ing with but someone else did it for me. After this I remember being tired and wanting to lie down on one of the ceremonial couches but I didn't. Two girls were lying on these, however.

Scoring Card for Dream 6

O	S	Char	Aggressive	Friendly	Sexual	Activities	Success
AV	OU	2JOA		1IOA 4>D		M	
NA	IU	1FOA				P, 1IOA	
NA	OU	1IOA					
AE		1IUA					
FO		2FUA					
FO							
NA							
HH							

O	Failure	M-Fort	G-Fort	Emot	M	T	N	OI	OE	CA	CW	PE	Activities	LI	WD
	D (GF)		D		S+	4	2								
					I+			x	x						
					E−			x	x						
					S+			x							
								x							

In the Object column for dream 6, the AV score was given for the college. Two NA scores were entered; one for the sea and one for the big rock. Water was not scored as NA because it was already included in the scoring for sea. School was not scored because this refers to the previously scored college, and the other schools referred to were not scored because the term is used in a generic sense. The question as to how to score the large room in which the class took place poses a problem. It appears to be a classroom, but it also appears to be a cafeteria where one can have dinner. Since more emphasis was given to the cafeteria aspects in terms of mentioning the foods, dinner, and mastodon meat, it was scored as AE. Two FO scores were given; one for the strange foods and the other for the mastodon meat. Another NA score was given for the rocks where the class took place, and the HH scoring represented the ceremonial couches.

The first setting was an outdoor one where the class was held on a big rock next to the water. The next setting is an indoor one which took place in the cafeteria-like room. Following that, the next setting occurs outdoors on the rocks. There is a possibility that another setting may have been involved when the dreamer mentions that he wanted to lie on one of the ceremonial couches. These were probably not located outside on the rocks, but since it is not clear that a definite change in locale was involved, no further settings were scored. All three of these settings were scored as being unfamiliar since the school was not named nor was the region identified, and the dreamer himself seems somewhat confused by the appearance of the cafeteria-like room.

The first character is the group of 50 students from the coed school. Since they are students, the O identification is used. The next character is the female professor who is also scored as O. The person with whom the teacher stopped was treated as a character because it was a specific person called upon by the professor rather than a generic character. The sex of the student was not specified, and an I score is therefore indicated. Another indefinite sexed individual appears when the dreamer mentions that someone else cleaned up the things that the dreamer was working with. This character was scored as U because there is a possibility that it may have been some sort of janitor or custodial person who cleaned up the dreamer's things rather than another student. The final character consists of the two girls lying on the couches who are not further identified. Since there is a possibility that this may have been a setting apart from the college, no great confidence could be placed in assuming that these girls were students, and they were therefore also scored as possessing uncertain identity.

One social interaction occurred in this dream. An F4 was scored for the person who performed a helping act in cleaning up the dreamer's things. There are only two scorable activities and these develop from this same situation. The first involves an M score for the dreamer when he left class and the other a P for the person who cleaned up. An M score was given rather than an L for the dreamer leaving because it seems implausible that he could have arrived outside on the rocks in any way except through a physical movement on his part.

A failure was attributed to the dreamer because he acknowledged that he did a very poor job in preparing for his classroom assignment. The dreamer, however, did not have to face up to the failure because he was "lucky" and saved by not being called on. A consequence of good fortune was therefore included as part of the overall scoring for this situation. Since this latter scoring represents an additional type of score, a primary GF score must also be listed in the good fortune column. Any consequence score must also appear as a primary scoring in some other column.

For modifiers, an S+ was given for the "big" rock but an S— was not given for the short talk, since short refers to temporal duration and not to physical length. An E— score was given for the poor job of preparing, and an I+ was also included because it was described as a very poor job. This lack of preparation is socially inappropriate, thereby qualifying for a "moral" type of evaluation. An S+ was included for the description of the cafeteria-like classroom as being large.

No temporal reference was scored because the dreamer did not refer to any specific unit of time nor attempt to date any event. His mention of leaving class early would therefore not qualify for a temporal score. Four negative scores were given. These were for mentioning that the dreamer "cannot" remember the subject, being sure he would "not" be called, "not" cleaning up the things, and he "didn't" lie down on one of the couches. OI was scored twice; once for the eating setting, i.e., the cafeteria-type room, and the other for the dinner preparations. The references to the strange foods and the mastodon meat were not scored because food is scorable only when it appears in isolation, not when it appears with any other scorable OI items.

DREAM 7

I cannot remember the beginning of this dream, but in the first part I can recall I was back in the country in Michigan talking with two girls. One was unattractive and the other was fairly nice-looking. I began to get friendly with this one, but not too enthusiastically. She took my display of affection to mean more than I had intended and started trying to get me aroused by pushing her breasts into me. At this point the thought came to my mind that her mother had taught her to do this to enable her to get a boy to marry her. However, I wasn't too concerned with this as I was rather enjoying her. Then we stopped because another girl, a very cute one, came on the scene. I liked her at once and knew that she was a girl I could love. I went over and talked with her for a while and soon was kissing her as the other two girls and the mother looked on sadly. She was great and I remember I wished I could have dreamed more about her or remembered more about her when I woke up.

Scoring Card for Dream 7

O	S	Char	Aggressive		Friendly		Sexual		Activities		Success
RG	AG	1FSA	D 3>1FSA		D 5>1FSA	1FSA	4>D		D V=1FSA+		
BS		1FSA			D 2>1FSA	D	3>1FSA		1FSA		
		1FSA			D 1>1FSA				1FSA P>D		
		1FSA							C		
									L, 1FSA		
									M		
									D V=1FSA		
									D P>1FSA		

O	Failure	M-Fort	G-Fort	Emot	M	T	N	OI	OE	CA	CW	PE	Activities	LI	WD	
				AP	E−	1	4		1				S, 1FSA+			
				HA	E+	x	x		x				1FSA+			
				SA 1FSA+	I−		x						1FSA			
				1FSA+	I−		x									
				1FSA	E+		x									
					E+											
					I+											

Only two objects were scored in Dream 7. The first was an RG score for mention of Michigan and the other a BS score for breasts. The reference to "in the country" is too indefinite to warrant scoring as a region.

Only one overall setting is involved in this dream. It is scored as ambiguous because it is unclear whether the activities are taking place outdoors or indoors. When the dreamer says that he was back in the country, this would suggest an outdoor setting was involved, but it is also possible that some sort of shack or cabin may have been the setting for the dream. The setting is scored as a geographical one because it is identified as taking place in Michigan and the dreamer does not indicate any greater degree of familiarity with the locale.

Four female characters are involved in this dream. They are an unattractive girl and a fairly nice-looking one with whom the dreamer was initially talking, the mother of one of these girls, and the cute girl who later arrived on the scene. Since these girls were never referred to by name and there is nothing in the dream report to indicate that the dreamer had ever met them before, all four characters were scored as strangers.

A large number of social interactions takes place and it is exceedingly difficult to disentangle them and assign them to their appropriate classes. An A3 score was given to the dreamer because he appeared to be rejecting the one girl whom he was initially with, since he left her when the cute girl appeared on the scene. This was also apparently perceived as a rejection by the other characters, because the dreamer describes them as looking on sadly. The dreamer says that he began to get friendly with the nice-looking girl. His words were taken at face value and therefore an F5 was assigned for taking the initiative in visiting or dating another character. From later remarks that the dreamer makes, it is quite probable that he was actually making sexual overtures to this girl since he elicited a sexual response from her, but this was thought to be too great an inferential jump and the dreamer's own words about getting friendly were therefore accepted. The dreamer was also credited with verbal friendliness (F2) for talking to the cute girl, but once again it is probable that he was making some sort of overtures to this girl because soon afterward he was kissing her. However, since a sexual response may unexpectedly follow an initial friendly response, it was decided to preserve his talking with this girl as a separate friendly act. The dreamer was also credited with a covert feeling of friendliness (F1) toward this same girl when he says that she was great and he wished he could have dreamed about her more. Under the sexual interactions, an S4 score was given to the first girl for taking the initiative in trying to arouse the dreamer through pushing her breasts into him. The dreamer is also credited with an S3 score for kissing the cute second girl.

The first activity which occurs is a mutual verbal activity between the dreamer and the two girls. No score was given for the dreamer becoming friendly since it was not specified how this was accomplished. The girl received a P for pushing her breasts into the dreamer. The C score was for the thinking that the dreamer engaged in concerning the mother and the intentions that the girl had toward him. The cute girl who came on the scene received an L score since it was not specified how she arrived. An M was scored for the dreamer going over to her since this seems to have been effected by his walking over. The dreamer then engages in a mutual verbal interaction with this girl, followed by a P for the dreamer kissing her. The final activity is a seeing one which is engaged in by the two girls and the mother.

In contrast to most of the other reports, some emotions are mentioned in this dream. The AP was scored for the dreamer mentioning he "wasn't too concerned." Since intensity is not a prerequisite for an emotion to be scored, not being too concerned is scored as readily as being very concerned. The HA was scored for the dreamer "rather enjoying" the girl. The two girls' and the mother's emotions as they looked on the kissing scene constituted the SA score, since they were so described by the dreamer.

Several aesthetic modifiers are contained in this report. The first one, an E−, was for the description of one of the girls as unattractive; the other girl who was fairly nice-looking was represented by an E+. An I− score was given for the mention of not too enthusiastic, since what is conveyed by this expression was that the dreamer was only slightly or minimally enthusiastic. The same rationale holds for the description of not being too concerned, so this was also scored I−. The mention in the same sentence of "rather enjoying" is ambiguous as to whether he was slightly or greatly enjoying this experience and so was not scored as an intensity modifier. The two E+'s were scored for labelling the girl as cute and being great. Since the girl was described as very cute, an I+ score is also indicated.

The temporal reference occurs in connection with talking to

the cute girl "for a while." The first of the four negative scores appears in the first sentence when the dreamer mentions that he "cannot" remember the beginning of the dream. It will be recalled that the negative scale is the only scale wherein general comments about the dream are also scored. The next N score was for the "unattractive" girl. The remaining two N scores are for "not" too enthusiastically and "wasn't" too concerned. The oral emphasis score was for the kissing activity.

DREAM 8

I was in an apartment building and I hinted something to my boss that I might quit Fuller Brush. He said nothing but went down to the patio and started talking with two other Fuller men, one of them the branch manager, and the other a German. When I came in the German began talking about quitting and the others tried to get him not to. They showed him how much money he was making, etc. and how foolish it would be to quit. Then they turned to me to ask if I didn't agree with all this. I said I did, and then he asked me why I wanted to quit. The little act they had been putting on was just to show me how foolish I would be if I did quit. I said I wouldn't quit until I was not making any money or my school work was hurt. They said OK. But then the manager began talking about my sales record. He said he wanted to see more than the $65 I turned in last week. I really turned in over $100 but my boss needed some of it to fill his quota. At this point I walked away, but I heard my boss saying that I had worked for him and earned another $50. This seemed to satisfy the men.

The first two objects in Dream 8 are AR and are scored for the apartment building and the patio. Four MO scores were assigned; the first for the mention of how much money the German was making, and the remaining three for the specific sums of money mentioned, i.e., $65, $100, and $50.

Only one setting was scored, an indoor one for being in the apartment building. Although mention is made of going down to the patio, it is not clear that this was located outside, and it was therefore treated as if it were a part of the building itself. With

Scoring Card for Dream 8

O	S	Char	Aggressive	Friendly	Sexual	Activities	Success
AR	IQ	1MKA	D 3>1MKA	1MKA 4>D		D V>1MKA	
AR		1MKA	1MKA 3>D			L, 1MKA	
MO		1MOA				1MKA V=1MKA+	
MO						MOA	
MO						M	
MO						V, 1MOA	
						P, 1MKA+	
						1MKA+	
						1MOA	

O	Failure	M-Fort	G-Fort	Emot	M	T	N	OI	OE	CA	CW	PE	Activities	LI	WD
						1	5						1MKA+		
					x	x							1MKA+		
						x							1MKA V>D		
						x							D VR1MKA+		
						x							1MKA+		
						x							1MOA		
													1MKA VRD		
													D VR1MKA		
													1MKA+		
													1MKA+		
													1MOA VRD		
													V, 1MKA		
													M		
													A		
													1MKA V>1MKA+		
													1MOA		

regard to familiarity, it might appear that the apartment building was not too familiar since it is only described by the word "an," but the patio is described by the definite article "the," suggesting that the dreamer may have had some experience with this building. A Q score therefore seemed best to handle this ambiguity. In the latter part of the report the dreamer describes walking away, but it was never stated how far away he walked or to where, so no additional setting was scored.

The three characters appearing in this dream are all individual male characters. The boss and the branch manager were both scored as being known, because the dreamer did work for the Fuller Brush Company and it was felt that he could name both of these individuals if he were so requested. The German could have been identified on the basis of his accent and may not have been known to the dreamer personally. Since the German was also identified as a Fuller Brush man, he was scored as O because this takes precedence over an ethnic scoring.

Scoring of social interactions in this dream presents some problems. The dreamer's hint that he might quit Fuller Brush sounds as if it might be an aggressive action involving rejection by the dreamer. Yet whom is he rejecting? Is it an actual character such as the boss or branch manager, or should it be scored with a question mark for the impersonalized brush company? We decided that his boss would be the probable victim, so the victim was scored as 1MKA. In actuality, this scoring does not distinguish between the boss and branch manager, which is preferable in this particular situation. A more specific aggression is involved when the branch manager begins to discuss the dreamer's sales record and says that he wishes to see more money turned in. This apparent aggression was scored as an A3 with the dreamer as the victim of the manager's remarks. Things become a bit tangled again as one tries to unravel the boss's actions in filling his quota. With some hesitation, a helping friendly act was scored for the boss because of his speaking in defense of the dreamer and satisfying the others that the dreamer had been doing a satisfactory job. Of course, it could be said that the boss had also behaved aggressively in using some of the dreamer's money initially, but it is not clear whether this may have been company policy. What is clear, however, is that without being requested to do so, the boss did spontaneously exonerate the dreamer, regardless of the preceding events.

The first activity was a verbal one from the dreamer to his boss when he hinted about quitting. The next activity was the boss going down to the patio. This was scored as an L rather than M because it was not specified that the boss walked down. It is possible that he might have taken an elevator. A mutual verbal activity was scored for the boss talking with the branch manager and the German. The dreamer received an M score for coming into the patio, since this would have involved walking. No score was given for the dreamer coming down to the patio as there was for the boss, since the dreamer's trip was not mentioned in the report. A score of V was listed for the German when he began talking, but the others trying to get him to remain and showing him about the money he was making did not receive a score because it was not clear what methods they used to accomplish this. The three characters received a P score for turning to the dreamer, and all three are credited with a verbal activity directed toward the dreamer for asking him why he wanted to quit. In actuality, probably only one person asked him but since the report states that "they" turned to ask, all three are represented in the scoring. A series of reciprocal verbal replies follows. First the dreamer is credited with a VR when he replies to them that he did agree, then another is entered for someone, probably the boss, asking why the dreamer wanted to quit. The dreamer then receives a VR for replying that he won't quit and the final VR appears when they, presumably all three, reply by saying okay. The preceding scoring is intended to reflect that there was one continuing verbal activity going on, and the various questions and replies that made up the bulk of this conversation were scored as reciprocal activities. Then a V was scored for the manager who began talking about the sales record. This introduced a new topic of conversation and was scored separately from the preceding conversation. No S score was given for the boss mentioning that he wanted to see more than $65, because this does not refer to any current or completed activity but to a colloquial way of speaking. The same explanation holds for why the dreamer "turning in" money was not scored. The dreamer walking away received an M score and an A score was recorded for hearing his boss. The last V appears for the boss explaining to the other two men about the other $50.

A temporal score was entered for the reference to last week. The negative scores were given for the boss saying "nothing," the others trying to get the German "not" to quit, asking the dreamer if he "didn't" agree with this, the dreamer saying he "wouldn't" quit, and the dreamer "not" making any money.

DREAM 9

The first part of the dream I can remember started in a monstrous hunting lodge which, for some reason, had live deer walking around. This did not seem to excite me or the others who were there (all male and only one I knew in real life—a man I used to hunt with). The deer were mostly doe, but there were a few buck. Only spike horns however. Later, I went outside and saw two hunters and told them about the deer. Then a doe came out and one of the hunters shot it, but only I could see this since it went behind a tree right after he shot. I heard him say "I missed" and then the next thing I knew, he had hit me in the ankle, but only with a couple pieces of buckshot. I went to a hunting store to get a First Aid kit but ran into a Spanish speaking saleslady that couldn't understand me. Finally, I got the kit and fixed myself up.

Scoring Card for Dream 9

O	S	Char	Aggressive	Friendly	Sexual	Activities	Success
AE	IU	2ANI	D 3>2ANI	D 4>2MOA		M, 2ANI	D
BH	OU	1MKA	1MOA 7>1ANI			M	
NA	IU	2MSA				S	
BE		2MOA				D V>2MOA	
IW		1ANI				M, 1ANI	
AV		1MOA				MOA P>1ANI	
HH		1FOA				S	
						M, 1ANI	

O	Failure	M-Fort	G-Fort	Emot	M	T	N	OI	OE	CA	CW	PE	Activities	LI	WD	
	1MOA	M5, D			S+		2				1	1	A			
		M1, D(SU)					x				x	x	V, 1MOA			
							x						L			
													P			

In Dream 9, the AE was scored for the hunting lodge and the BH for the mention of the spikehorns on the buck. An NA score appears for the tree and a BE for the dreamer's ankle. The pieces of buckshot were placed in the weapon subclass and the hunting store was scored AV. The difference between a hunting lodge being scored AE and a hunting store being scored AV is that the former is used for recreational purposes while the latter is a place where business transactions occur. The first aid kit was scored HH since medicines are considered household items.

The initial setting was an indoor one located within the hunting lodge. The dreamer then went outside and talked to the hunters, so the dream locale shifted to an outdoor one. Eventually the dreamer enters a hunting store, so a final indoor setting is indicated. All three settings were scored U because no indication was given that the dreamer had ever seen any of these settings in real life.

The first character mentioned in this report is the live deer. Although later on the dreamer distinguishes between them on the basis of sex, only one group of deer is listed because scoring distinctions are not made within the animal subclass with regard to age, sex, or familiarity. The man the dreamer knew in real life was given a K score. The other males that the dreamer did not know were scored as strangers. They would have been scored as O if they were identified as hunters. The two hunters were scored as O. An individual score was given for the one doe that came out and an individual score for the one hunter who attempted to shoot it. Individual characters differentiated from a larger group are scored separately. The Spanish-speaking saleslady was scored as O rather than E, because occupational identification takes precedence over ethnic identification.

As in the last dream, social interactions pose some scoring problems. The difficulties are encountered in handling the dreamer's activities when he tells the hunters about the deer. We decided that to inform hunters where they might be able to obtain their sought after goal of deer would be a friendly thing to do and scored it as an F4. However, in doing so, the dreamer must play the role of accomplice or intermediary in causing the expected death of the deer. The dreamer was therefore also credited with an aggressive act (A3) against the group of deer. The hunter who shot at the one doe clearly displayed aggressive behavior toward this animal. Even though the hunter in this case missed hitting the deer, his aggression qualifies as A7 because he engaged in a threatening act with a weapon.

Under activities the M score was given for the group of deer walking and an M score was also given for the dreamer when he went outside. The S score is for seeing the two hunters and the V is for the dreamer telling the hunters about the deer. The doe who came out of the lodge was given an M, and a P was credited to the hunter who shot at it. The dreamer receives another S score for seeing this. Another M was given to the deer for going behind the tree, because this seems to represent a different activity than coming out of the lodge since it did not occur until after the hunter had shot. An A was credited to the dreamer for hearing the hunter and a V to the hunter when he said he missed. It was not explained how the dreamer arrived at the hunting store, so this was scored with an L. It is not clear exactly what was involved in the dreamer fixing himself up with the first aid kit, but it would seem to necessitate some physical activity and was therefore scored as a P.

In the achievement outcome classification, a success score was given to the dreamer for finally obtaining the first aid kit and fixing himself up. This was the task that he set for himself in going to the hunting store, and after overcoming the obstacle of the saleslady that couldn't understand him, the dreamer did manage to achieve his goal. An FL score was recorded for the hunter who failed to hit the deer he was attempting to shoot, and who acknowledged his failure by saying he missed. For the environmental press classification, an M5 was scored for the dreamer because of the injury he accidentally received. It is true that he was shot by one of the hunters, but this was not a deliberate intentional act on the part of the hunter and therefore qualifies as a misfortune. An M1 was also scored for the dreamer encountering the obstacle of the Spanish-speaking saleslady who couldn't understand him. Again the misfortune occurs indirectly as the result of another individual, but the saleslady was not being intentionally unhelpful to the dreamer, so a misfortune rather than an aggression should be scored. Since the dreamer was able somehow to secure the kit, an additional successful consequence is recorded as part of the M1 scoring. There is a question as to whether a good fortune was present in terms of the bountiful environment provided by the lodge full of deer, but since neither the dreamer nor the others in the lodge had any apparent intentions of hunting, this would not constitute any special good luck for them. Had the two hunters come upon the deer themselves, a GF could have been scored for them. Since their awareness of the group of deer was made possible through the dreamer's information, they do not encounter any impersonal good luck but rather a friendly act on the part of another person.

The only modifier present in this dream is the S+ for the description of the hunting lodge as monstrous. Two negative scores were present: this did "not" seem to excite me, and the saleslady "couldn't" understand the dreamer. For two reasons, no score for emotion was given to the dreamer's statement that this didn't seem to excite him. First, the verb excite is too nondifferentiating in describing the type of emotion involved for it to be classified as one of the five scorable emotions. Second, the dreamer has effectively negated the presence of any emotion through the wording of his report. Note that this wording is different from saying something such as "I did not seem to be very excited," which would indicate that the dreamer was at least slightly excited. Two scores were given for the castration complex scales. The CA score was listed for the dreamer being injured in the ankle, and the CW was listed because another character, the hunter, was unable to handle his rifle successfully and missed the deer that he was shooting at.

DREAM 10

I was in a bar drinking beer with my roommate. The bar was in Ft. Carson, but did not resemble any one we had been in. It most closely resembled a little lunch counter. In fact, the more I think of it, it was exactly the same. My roommate and I were fairly high on the beer we had been drinking. A friend we had brought with us was asleep on the floor between us. We were talking and joking about various things. The subject of age came up and my roommate was telling me how lucky I was because I never had to worry about I.D. cards now that I am 21. The bartender heard this conversation and thought it was I who was underage. He asked for my I.D. so I gave it to him, sure that he would find it OK. He didn't, however, and thought the card was a fake so he booted me out. My roommate was laughing so hard it was all he could do to keep his seat. I, too, was laughing but was a little mad at the bartender, so I started beating on the door. The bartender finally came and this time looked at all my identification. Then he let me back in. I went over to my roommate, hit him on the back and bought him a beer.

Scoring Card for Dream 10

O	S	Char	Aggressive		Friendly		Sexual		Activities		Success
AE	IU	1MKA	1MOA 7>D		D 6>1MKA				P, D +		D
RG	OU	1MKA		D2R1MOA	D 3>1MKA				1MKA		
AE	IU	1MOA							D V=1MKA		
FO									1MKA V>D		
AD									A, 1MOA		
CM									1MOA V>D		
HH									D P>1MOA		
AD									C, 1MOA		

O	Failure	M-Fort	G-Fort	Emot	M	T	N	OI	OE	CA	CW	PE	Activities	LI	WD
BT				AN	S−		3	3	2	1			1MOA P>D		
FO					I+		x	x	x	x			E, 1MKA		
					I−		x	x	x				E		
					A−		x	x					P		
					E−								M, 1MOA		
													S, 1MOA		
													M		
													D P>1MKA		

In Dream 10 the score of AE appeared for the bar and RG for Fort Carson which is a city. Another AE was scored for mention of the lunch counter. FO was recorded for the beer and the floor was scored as AD. The I.D. card was scored as CM. The HH was scored for referring to seat, although it is a little vague as to whether seat means bar stool, or whether it means that the roommate had difficulty keeping his balance. A second AD was included for the door and a BT for the roommate's back. Another

FO score was given for the beer that the dreamer bought since this represented a different beer.

Three settings were involved. The first consisted of an indoor setting when the dreamer and his roommate were in the bar or lunch counter. The second occurred when the dreamer was booted out and he was standing outside beating on the door. This was scored as an outdoor setting. Finally, the dreamer was able to re-enter the bar and some of his activities after returning inside are described. The dreamer specifically said that the bar did not resemble any that he had visited in real life so both indoor settings were scored as unfamiliar. It appears probable that the area immediately adjacent to the bar or lunch counter, i.e., the area around the front door where he stood, was also unfamiliar to the dreamer so the outdoor setting was also scored U.

Three individual male characters were described in this dream. The first was the dreamer's roommate, the second a friend they had brought with them, and the third was the bartender. The roommate and friend were scored as K because they would be familiar to the dreamer, and the bartender was scored as O.

The bartender was being aggressive when he forced the dreamer to leave the bar. There is some question as to how this was accomplished. Since the dreamer did use the words "booted me out," the bartender's act was scored A7. The dreamer reciprocated with a mild form of aggressive activity when he began beating on the door. The language of the report structures this as the consequence of the dreamer being a little mad at the bartender. If the dreamer had only felt a little mad without doing anything about it, it would have been an A1, but since the dreamer did attempt to express his aggression in some more overt fashion, it was scored as an A2. This subclass can be used for such indirect expressive behavior as slamming a door to show one's anger. The dreamer initiated two friendly acts toward his roommate: one when he hit him on the back and the other when he bought him a beer. The back slapping is a form of expressing friendliness through physical means and is therefore an F6, while the purchasing of the beer is similar to offering a gift and was scored as F3.

Under activities, a score of P was used for the dreamer and

his roommate drinking beer. A mutual V appears for the dreamer and his roommate talking and joking. The roommate then initiates a V to the dreamer and an A score is given to the bartender for hearing this remark. The bartender then receives a V for asking the dreamer about his I.D. card and the dreamer interacts in a physical activity with the bartender when he hands him his card. The C is credited to the bartender for the thinking activity that he engages in when he first thinks that the dreamer is underage and then later when he decides that the dreamer's card is a fake. Following this the bartender performs a physical act to the dreamer when he puts him out. The roommate laughing was scored as E, and an E was also included for the dreamer laughing. The next P is scored for the dreamer beating on the door. The bartender's arrival at the door is scored as M since he would have to walk to reach there. An S score is given to the bartender for looking at the identification, and the dreamer receives an M for going over to the roommate, after which a P is scored for the dreamer slapping the roommate on the back.

A successful achievement was scored in this dream for the dreamer being able eventually to get back into the barroom. He had made this his goal, and after engaging in beating on the door, he was able to prove his age and be readmitted as he intended. The emotion of anger was scored for the dreamer because he stated that he was a little mad at the bartender.

Reference to the lunch counter being little received an S— score, but no score was given for mention of being fairly high on beer. In some ways this sounds as if a reference to intensity is being made, but both the terms of fairly and high are too vague to be scored in this case. An I+ was scored for the roommate laughing so hard, and an I— was scored for being a little mad at the bartender. The reference to being underage was scored as an A—. It will be recalled that mention of a specific age is not scorable as an age modifier, but the term underage here has the meaning of being too young. An E— score was given for the bartender initially judging that the card was a fake.

Three negative scores appear for this dream. The first was for the bar which did "not" resemble any they visited, the second was for "never" having to worry about I.D. cards, and the third for when the bartender "didn't" find the card OK. A score for CA was assigned to the dreamer for the overall situation of being ejected from the bar. In effect, the dreamer was found not to be a man, and he did not have the proper identification and credentials to be considered an adult like his roommate. Although it is true that the dreamer is eventually able to gain entrance to the bar, the damage can be said to have been done. Three OI scores were given for this dream: one for the overall setting of being in a bar or lunch counter, another for the activity of drinking beer, and the third for the activity of buying the roommate a beer. Mention of the word beer itself was not scored in this case, because food or drink are not scored separately if they appear as part of the scoring for any of the OI subclasses.

Two OE scores were given, one for the roommate laughing and one for the dreamer laughing.

APPENDIX C

Mechanical Recording and Processing of Dream Data

In Appendix B it was pointed out that the 5" x 8" scoring card we use contains sufficient space for recording all the scores derived from even a rather lengthy dream. Since all the information pertaining to a particular dream is retained on a single card, very little filing room is needed to store all the dream data from a large scale study. When the investigator reaches a point where he wishes to analyze, correlate, and evaluate his data, however, he will find it to be extremely time consuming if he attempts this task with these cards.

The format of our scoring card was developed in order to facilitate mechanical processing of the data. Once the data from the scoring cards has been transferred to punched cards, the investigator can very quickly tabulate the frequency of any score in isolation or in any desired combination with other scores. He may then ask rather simple questions such as "How many good fortunes appeared in my dream sample?" or more involved questions such as "Do aggressive scores predominate over friendly scores in dreams where animal characters appear?" or "Are chromatic colors reported more frequently in dreams when the emotion of happiness is described and achromatic colors when the emotion of sadness is described?"

In our classification system, capital letters, numbers, or typewriter characters are used for scoring symbols. This enables the entire system to be transferred to IBM, Fortran, or other standard types of punched cards. Some suggestions as to how one might proceed to record our scoring symbols on punched cards will be made below.

It will be noted that our scoring card (see Appendix B) is divided horizontally into two sections. The top section will be referred to as the A section and the bottom half as the B section. With the exception of Objects and Activities, the A and B sections are used to record the scores from different scales.

A punched card contains provision for 80 vertical columns of information to be stored. Five of these columns can be used for identification purposes and the remainder for scale scores. One of the five identification columns must be reserved for identifying whether the punched card contains scores from the A or from the B section of the scoring card. A simple way to indicate the identity of a subject is by number. The name of each subject is kept in a master book and a number assigned next to the name. In this way, 1,000 subjects could be differentiated through the use of three identification columns, as each subject can be assigned a three digit number ranging from 000 to 999.

The number of columns needed to contain the symbols appearing on the scoring cards will vary from scale to scale. The Negative and Temporal Scales require a single column apiece while Objects, Settings, and Modifiers need two columns each. Characters can be handled with four columns. Success, Failure, and Good Fortune each require five columns while Misfortunes and Emotions each need seven columns. The Social Interactions and Activities require thirteen columns.

The thirteen columns for Aggression are divided in the following fashion: four columns for the aggressor, four columns for the victim, one column for the aggressive subclass number, one column to indicate whether it is an initiated, mutual, or reciprocal aggression, one column to indicate whether a "linked" aggression is involved (a series of sequential aggressive acts between the same aggressor and victim indicated by a { mark on the scoring card), one column to indicate whether a joint aggressor is involved, and one column to indicate whether a joint victim is involved. These latter indications of joint characters are shown by a plus mark appearing in the column. The manner of representing a social or activities interaction can be seen by examining the scoring cards appearing in Appendix B. In order to keep within the prescribed number of columns, it will be noted that joint characters must be listed vertically on the scoring card, rather than horizontally as they were when scoring symbols were first introduced in the scoring chapter. It is, of course, imperative that the same type of information always appear in the same column. Thus, the subclass numbers must be aligned so that they are always represented in the identical column on all Section A cards.

Each punched card will contain all the information appearing on a single horizontal line of the scoring card. As many punched cards will be needed to represent a single dream, therefore, as there are lines containing scoring information on a scoring card. If Objects occupy more lines on the scoring card than any other classification and there is a total of 12 Objects scored, a total of 12 punched cards will be needed for that dream.

In preparing punched cards from the scoring card for Dream 1 in Appendix B, a total of nine cards would be needed. The first card would be punched for the Objects columns, the Settings columns, the Characters columns, the Friendly Interaction columns, and the Activities columns. The next six cards would only be punched under the two columns reserved for Objects. The eighth and ninth cards, representing the B section of the scoring card, would only be punched under the Modifiers columns.

A professional punching machine operator can quickly transfer the information from the scoring card to a series of punched cards. The machine contains a keyboard similar to a typewriter and spacing tabs can be arranged so that the operator can quickly locate the appropriate columns as she moves across a line on the scoring card. The operator can place a ruler across the scoring card so that the information appearing on an individual line can be readily followed. All of the scoring cards should have the Section A data transferred first. The spacing tabs can then be adjusted for the Section B columnar arrangement before transferring that data.

Once transferred to punched cards, the investigator can process his data in almost limitless ways. He can obtain frequency totals for any class or subclass in a matter of seconds. Contingency analyses can be carried out in order to discover what types of dream elements are associated together. It is also possible to take the original set of punched cards and quickly duplicate as many additional sets as may be desired.

We hope that this brief discussion of some of the obvious benefits accruing from the usage of mechanical data processing will stimulate dream researchers to quantify their data in ways which will allow them to take advantage of this technique. There are many exciting discoveries to be made about dreams and their relationship to other forms of behavior. If substantial progress is to be made in this area, we must equip ourselves with every available scientific tool that holds promise of aiding us. Gadgetry, of course, is no substitute for good theorizing. We need to advance carefully constructed hypotheses that can be tested against the hard reality of data. It is possible, however, that more efficient means of data analysis may uncover relationships which would otherwise have gone unsuspected and thereby cause us to propose new theoretical formulations to account for their presence.

APPENDIX D

A Sample Dream Report Form

After having experimented with several types of forms used for recording dreams, we have come to prefer a 5″ x 8″ card for this purpose. An advantage of having dreams recorded on this size card is the great ease of storing or filing them. They are also a convenient size to work with when scoring. The following instructions are printed at the top of the card.

Name or code no.   Place
Date of dream   Date of this report   Age   Sex

Please describe the dream exactly and as fully as you remember it. Your report should contain, whenever possible, a description of the setting of the dream, whether it was familiar to you or not, a description of the people, their sex, age, and relationship to you, and of any animals that appeared in the dream. If possible, describe your feelings during the dream and whether it was pleasant or unpleasant. Be sure to tell exactly what happened during the dream to you and the other characters. Continue your report on the other side and on additional cards if necessary.

Each investigator must decide for himself what type of instructions to provide for his subjects. Such factors as age or literacy level will need to be taken into account. If too much emphasis is placed upon a particular element in the instructions, the investigator runs the danger of "leading the witness" or else of having most of the report focusing only on that element, with the result that other details are omitted. If too little structure is provided and the investigator simply asks the subject to "report your dream," the subject may fail to mention items or events that he

313

was capable of reporting but did not, because he thought the investigator was not interested in this information. Emotions are a good example of the latter. Unless subjects are requested to indicate the emotions they experienced during their dreams, they frequently neglect to include such descriptions.

Our instructions are intended to obtain the information needed to score most of our scales, but they are also sufficiently open-ended so that the dreamer can proceed to organize and detail his report in whatever manner seems most appropriate to him.

Author Index

315

Subject Index